BTP.

CELT. 57.

£11.99
£8

D1146849

THE COMING *FIN DE SIÈCLE*

This book attempts to show the relevance of Durkheim's sociology to the debate on modernity and postmodernism. It does so by examining how Durkheim's ideas can be applied to current social issues. The author argues that there are striking parallels between the social context of the 1890s, when Durkheim began to publish in book form, and today. Communism and socialism are in turmoil, as they were a century ago. Now, as then, stock markets are in constant danger of 'crashing'. AIDS has become the new syphilis. Medjugorje has become the new Fatima, and the Virgin Mary is predicting terrible punishments for humanity again.

The book reexamines the *fin de siècle* spirit of the nineteenth century and applies the conclusions which emerge to the coming *fin de siècle*. It argues that the fruits of the Enlightenment are either dead or dying. It concludes that a new liberalism can be founded on Nietzsche's and Durkheim's 'cult of feeling', a benign irrationalism.

Timely and assured, the book will appeal to readers of sociology, as well as the related disciplines of philosophy, psychology, cultural studies and history. It is also intended for anyone interested in the issues and questions that will be raised as humanity approaches the coming end of the century and the end of the millennium.

THE COMING
FIN DE SIÈCLE

*An application of Durkheim's sociology
to modernity and postmodernism*

STJEPAN G. MEŠTROVIĆ

LONDON AND NEW YORK

First published in 1991
by Routledge
11 New Fetter Lane, London EC4P 4EE

Simultaneously published in the USA and Canada by
Routledge
a division of Routledge, Chapman and Hall, Inc.
29 West 35th Street, New York, NY 10001

First published in paperback in 1992

© 1991 Stjepan G. Meštrović

Typeset by NWL Editorial Services

Printed and bound in Great Britain by
Biddles Ltd., Guildford and King's Lynn

British Library Cataloguing in Publication Data
Meštrović, Stjepan G.
The Coming *Fin de Siècle*: Application of Durkheim's Sociology to
Modernity and Postmodernism. – New edn
1. Sociology. Theories of Durkheim, Émile, 1858–1917
I. Title
301

Library of Congress Cataloging in Publication Data
Meštrović, Stjepan Gabriel.
The Coming *fin de siècle*: an application of Durkheim's sociology to
modernity and postmodernism/Stjepan G. Meštrović.
p. cm.
Includes bibliographical references.
1. Postmodernism—Social aspects. 2. Durkheimian school of
sociology. 3. Rationalism. 4. Irrationalism (Philosophy)
I. Title.
HM73.M48 1990   90–8468
301'.01 – dc20   CIP

ISBN 0-415-08526-8

To David Riesman

CONTENTS

PREFACE AND ACKNOWLEDGEMENTS

Nowadays, so many books and papers are being written about modernity and postmodernism that these terms have gained cliché status. And their use has given rise to great confusion. Some authors understand postmodernism as an extension of modernity, while others see it as the antithesis of modernity. The interested reader may find it helpful for me to summarize in this preface how I compare with and differ from some other authors writing on these topics, and what is distinctive about the present book.

The gist of the argument presented in this book may be summarized as follows. The previous *fin de siècle* spirit and the current wave of postmodern culture share a common rhetoric of rebellion against the Enlightenment narrative. In this sense, the coming *fin de siècle* and the previous *fin de siècle* also seem to share cultural values and traits: a sense of anxiety, uneasiness, and excitement; a deliberate breaking away from the seriousness of tradition in favour of play, impulse, and fun; and a seemingly liberal concern with what might still be termed socialist, democratic, humanistic ideals of justice and equality. How many dictatorships have been toppled since the late 1970s and 1980s! No doubt these are among the many reasons that many authors today depict postmodern culture as a reaction against cold-hearted modernity.

But the present book will conclude that despite the apparent overlap between the *fin de siècle* spirit and the postmodern spirit, postmodernism is, in fact, an extension of modernity – the very same bloodless Enlightenment modernity that the previous *fin de siècle* spirit rebelled against. Thus, the previous *fin de siècle* is depicted as a genuine reaction against Enlightenment narratives and a genuine search for the irrational bases of social order, primarily in the notion of human compassion. The coming *fin de siècle* will be understood as an imperfect, ambiguous, confused, and contradictory effort to replicate this genuine rebellion from the previous century. It will be argued that postmodern philosophy never truly rebels at the notion of rationality, never embraces compassion, and always maintains the commercialist, bourgeois status quo.

Thus, similarities and differences exist between the former and coming turns of the century. Perhaps important similarities are shared by all turns of the century – this is something that is important to determine at some point, but will not be of any concern in the present book. Nor shall we be concerned with the questions of whether the *fin de siècle* may be considered as an archetype, a state of consciousness, a collective representation, nor with other philosophical, psychological questions that pertain to this topic. Rather, the present discussion will begin with an examination of empirical facts from current events that illustrate that, in fact, there do exist striking similarities between the former and coming *fins de siècle*. A more thorough search will uncover the differences. The method to be followed is primarily inductive and empirical, not deductive and speculative.

Perhaps the most important tradition to consider in a discussion of this sort is that of German *fin de siècle* intellectualism. This view is found, implicitly or explicitly, in the works of a number of contemporary writers, among them Jürgen Habermas, Allan Bloom, Hans Joas, David Frisby, Simon Deploige, Peter Sloterdijk, and Robert Bailey. David Riesman, in particular, pushed me gently into this direction. Like Habermas (1987), I travel back to the crossroads of the previous turn of the century to re-examine the roads taken by Western modernity, as well as the roads not taken. (Here is another fruitful and interesting point of intersection between the concepts of modernity and the *fin de siècle*.) But I disagree with Habermas that despite the shortcomings of the Enlightenment, the Enlightenment 'project' must be completed. Like so many modernists, Habermas manages to march from Kant and Hegel to Nietzsche and the Frankfurt School while ignoring Schopenhauer and the *fin de siècle* rebellion against the Enlightenment. In contradistinction to Habermas, I propose that this *fin de siècle* spirit needs to be re-examined for clues as to what might be alternatives to the Enlightenment 'project'.

Allan Bloom (1987) deserves credit for exposing the other, darker side of Enlightenment liberalism, its paradoxical nihilism despite its avowed openness. Despite the criticisms levelled at Bloom on ideological grounds, everyone knows that he is correct to claim that extreme cultural relativism leads to a dead-end. If things are true only in relation to specific social contexts, then nothing is really true, and then everything seems rather pointless. Compared to Bloom, Habermas seems naive. Nevertheless, I reject Bloom's conservative ideology as well as Habermas's conclusion that those who do not wish to complete the Enlightenment project must be neoconservatives. I seek a third alternative between classical enlightened liberalism and irrationalist conservatism. This alternative is a liberalism that is derived from irrationalism, from the 'heart' emphasized by the *fin de siècle* spirit as opposed to the 'mind' glorified by the Enlightenment. My book is an attempt to explicate this alternative, to argue that if the next millennium is to grant more rights and dignity to individuals, the weak, and the powerless, this will occur not from cognitive development but from a development of compassion.

This is an important point to consider. Postmodernism is typically depicted as a radical departure from historicism, traditionalism, and any semblance of permanence in any sphere, intellectual, artistic, or mundane. This anomic state is welcomed by some as liberating, and deplored by others as immoral, yet everyone is left hungry for something permanent. In either case, anyone who invokes historicism and postmodernism's other antitheses risks being labelled a conservative, or worse. Irrationalism has been given a 'bad press'. One automatically associates it with fascism and other attacks on liberalism not with compassion or socialism. Descendants of the Enlightenment in the USA and Western Europe have forgotten that irrationalism can and typically did denote benign phenomena like compassion, sympathy, and other derivatives of the heart. In fact, in contradistinction to Lukács (1980), Habermas (1987), and many other writers in this field, I believe that fascism and all totalitarianisms may be understood better as refractions of extreme, heartless *rationalism*, not irrationalism.

Another distinctive aspect of the present project is that I make connections between and among important intellectuals that are not typically invoked: Arthur Schopenhauer, Georg Simmel, Émile Durkheim, Charles Baudelaire, and others. It seems to make sense that even if many of these intellectuals were not or could not be aware of each other explicitly, their works were informed by a similar *fin de siècle* spirit, ethos, 'climate of opinion', or 'collective consciousness'. In this manner, I bring to the discourse on modernity and postmodernity authors that are not typically invoked – especially Durkheim and Schopenhauer – and all this in the context of the previous *fin de siècle* spirit as it is refracted in the coming *fin de siècle*.

Yet, without wanting to reproduce the argument that is made in subsequent pages, we can see that it is important to isolate precisely in what ways some of these intellectuals are important for understanding modernity and postmodernism. I hope to engage readers who do not necessarily regard themselves as professional intellectuals (although I must keep my colleagues 'in mind' as well, of course). To the reader who finds the names of many of these nineteenth-century authors unfamiliar, I wish to offer the following summary.

Arthur Schopenhauer (1818) argued that the 'heart' was more important than the 'mind', and in this regard, he self-consciously offered a distilled version of the essential message found in Hinduism, Buddhism, Plato's philosophy, and Christianity. His philosophy was apprehended by Simmel and others as representative of the previous *fin de siècle* spirit. Thus, he represents Western (and Eastern) 'narratives' at the same time that he is an iconoclast with regard to the modernist faith in mind over heart. It will be argued that Schopenhauer influenced Durkheim, that he foreshadowed socialism and other humanistic doctrines that blossomed around the turn of the previous century, and that he is still relevant to moral issues and concerns as humanity heads towards the next *fin de siècle*.

Similarly, the lyric poet Charles Baudelaire, immortalized by Walter Benjamin (1973), depicted modernity as existing under 'the sign of suicide', and claimed that the modern hero is the ordinary person. Baudelaire is known as the father of the modernity concept, and he was one of the most important literary influences in the previous *fin de siècle*. Yet his legacy lives on. Ordinary persons are still heroic: stress is on everyone's lips today. Everyone is constantly tired, and true to Baudelaire's dictum, the act of enduring, day in and day out, a modern marriage and modern job seems to be a heroic act for most persons. Ever-increasing statistics of suicide, divorce, and symptomatology of all kinds testify to the truth of Baudelaire's Schopenhauerian observations.

Out of sociology's many founding fathers, Simmel (1893) and Durkheim (1893) were the ones who wrote with the most pathos on the need to establish morality on a scientific basis, in response to the horrifying portraits of modernity offered by Schopenhauer and Baudelaire. This may seem like an endorsement of Habermas's Enlightenment 'project' at first blush, but it is not. Their version of scientific morality was to be rooted in Schopenhauerian compassion in direct opposition to dry, Kantian duty. The average person today can relate to their concerns even if he or she has never heard of them. Everyone has become cynically used to the constant stream of greed, corruption, deceit, and other sorts of immorality that pour forth from public and private life. Nobody *really* believes that the enlightened, educated, intellectuals are more moral than the backward and uneducated masses. More than ever, the next millennium needs a revival of the forgotten *fin de siècle* project of instilling a mutual sympathy among all the world's inhabitants for each other and for our common fate. Again, this project does not fit the conservative nor liberal mould, but is something radically new and different. It deserves to be taken seriously.

Some readers may feel that my use of the terms modernity and postmodernism sometimes borders on reification. Where possible, I have tried to refer to modern and postmodern culture, theorists, philosophies, and intellectuals. However, at times I deliberately use these terms as 'things', in Durkheim's sense of social facts as things. Of course, Durkheim has also been criticized for reification in this regard. But having cast my lot with Durkheim's sociology, I believe good reasons exist for maintaining some degree of social realism despite the critics who are wary of reification. These reasons are explained in subsequent chapters, especially chapter 6.

The most important influence on me in developing this project has been David Riesman. While I express my gratitude to him for the many ways he has guided me through our correspondence ranging over fourteen years, I am solely responsible for the arguments put forth here. I am also deeply grateful to Chris Rojek for the active guidance he has given me in writing this book. Thanks also to an extremely erudite anonymous reviewer, and to David Frisby for reading the manuscript prior to publication.

A separate note of thanks goes to Geoffrey P. Alpert, Harry Alpert's son, for making available to me his father's unpublished notes on Durkheim. These notes are a trajectory of Alpert's (1938a) forgotten but brilliant study of Durkheim, and they stimulated my thinking.

While the present project is a unique blend of various influences, mentioned above, there exists some overlap with some of my previous publications. In particular, I acknowledge that various portions of my argument were found in articles published by *The British Journal of Sociology* (1989a), *The Sociological Review* (1988b, 1989b), and *The Journal for the Theory of Social Behaviour* (1989c).

Chapter One

BACK TO THE FUTURE

Humankind is fast approaching another *fin de siècle*. This French phrase is difficult to translate accurately into English, because it carries connotations of end of the century, end of an era, end of the world, and in this particular case, the end of a millennium. It also connotes the end of modernity conceived as the rationalistic child of the Enlightenment, and the movement into something that is vaguely called postmodernism, the popular opinion that everything is relative and therefore as good (or bad) as anything else.

The term *fin de siècle* came into prominence as the calendar moved from the nineteenth to the twentieth century, but is somewhat difficult to date precisely. Scholars generally refer to the years from 1880 to 1900 as the *fin de siècle*, yet in these same discussions, they also invoke intellectuals and social movements that do not fall neatly into this time frame. For example, Arthur Schopenhauer's *The World as Will and Representation* was first published in 1818, but was not read widely until the 1880s, long after his death. Nevertheless, Schopenhauer is typically cited as an important figure in the *fin de siècle* (Ellenberger 1970). Scholars also disagree on the extent to which the *fin de siècle* may be characterized as optimistic or pessimistic, rationalist or irrationalist (Bailey 1958; Weber 1987).

It is only in the past few years that the term *fin de siècle* is being applied by the media to the coming end of the millennium. This is a strange oversight if one uses the previous *fin de siècle* as a guide, because in that case, one should have been concerned with this coming event starting with the 1980s. Instead, the 1980s were the years of the 'me-generation', and the coming *fin de siècle* seems to be an afterthought, one more postmodernist spectacle to endure.

1

Despite these conceptual problems, something referred to as 'the *fin de siècle* spirit' refers generally to the pessimism, cynicism, and ennui felt by people in the 1880s and 1890s, along with the widespread belief that civilization leads to decadence. This is true especially with regard to the intellectuals and literary figures from Baudelaire to Nietzsche who looked back upon the sometimes bitter fruits of the Enlightenment with disgust.

In this regard, the coming *fin de siècle* is not essentially different from the previous one. Irrationalism, cynicism, and disenchantment are in vogue as humanity approaches the year 2000, only these things are disguised under the rubric of 'postmodernism'. In the present *fin de siècle*, we have more technological advances and gadgetry than before at the same time that the word stress is on practically everyone's lips. The cynicism and other elements of the *fin de siècle* spirit are better camouflaged today; nevertheless, humankind has lost its collective innocence. Ideas and social movements debated by the nineteenth-century precursors of many intellectual disciplines are being reinvoked and re-examined: communism, socialism, feminism, nationalism, and human rights. Eastern Europe is in turmoil, and looks to Western Europe (not the USA) for guidance in establishing the 'right' kind of socialism. Yet Western Europe suffers from cynicism and anomie. All European nations are rediscovering their ethnic identities, which were forged in the previous *fin de siècle*, at the same time that they dream of a united and cosmopolitan Europe. And beneath all the turmoil, there is the burning question left over from the 1880s: how to secure a humane, decent, and just society and government?

As I write this book, humankind is passing the one hundredth anniversary markers for a variety of phenomena: the invention of the bra, the construction of the Eiffel Tower, the invention of pizza pie, the establishment of the *Wall Street Journal*, even the establishment of sociology as a recognized profession, among many other cultural landmarks. Still other milestones will be passed as we approach the year 2000, and many of them are worthy of separate social scientific study. Each landmark represents a decisive break with the past as well as earnest hope for a better future. Now as then, intellectuals and laypersons alike will increasingly look back as they look to the future.

Apocalyptic themes are already upon us in religious and popular culture. Some fundamentalist Protestant cults await eagerly a nuclear holocaust and the subsequent second coming of Christ. In the Deep South of the United States, especially, one finds bumper stickers on cars and posters on highways that proclaim, 'Jesus is Coming – Are You Ready?' Some of the most popular films in recent times refract this religious theme, from *The Seventh Sign* to the *Road Warrior* series. In fact, one can scarcely think of a popular film from the 1980s that does not refer, in some fashion, however obliquely, to the theme of the destruction of the world (or its salvation through postmodernist magic). A more hopeful and optimistic twist to the apocalyptic theme is presented in the typically postmodernist film, *My Stepmother is an Alien*. Therein, a hyper-rational alien is converted to 'old-fashioned' (nostalgic and fictitious) human love and compassion, and thereby saves the world from annihilation.

A 1980s film that perhaps best represents the strange confluence of postmodernist play, fun, cynicism, and hedonism in the face of probable destruction of the world is *Bill and Ted's Excellent Adventure*. The two young protagonists, Bill and Ted, travel through time to kidnap Napoleon, Billy the Kid, Socrates, Lincoln, Freud, Genghis Khan, Beethoven, and Joan of Arc, and bring them to a 1980s shopping mall. They do this so that they can pass a history course, so that they can become famous musicians, so that their music can save the world! At the end of the film, Abraham Lincoln tells his postmodernist audience: 'Be excellent to each other, and party on, dudes!' The important point is that postmodernist audiences are exposed routinely to apocalyptic themes that are camouflaged in 'fun' images, so that they are not permitted to feel indignation, outrage, real concern, nor even a desire to act. The threat of the apocalypse is converted into entertainment.

Everyone has noticed the repackaging of *fin de siècle* heroes in the popular media. The *Superman* series of films refracts an old cartoon character and more obscurely, Nietzsche's 'overman'. Riesman (1950) has remarked that compared to traditional fairy tales, comic book heroes do not permit the listener or reader (today, the viewer) to identify with the superhuman hero. The postmodernist viewer becomes the passive consumer of images whose imagination atrophies, because the media supplies the images ready-made. For example, the 1988 film *Batman* became a craze in the sociological sense, even though many viewers could not comprehend the film, nor did they like it. Like many popular films in the 1980s, it portrays the city as a cesspool of evil and decadence, with no time frame and out of context. Distinctions between good and evil in the heroes and villains of popular culture are becoming increasingly blurred, and gratuitous violence has become a norm. From Ayn Rand's ice-cold, rational heroes to Bugs Bunny and other cartoon characters, modern heroes are typically single, aloof, and hyper-objective, refractions of Hesse's *Steppenwolf*. The postmodernist mixing and borrowing of diverse themes from scattered contexts ensures that no one can ever distinguish fully the sinister from the benign themes. In responding to the popular media, we laugh at the same time that we are filled with horror. Much the same difficulty exists in everyday relationships among persons.

The previous *fin de siècle* introduced a radically new conception of heroism: civilization and enlightenment became such heavy burdens that the ordinary person surviving an ordinary life became heroic. It is difficult to endure modernity! The next *fin de siècle* will only accentuate this new heroism. Stress is on everyone's lips, and stress is the modern person's road to Baudelaire's (1863) type of heroism. Again, the popular media refracts this modern theme in its typically unconscious way. For example, Batman, Superman, Mighty Mouse, and most fantasy heroes are heroes in the modern, not the classical sense of being Herculean. They all lead double lives of ordinary, humdrum existence (consider Clark Kent) contrasted with the secret life of superhuman powers. Contrary to Riesman's (1950) claim that comic book heroes do not permit identification, it seems that many persons living in the coming *fin de siècle* can relate to the postmodern hero, because they feel that postmodernity requires something superhuman from them.

Despite the postmodernist camouflage of fun and play, a feeling of gloom and doom is associated with the notion of the *fin de siècle* (including the forthcoming one). Viewed objectively and critically, most postmodern cultural products address extremely depressing, disturbing, sad, and violent themes, from children's toys to popular films (see Denzin's 1988 analysis of the film *Blue Velvet*). For example, Freddy Kruger's 'hand' was a best-selling toy

4

during the 1989 Christmas season. (This 'hand' is used by Freddy to kill people in their dreams, and has been depicted in a series of popular films as well as a television series.) Consider the gloomy predictions concerning the environment, politics, and the economy in *The Year 2000* by Raymond Williams. Daniel Bell (1976, 1977) has published a long list of books and articles that forecast what social life will be like in the next century, and they are anything but upbeat. Government, corporate, military, and industrial institutions are making and have already made plans for the next century. Not all of these plans have been made public, but when they 'leak' through to the public, they evidently assume catastrophes from nuclear holocaust to economic meltdown. Thus, the Internal Revenue Service (the 'tax man') in the United States has drafted contingency plans for collecting taxes after a nuclear war.

As I write this book, the media is reporting the alleged death of communism in Eastern Europe, the Soviet Union, and China. For example, Zbigniew Brzezinksi (1988) has declared the birth, death, and 'grand failure' of communism in this century. Marxism may be dead, but what will take its place? Capitalism? Efforts by Ronald Reagan, Margaret Thatcher, and some others to make capitalism a substitute for the religion of Marxism seem feeble. Capitalism may be expedient and useful, even inevitable as some aspects of it penetrate into previously Marxist countries, but it provides no faith of any kind compared to the faith, even fanaticism, that Marxism inspired. Moreover, capitalism itself is decaying and decadent, even though the institutions it shaped persist.

Socialism is cited by many as an alternative to communism. But Martin Jay (1988) is correct to point to the present crisis of socialism as one of the most important links between the coming and previous *fin de siècle*. Western European socialism has unwittingly reproduced the capitalist production of cynicism, malaise, high suicide rates, and anomie. Alvin Gouldner had foreshadowed this concern in his neglected 1958 introduction to the English translation of Émile Durkheim's (1928) *Socialism and Saint-Simon*. In this obscure but important book, Durkheim had predicted the eventual demise of socialism and communism even as he witnessed their formation in his time, because he felt that these doctrines had been erected on the incorrect, overly optimistic premiss that

5

human passions will regulate themselves of their own accord, and that human compassion for fellow humans can be induced through rational social planning. He criticized severely thinkers from Saint-Simon to Karl Marx for this Enlightenment delusion.

Moreover, Durkheim ([1928] 1958: 53) observed that 'communism is nothing other than charity raised to a fundamental principle of all social legislation', a sort of 'compulsory fraternity'. Durkheim argued that charity without justice merely maintains the conditions that made charity necessary in the first place. Yet *Socialism and Saint-Simon* remains one of Durkheim's least known and least appreciated works, but its importance for today's political, social, and economic crises in much of the world should be obvious finally (see also Filloux 1970, 1977; Hayek 1988).

As the political fruits of the Enlightenment are dying, religion is gaining strength. The end of the present century has witnessed evangelicism on a grand scale, and even fundamentalism continues to gather increasing numbers of converts (Hunter 1983). Especially in communist countries, young people are attending church again, and in droves. Why should Christianity – which should have died out long ago according to Marx, Comte, and a host of other rationalists – be enjoying a resurgence? One answer out of many may be found in Arthur Schopenhauer's (1818) strongly expressed affection for Christianity's pessimistic symbols and teachings: the cross as the symbol for torture, the belief that life is a vale of tears, the constant emphasis on asceticism and suffering. In a word, Christianity is really quite modern, if not postmodern. It encapsulates the serious side of life that postmodernism distorts into the ethos of never-ending fun and play, and thereby fills the vacuum left by excessive optimism. This connection between Christianity and postmodern pessimism may seem paradoxical at first, but is worth considering. For example, the controversial 1988 film *The Last Temptation of Christ* captured the agony and suffering of the humanized, modern Christ, as opposed to the many Renaissance depictions of Christ (in art as well as theology) in which he never seems to have felt the pain of the crucifixion.

Mikhail Gorbachev has emerged as one of the world's foremost leaders, a representative of the cosmopolitanism that was born in the previous *fin de siècle*. Consider the books on peace, progress, and the dawning of a new era of hope that this politician has

6

published (see Gorbachev 1986a, 1986b, 1987). If he is different from Marx and Lenin in that he perceives the limitations of their modern utopian visions, he shares with them the profound knowledge that the need for faith moves the masses. It must be emphasized that Gorbachev presents himself and is perceived by Eastern Europeans as a zealous socialist who turned against communism because of its excessive bureaucracy and failure to realize socialist ideals, not because he is a closet capitalist. Many in the USA would like to think that Soviets and Eastern Europeans will embrace their political and social brand of 'capitalism' now that communism is dying. Nothing seems to be further from the truth: Eastern Europeans admire both Gorbachev and Reagan for their stands against bureaucracy, but they do not admire the Americans.

Marxism is dead, but it has left a void in Marxist as well as capitalist nations. Consider the enormous yet hidden anxiety in the United States and United Kingdom in particular concerning both Gorbachev and this void: Is Gorbachev a 'good guy' or a more 'slick operator' than his predecessors? And how shall we manage without the Cold War? When so much cultural expenditure – emotional, financial, and otherwise – has been devoted to enmity between Marxism and the bourgeois West, this rift is not going to be eliminated without enormous cost. It entails a major change, and we have learned that all change is stressful. Unemployment is already being felt in many regions of the USA that made a living off of 'defence'.

An economically united Europe will exist as of 1992. It is an achievement that will affect not only the economies of many nations. It is also a huge step in the direction of achieving the *fin de siècle* dream of a cosmopolitan unity of world nations under one government. The world is being internationalized in many other respects: blue jeans, VCRs, colas, and Christianity are spilling over diverse borders, even behind what used to be the Iron Curtain. Music Television (MTV), in particular, is broadcast into Eastern Europe as of the late 1980s. MTV is a typically postmodern phenomenon: an endless stream of images that distorts violence, sexual licence, and the ethic of anomie into 'fun' themes, mixed in with rock and roll. One obvious effect is that young people's cultural tastes, values, and fashions from the Soviet Union to California have been homogenized.

Democracy is erupting in totalitarian nations, seemingly in a spontaneous fashion, without CIA or other Western intervention. From the fall of Marcos to the fall of Ceausescu, the 1980s have made totalitarianism and dictatorship seem obsolete. Again, Durkheim had already declared in his neglected *Leçons de sociologie*, first published in 1950, that democracy is not a Western discovery nor a revival in our own century. Rather, democracy has been evolving since the beginnings of social solidarity, despite its obvious setbacks, because it is intimately linked to the inevitable progress of the division of labour and individualism. Durkheim's views on democracy seem to resemble the Enlightenment narrative that postmodernism rebels against. But unlike the Enlightenment philosophers, Durkheim (1950) had argued – to deaf ears – that democracy is the inevitable outcome of humankind's *irrational* movement towards a respect for human dignity and individualism, what he called the cosmopolitan 'cult of the individual'. (The parallels between Gorbachev's and Durkheim's cosmopolitanisms in this regard are striking.) Along with democracy and religion, nationalism has become more, not less, noisy and important as the twentieth century draws to a close – in direct contradiction to Marx's and other Enlightenment predictions. Various ethnic groups are demanding independence or at least a stronger voice, from the Soviet Union to French Quebec. Again, Durkheim (1958) had predicted as much, despite the fact that Marxism eclipsed completely the tiny movement called Durkheimianism.

These and other *fin de siècle* themes connote hope as well as fear and cynicism, represented well by the contrast between Ernst Bloch's *Principle of Hope* (1938) versus Peter Sloterdijk's *Critique of Cynical Reason* (1987), respectively. In modernity, one hopes for greater democracy, equality between the sexes, justice, and other good things for cosmopolitan humankind at the same time that one is filled with an existential 'sickness unto death' made popular by Kierkegaard almost every time one tunes to the evening news. Despite this dualistic aspect to the *fin de siècle* spirit, scholars seem to agree that its overriding characteristic is negative: disenchantment, boredom, cynicism, malaise, and decadence (Calinescu 1987; Ellenberger 1970; Weber 1987).

Other linkages between the coming *fin de siècle* and the previous one are obvious. Since the last turn of the century, humankind has witnessed an increase in alternating economic crises and periods of prosperity that alarmed nineteenth-century social thinkers (Etzioni 1988); the spread of cynicism and lack of ethics in professional and personal life that caused nineteenth-century philosophers to respond by trying to establish a science of morals (Hall 1988); and the institutionalization of cultural relativism that has practically crippled the social sciences as well as moral institutions (Hazelrigg 1989).

The ordinary person today is concerned with holes in the earth's ozone layer, the destruction of the ecosystem, contamination of the water supply, nuclear proliferation, and chemical contamination of Nature in general that resonates with similar concerns about the environment by nineteenth-century individuals who invented personal hygiene, recreational parks, sewage treatment, and other aspects of the modern medical revolution (see Dubos 1959). Practically everyone recognizes the words 'greenhouse effect', and celebrities take up media time to plead for us to grow trees in a desperate effort to offset its effects, already linked to droughts and 'strange winters'. Ecology is one of several competing phenomena striving to become a 'natural' religion as the old gods are dying. It has some disagreeable links with postmodernist, anti-science movements that seek not to reform science, but dismiss it. Ecology is not linked up, among most of the American population, with nuclear proliferation – this, despite the popularity of Gorbachev. Another strange contradiction is that while many citizens of the USA express concern over the cost and safety of nuclear reactors used for electric power, they tolerate the high cost and potential threat of reactors used to make nuclear weapons.

Even the closely related animal rights movements never target needlessly cruel activities such as rodeos, hunting, bullfighting, horse-racing, dog-racing, bird-stuffing orgies in Malta, and so on – only animals used for science and baby seals used for furs. The fur industry is in trouble, but still strong. Postmodern fashion, despite its pretence of environmental concern, uses leather and fur extensively to achieve 'the look'. Thus, the new gods that are springing up to replace the dead ones are still mired, to some extent, in the hypocrisy, cynicism, and other negative aspects of postmodernism.

In the previous century, syphilis spread terror among humanity, because it was considered incurable, and because it touched on one of the most intimate and important aspects of being human – sexuality. Today, AIDS is the new syphilis in this symbolic sense. Susan Sontag and the de-constructionists seek to strip AIDS of its mythical connotations of 'epidemic' in a vain, positivistic effort to have us think of it as just a virus (if that is what it is). But the fact is that the public reacts to AIDS in a non-positivistic, mythical way, as a plague. (Even the concept of 'virus' is hardly value-neutral, but insidious – consider 'computer viruses'.) In the previous century, individuals were alarmed by cocaine addictions and drug abuse, homosexuality, divorce, stock market crashes, apparitions of the Virgin Mary that predicted terrible punishments for collective sins, satanism, occultism, creationism, and ever-present political scandals (Weber 1987). We are even more alarmed by these same things, and frightened by many more. Consider that most things that are purchased in the West are 'child-proof' or otherwise 'tamper-proof' – we live in constant yet hidden fear of the irrational, of killers in the form of human agents or inhuman dangers. To repeat, postmodernist culture exploits these fears in media and advertising at the same time that it neutralizes them with the themes of nostalgia and fun.

In the previous era, neurasthenia was so widespread it was almost fashionable. Today, we have our chronic fatigue disorders, and doctors get annoyed with patients who claim they're always tired. It seems that everyone is always tired! Rich young people, bored, self-destructive, and overtly suicidal, make up the staple of 'soap operas' on television as well as films, and statistics indicate that these 'soaps' reflect the fact that violent death is, indeed, the leading cause of death among young people. In the 'good old days', films portrayed endings in which one lived happily ever after. By contrast, it is rare to find a contemporary film in which the main characters do not end up as victims of some sort of gruesomely depicted violent death, usually carried out to the tunes of nostalgic songs taken from the 1950s (witness the films *Diehard* and *Blue Velvet* as illustration).

Suicide deserves special mention. It is one of the most important *fin de siècle* themes in literature as well as scholarly works. Walter Benjamin's (1973: 75) horrifying claim that 'modernism must be under the sign of suicide' can hardly be surpassed for its truth-value. Schopenhauer (1818) had argued that suicide is the outcome of the infinity of desires unleashed by modernity, such

10

that the more material objects of desire one obtains through rational calculation, the more one desires. In his *Suicide and the Meaning of Civilization* (1881), Thomas Masaryk had indicted civilization as the ultimate cause of the rise of suicide rates, already alarmingly high in the nineteenth century. When Durkheim came on the scene and published *Suicide* in 1897, a work in which he referred to suicide as the 'ransom money' of civilization, he wrote to a receptive audience. As of this writing, suicide rates have surpassed nineteenth-century rates; they are *still* outrageously higher in Western, 'civilized', modern nations than in developing nations; and are constantly increasing. In addition to suicide proper, Durkheim referred to the insidious forms of self-destruction found in poor hygiene, lack of exercise, lack of proper nutrition, and a variety of other acts in which death is accelerated by negligence. Currently high death rates from cancer, heart disease, stroke, and cirrhosis indicate that Durkheim's warnings were on target. More than ever, we live in the shadow of the question posed by Albert Camus (1955), 'Why *not* commit suicide'?

The happy face that postmodernism paints on everything cannot change the horrifying fact uncovered by Freud and Durkheim that modernity entails a shift in the displacement of aggression from the external to the internal environment. Pre-modern people express aggression through murder and violence inflicted on others more often than through suicide. The reverse is true for postmodern persons who, by contrast, implode with aggression. The coming *fin de siècle* is the age of suicide, stress, and high blood pressure.

In addition, the costs of litigation, insurance, and merely existing in a 'rational' world of bureaucracy – phenomena that hardly existed on a wide scale until the previous *fin de siècle* – have led to wholesale cynicism and exasperation that is expressed by juries through the awarding of outrageous settlements, professionals by avoiding certain specializations out of fear of such settlements, and the common person by a general 'I don't give a damn' attitude. Litigation is a drain on Western societies in many ways: the law profession syphons some of the best talent that might have gone into other professions, because the West continues to hold the record for an ever-increasing per capita rate of lawyers. And litigation is hardly the way to solve the real problems of justice or redistribution.

11

In fact, cynicism is one of the hallmarks of postmodernity, as Peter Sloterdijk (1987) argues convincingly in his popular *Critique of Cynical Reason*. I find the following passage from Sloterdijk (1987: 5) to be as disturbing as it is true:

> Psychologically, present-day cynics can be understood as borderline melancholics, who can keep their symptoms of depression under control and can remain more or less able to work. Indeed, this is the essential point in modern cynicism: the ability of its bearers to work – in spite of anything that might happen, and especially, after anything that might happen. The key social positions in boards, parliaments, commissions, executive councils, *publishing companies*, practices, faculties, and lawyers' and editors' offices have long since become a part of this diffuse cynicism. A certain chic bitterness provides an undertone to its activity. For cynics are not dumb, and every now and then they certainly see the nothingness to which everything leads.... Others would do it anyway, perhaps worse. Thus, the new, integrated cynicism even has the understandable feeling about itself of being a victim and of making sacrifices. Behind the capable, collaborative, hard facade, it covers up a mass of offensive unhappiness and the need to cry. In this, there is something of the mourning for a 'lost innocence,' of the mourning for better knowledge, against which all action and labour are directed.

Thus, for Sloterdijk, 'cynicism is enlightened false consciousness', a 'modernized, unhappy consciousness' in which persons are 'well-off and miserable at the same time' (ibid.). Enlightenment only makes the situation worse. Sloterdijk's book is an incredible revival of a significant intellectual theme of the late 1800s in the 1980s. Sloterdijk's cynic is Baudelaire's (1863) dandy, Simmel's blasé urbanite, Durkheim's (1897) irritable and disgusted anomic type, even Freud's clever neurotic, who derives benefit from sickness. Additionally, Sloterdijk refracts, unwittingly, the 'inside dopester outlook' of the modern, other-directed type portrayed by Riesman in *The Lonely Crowd* (1950: 199–210). All these varieties of the cynic share the trait of refusing to be moved or touched emotionally by events or persons in their lives. One wonders whether this cynicism is stronger among males, whites, and urbanites than females, minorities, and those who still live in rural settings, along the lines of Riesman's, Durkheim's, and other *fin de siècle* analyses of cynicism and pessimism.

'The times of *naiveté* are gone', Sloterdijk concludes (1987: 5). Even if that is an extreme assessment – even if one has been able to nurture a secret *naiveté*, and prefers the Disney Channel on cable television to the violent shows on other channels – one does not dare display this *naiveté*, nor innocence. One does not hope too openly, for fear of ridicule, and also because excessive trust of anyone or anything is simply dangerous in the postmodern world. We always prepare for disaster, from signing a marriage contract to a house contract (if we can afford either). And after the disaster, we go on, because we must.

One can sense a turn to Sloterdijk's portraits of cynicism with Simon and Garfunkel's popular song 'I am a Rock' and the long-lasting popularity of the television series 'M.A.S.H.'. The hero of this series, 'Hawkeye', is based on a similar character in Heller's *Catch-22* (which was also turned into a motion picture). Hardly a sentence uttered by this hero did not betray a corrosive cynicism. Yet the character Hawkeye, the actors who portrayed him (Donald Sutherland and Alan Alda), and the phrase 'catch-22', are instantly recognizable in America as well as in much of Western Europe.

In addition to Sloterdijk's (1987) distressing book, the present generation's mood is captured accurately by Bailey's book entitled, simply and arrestingly, *Pessimism* (1988). Bailey argues that despite our avowed yet shallow optimism, we are constantly taking precautions against possible future dangers and catastrophes in practically every aspect of our lives, thereby betraying a deep-seated anxiety and pessimism. Postmodernists do not want to discuss pessimism or admit its existence (it's so non-modern), but pessimism rules the details of our lives.

THE STARTING POINTS FOR THIS ANALYSIS

Every analysis has its starting points, by far the most important part of any argument, and I intend to make my premises explicit here. The first six chapters of this book will elaborate on these premises. In subsequent chapters I will move to an application of these premises to the neglect of compassion in modern and post-modern studies of moral development compared to former attempts to establish a science of morality; to the sociological significance of the apparitions of the Virgin Mary at Medjugorje in relation to her appearances since the previous century; to an analysis of the stock market crash of 1987 in relation to the state of chronic economic crises that have plagued us since the previous *fin de siècle;* and to the general theme of civilization and its discontents – seemingly *the* theme of the previous *fin de siècle*. The concluding chapter will look to the future based upon this analysis of the past.

I take as my most basic starting point the opposition between 'heart' and 'mind' found in thinkers as diverse as Plato, St Augustine, Saint-Simon, and Schopenhauer, among many others. In line with most precursors of the social sciences writing at the turn of the previous century, I assume that the most important aspect of modernity is that it causes humankind to suffer from an excess of 'mind' at the expense of the 'heart': a virulent abstractionism that abhors anything permanent (see Rochberg-Halton 1986). Paradoxically, this excessive intellectualism has caused an unleashing of desire in modern times, a condition that Durkheim called anomie, although most people do not recognize that this has occurred. We are filled with wants, but are never truly satisfied, truly the personification of *fin de siècle* themes of life as constant, unquenchable thirst. Most of this book is devoted to explaining this paradox, so I will do no more than refer to it at this point.

Many precedents exist for criticizing modernity on the basis of its excessive abstractionism and neglect of the passions, feelings, and sentiment (see Frank 1988; Grunbaum and Wesley 1988; Hayek 1988; Hollis 1987; Katz 1988; Margolis 1989). However, unlike many of these other critics of modernity, I will be more forceful in my emphasis on the 'heart' as an alternative to modernity's vicious intellectualism, and my book will approach this problem from a sociological perspective, in particular the sociology of Émile Durkheim. It may be useful to compare and contrast my approach with Habermas (1987). Both of us hark back to the previous turn of the century for a re-examination of the crossroads and roads that modernity took. But unlike Habermas, I do *not* believe that·a solution to the problems generated by the Enlightenment lie in completing the Enlightenment project. Rather, I believe that an important road not taken by post-

14

modernists is the completion of the *fin de siècle* spirit, a solution that seeks to reconcile the Enlightenment with metaphysics. All this will become clear as the present book progresses.

I treat postmodernism as an extension of modernity's abstractionism, despite the rhetoric of rebellion against Enlightenment narratives. Postmodern themes of impulse, play, fun, and fantasy (see Featherstone 1988) are shallow, kitsch imitations of genuine compassion and emotionality expressed by the Romantics. Cold-hearted, decadent commercialism almost always lurks beneath the façade of postmodernist 'fun'. Despite its rebellious rhetoric, postmodernism, like modernity, takes a disparaging attitude towards the irrational aspects of life.

My book is *not* intended to be read as a mere history of ideas, but as a theoretical treatise with contemporary applications. It is a book about modernity and postmodernism despite the fact that it refers to the ideas of thinkers who have been dead for more than a century. (In any event, the words modern and contemporary are not synonymous according to most writers in the field of modernity.) An unfortunate byproduct of the modern attitude is that one regards thinkers from the previous century as relics that are irrelevant. On the contrary, I regard the works of Durkheim, Marx, Simmel, Mead, Tönnies, and other giants from that era as the only genuinely relevant theorists that can help us comprehend modernity in an objective fashion. They were still innocent, born and raised in pre-modernity. This gave them the perspective of being Simmel's 'strangers' to modernity, simultaneously in and out of modernity.

The concerns and needs of *fin de siècle* intellectuals are still very much with us: pragmatism, positivism, cultural relativism, and nihilism, among many others. We still need a science of morality and moral education. The business and government professions are still perceived by the public as being essentially and routinely amoral, in capitalist, socialist, as well as formerly communist nations. Contrary to Enlightenment predictions, religion has not disappeared and has not been replaced by cold-blooded rationalism in communist or Western nations. Moreover, the Virgin Mary, the only female goddess left in Western culture, 'appears' only during times of extreme social and economic crises. Her appearances at Medjugorje are a representation or symbol, albeit unconscious and mostly unrecognized, of such deep-seated crises and fears of further crises at the present time, particularly the forthcoming death of Marxism and perhaps even the last vestiges of the Enlightenment. Her 'appearances' have been the most frequent since 1838 in Paris, the city that stood as one of the foremost previous symbols for modernity. Catholic theologians have interpreted her 'appearances' as warnings to turn back to faith, to the 'heart'. Durkheimian sociology allows us to re-represent this dogma in a sociologically relevant manner.

Habermas (1987) emphasizes the importance of Hegel and Nietzsche for understanding the course taken by modernity and postmodernism. Granted, these are two extremely important philosophers. But one must take account of Hegel's rival and Nietzsche's master, Arthur Schopenhauer, if discussions of this sort are to be complete. Habermas and most writers on modernity and postmodernism simply ignore Schopenhauer. This fact is significant. Why should Schopenhauer's legacy be repressed? An answer is not difficult to find. Schopenhauer was a genuine rebel against the Enlightenment in that he asserted, simply and boldly, that the heart was more powerful and significant than the mind. For this reason, he threatens all narratives spun from the Enlightenment, including postmodern narratives. Schopenhauer's omission from discussions of this sort testifies to the strength and power of his argument. Schopenhauer criticized Kant's establishment of ethics on a rational basis by pointing out the simple fact that compassion is the true basis of morality, and that humankind is more motivated by passion than rational duty (see Cartwright 1989). The burning question for modernity that flows from this forgotten debate is the following: Do we need more cognitivistic morality as found in the works of Kohlberg, Piaget, Habermas, and their followers, or do we need to find a new morality based on compassion and desire, as Schopenhauer, Durkheim, and other *fin de siècle* thinkers advocated?

I have mentioned Émile Durkheim (1858–1917) several times already. He was the first 'real' sociologist in the sense that he was the first to be appointed to a bona fide professorship in sociology in France in 1887. All the other precursors of sociology made their living in some other profession (especially philosophy). Even though I will treat Durkheim's intellectual affinities with other thinkers in his time, his sociology shall be the central vehicle for this discussion. Why Durkheim, as opposed to Simmel, Marx,

Weber, Freud, or some other giant precursor of the social sciences from that era?

The choice of Durkheim can be justified. With the possible exception of Simmel, he is the least known and most misunderstood among the precursors of the social sciences. By contrast, Freud's name is a household word, Marx had the greatest impact on the world in this century, and Weber has given rise to the most articles and scholarly treatises. In chapter 2, I will focus on the affinities between Simmel and Durkheim, because I believe that these two thinkers should be regarded as the first sociologists of modernity, even though Simmel regarded himself primarily as a philosopher. The other precursors of sociology can be eliminated from consideration for the purposes of this study mainly on the grounds that they have been received and understood primarily in the rationalist and modern sense that is being critiqued here.

By this I mean that Freud is apprehended mainly as a rationalist of the irrational, even if it may be argued that this is a bastardization of his intentions (see Bloom 1987). Marx, despite the influence of Hegel, is a product of the Enlightenment, and Marxism is dying in the mundane as well as the intellectual worlds. At best, intellectual Marxism has been embroiled in sometimes bitter in-fighting about its true meaning for some time now (Descombes 1980; Kojeve 1969). While Weber is invoked frequently in discussions of modernity, recent scholars seem to agree that Max Weber's 'stand' on issues in general and rationality in particular is marred by an absolute refusal, if not inability, to reach a comprehensive, exhaustive answer to any problem he tackled in this regard (Käsler 1988; Segady 1987; Sica 1988; Whimster and Lash 1987). Weber's constant equivocations, his scrupulous circumscriptions and relativizations, probably explain why he was a failure in his lifetime, and also why he appealed so greatly to Parsons and neo-Parsonian modernists. His sociology is as mercurial as modernity itself.

Käsler (1988), in particular, cites Weber's excessive equivocations as the primary reasons why Weber was virtually ignored in his lifetime, and gained notoriety only after Parsons (1937) wed him to the rational social action paradigm. Overall, I agree with Käsler's severe indictment of Weber: Weber was an outsider whose influence was so negligible that he may be considered a failure in his lifetime who gained fame only after the Second

World War. Weber did not stand at the centre of the sociological discourse of his own age (this was achieved by the Durkheimians and Simmel). Weber did not discover any new problematic area nor methodology that had not been discussed previously. In sum, according to Käsler (1988: 214), 'Weber did not furnish sociology with *any* theory at all. In this respect, his work consists of an unending multitude of axioms, premises, suggestions, theses, hypotheses and a few theorems.'

By contrast, Durkheim, along with Simmel, took definite stands on modernity and related phenomena. In addition, Durkheim and Simmel ought to be considered as products of German Romanticism. Romanticism gives one leverage in analysing modernity, because Romanticism assumes social realism (an objective 'reality', ranging from the 'group mind' to the objective 'spirit' of Hegel), as well as the penultimate importance of the passions. Deploige (1911) claimed that Durkheim's sociology was more essentially German than French long ago, to deaf ears. To repeat, I shall elaborate on this importance of German Romanticism in the opening three chapters. Durkheim has been misunderstood because his Romantic underpinnings have been unrecognized or misunderstood. And the importance of German Romanticism for understanding modernity has been brought to the forefront recently by Allan Bloom's controversial *Closing of the American Mind* (1987). Despite Bloom's acidic and cynical style, some errors in scholarship, and some well-deserved criticisms brought out in reviews, Bloom deserves great credit for pointing to the obvious: most twentieth-century intellectual thought in many disciplines was more influenced by German Romanticism than any other source. The previous *fin de siècle* underwent the death pangs of the last stage of several stages of Romanticism that began with Goethe. Subsequent positivisms, pragmatisms, relativisms, and rational social action theories are victims of modernity.

In addition, I have already pointed to significant predictions by Durkheim that have proved to be more correct than the predictions of Marx. Durkheim predicted the eventual demise of socialism; the spontaneous growth of democracy; the rise of a new cosmopolitanism; the preservation of religious representations despite modernity; the gradual development of a 'cult of the individual' that would grant more and more rights to the oppressed, including women, children, and minorities; and the increase of anomie as the malignant counterpart to progress. He referred to suicide as the 'ransom money' of civilization, and a glance at social suicide rates in relation to a world map justifies this and many of his other predictions. Thus, he deserves to be taken seriously.

Finally, and not surprisingly, my intentions in this book imply a complete disavowal of positivistic methodologies. I certainly embrace empiricism, science, and objectivity, but do not believe that these things are even remotely related to twentieth-century positivism. Rather, positivistic methodology is the product of modern abstractionism and postmodernist kitsch in the sense that it borrows from the old masters, without any sense of context, what it needs to establish dreamed-up hypotheses. These hypotheses, in turn, are supposed to be 'falsified' (proven to be false) and not verified – one no longer seeks the truth, at least not since Karl Popper (1934). One deduces abstractions that one tries to show are false, and thereby piles up mountains of research articles that never satisfy the most basic need to distinguish truth from falsehood (on the limits of deductive methodology, see Grunbaum and Wesley 1988). Contemporary social scientists are trained to be cynics who search for falsehood, not truth. Not surprisingly, and in a typically postmodern fashion, many scientists follow Popper from the hours of nine to five and turn to fundamentalist, religious beliefs after work to satisfy their need for faith. Postmodernism allows one to live in such a contradiction. My intentions are to critique this monstrous, postmodernist version of science, not to succumb to scientism.

Chapter Two

DEFINING MODERNITY AND POSTMODERNISM

Well over one hundred books on modernity and postmodernism may be found in any adequate university library, and of course, the author of each book brings a subjective aspect to his or her definition of these phenomena. In a way, I hesitate to use these terms, because they have gained cliché status, and Zijderveld (1979) argues that clichés are an aspect of modernity. Thus, even the study of modernity is often reduced to tautologies. Nevertheless, reasons for these clichés must be found, and remarkably common themes exist despite the diversity. Most writers begin with Baudelaire as the father of modernity, pay much attention to Walter Benjamin, and end with Habermas as its most recent, famous inheritor. Most authors also tend to treat modernity as well as postmodernism as pejorative concepts.

A fundamental ambiguity, exposed by Scott Lash (1990) and others, with regard to the importance of Habermas (1987) to this discussion is whether postmodernism constitutes a deepening or undermining of the Enlightenment, rationalist project that constitutes modernity (see also White 1988). It seems very difficult to resolve this issue. According to Featherstone (1988), Harvey (1989), Kellner (1988), and Lyotard (1984), what is labelled as postmodernism includes the following diverse and often contradictory phenomena: neo-conservative ideology, reactionary sentiments, cynicism, a rejection of narrative structure, parody, stylistic promiscuity, pastiche, schizoid culture, excremental culture, a preference for visual images over words, fantasy, a 'post-tourist' search for spectacle, the epistemological equivalence of past and present, end of the Eurocentric perspective, commercialism, nihilism, and a penchant for 'hyper-reality' in which distinctions between the real and unreal are no longer valid. Above all, postmodernism is defined as an attack on the 'myth' of modernity, the belief that the progressive liberation of humanity shall occur through science. Postmodernist philosophy disregards historical and social contexts, and mixes contexts freely (see Murphy 1989). At the same time, it caters to nostalgia and images borrowed from the past! Postmodern beliefs co-exist with science and dogmatism, play and excrement, hope and cynicism, 'fun' with pessimism – in sum, with bipolar opposites of many sorts. But are all these strange aspects of postmodernist culture an extension of or a rebellion against modernity?

Consider a scene taken from the postmodernist film, *Bill and Ted's Excellent Adventure*, in which the kidnapped Socrates is brought to a 1980s shopping mall in California via time travel. The depiction of this idea corresponds to many of the contradictory categories described above. But even though it is a typical postmodernist tactic, it is not original. Dostoevski had already achieved a similar disregard for historical context in his pre-postmodern novel, *The Brothers Karamazov*, in which he transposes Jesus to the time of the Spanish Inquisition. Similarly, postmodern architects delight in borrowing from many different historical styles and using them to achieve a postmodernist style (Harvey 1989) – which, despite the rhetoric of individuality, is predictable and universal from Amsterdam to Los Angeles. Again, the Secessionist movement had already achieved this mixing of architectural styles during the previous turn of the century (see Janik and Toulmin 1973).

Long before the word postmodernism came into vogue, the sociologist Pitirim Sorokin (1957: 700) captured well the gist of postmodernism in his description of the last stages of decadent, sensate culture:

The place of Galileos and Newtons, Leibnitzes and Darwins, Kants and Hegels, Bachs and Beethovens, Shakespeares and Dantes, Raphaëls and Rembrandts will be increasingly taken by a multitude of mediocre pseudo thinkers, science-makers, picture-makers, music-makers, fiction-makers, show-makers, one group more vulgar than the other. The place of moral categoric imperatives will be occupied by progressively atomistic and hedonistic devices of egotistic expediency, bigotry, fraud,

21

and compulsion. The great Christianity will be replaced by a multitude of the most atrocious concoctions of fragments of science, shreds of philosophy, stewed in the inchoate mass of magical beliefs and ignorant superstitions.... Even the greatest cultural values of the past will be degraded. Beethovens and Bachs will become an appendix to the eloquent rhapsodies of advertised laxatives, gums, cereals, beers and other solid enjoyments. Michelangelos and Rembrandts will be decorating soap and razor blades, washing machines and whiskey bottles. Reporters and radio babblers will once in a while condescend to honor Shakespeares and Goethes by permitting them to 'make a line' in their papers and talks.

Similarly, most contemporary writers on modernity borrow some aspects of their definitions from 'totemic' figures that wrote in the previous century. Thus, Habermas (1987) depicts Hegel as the first philosopher of modernity and Nietzsche as the first postmodernist. Sloterdijk (1987) emphasizes that Nietzsche was the first great contemporary cynic. According to David Frisby (1986: 5) and many other commentators, Baudelaire (1821–1867) was the first to comprehend modernity with his famous phrase: 'Modernity is the transitory, the fugitive, the contingent, the half of art, of which the other half is the eternal and the immutable.' (Far more attention has been paid to the first half of this definition at the expense of the second.) Baudelaire (1863, 1869) was also among the first to link modernity to the theme of decadence, to cite the possibility that the ugly can be beautiful. Clearly, Baudelaire's understanding of modernity overlaps, at least somewhat, with contemporary understandings of postmodernity.

Frisby (1986: 5) also claims that 'Simmel is the first sociologist of modernity'. For Simmel (1858–1918), modernity finds its dynamic expression in the fragmentary, centrifugal, and arbitrary elements of what Simmel called 'life'. In Frisby's analysis, Baudelaire's vision of modernity was transformed into Georg Simmel's eternal present, such that 'the substantive element of the external world is reduced to a ceaseless flux and its fleeting, fragmentary and contradictory moments are all incorporated into our inner life' (1986: 46). In modernity, there is 'no final end in life, only the human will' (43). But is not this so-called modern vision similar to the postmodern rhetoric of rebellion against forms and narratives?

The Frankfurt School produced many distinguished intellectuals who elaborated on the decadence of modernity in a movement that has come to be known as critical theory: Horkheimer,
Fromm, Adorno, Marcuse, Benjamin, and others. Horkheimer
(1947) relied on Schopenhauer in his critique of the 'eclipse of
reason' (see Fox 1980). Erich Fromm, who became one of David
Riesman's most important mentors, attempted to find common
ground between Freud and Marx (see Fromm 1955, 1962). But in
my opinion, the writings of Walter Benjamin (1892–1940) still
deserve special mention, even though Benjamin's works have
definitely gained cliché status. Like so many writers on modernity,
Benjamin (1968, 1973) invokes Baudelaire frequently. Thus,
Benjamin (1973: 74) observes that for Baudelaire, 'the hero is the
true subject of modernism'. But this new, modern hero is the ordinary person, because 'the resistance which modernism offers to
the natural productive elan of a person is out of proportion to his
strength. It is understandable if a person grows tired and takes
refuge in death [suicide]' (75).

In his 'Work of Art in an Age of Mechanical Reproduction',
Benjamin (1968) argues that the very existence of reproduction
(printing, lithography, photography, and film, among other
kinds) destroys the aura of the original: 'Even the most perfect
reproduction of a work of art is lacking in one element: its
presence in time and space, its unique existence at the place where
it happens to be' (1968: 222). More significantly, Benjamin makes
the bold leap that modernity in general destroys aura in all areas
of life. Cold-hearted rationalism coupled with the repression of
aura leads to the horrifying state of affairs in which humanity 'can
experience its own destruction as an aesthetic pleasure of the first
order' (244). Consider all the Rambo, GI Joe, and other destructive children's toy figures that have captivated postmodernist
audiences since Benjamin wrote this essay.

For Rochberg-Halton (1986: 230), the essence of modernity
lies in its abstractionism:

> As the twentieth century enters its final years, it becomes in-
> creasingly clear that its chief distinguishing feature, though
> not, perhaps its enduring legacy, is the triumph of abstraction-
> ism, so rightly termed by William James 'vicious intellectual-
> ism'. Not only is the dominance of abstract forms of life

23

encompassing the whole range of existence characteristic of modernity, but so is the critique of this problem of overly rationalized existence.

Rochberg-Halton also describes 'the culture of modernism as a culture of nominalism', and this is another common theme found among writers on modernity. Much like Durkheim criticized the pragmatists in favour of a social realism that would act as an anti-dote to this excessive nominalism, Rochberg-Halton argues that Peirce's pragmatism was far more realist, in this objective sense, than the other, more modern versions of pragmatism that have taken root in this century. (Joas 1985 supports a similar view in his re-examination of George Herbert Mead's pragmatism.) Again, this modernist nominalism overlaps with postmodernist nominalism, and both succumb to abstractionism despite the fact that one would expect subjective nominalism to lapse into an orgy of emotions.

POSTMODERNITY, PLAY, AND IMPULSE

The concept of play is an important aspect of postmodernist narratives (one thinks of the popular 1980s song, 'Girls Just Want to Have Fun'). For Daniel Bell (1976), postmodern play becomes the domain of the anomic, untramelled self that opposes the work ethic that supposedly operates during the hours nine to five – this is part of the cultural contradiction of postmodern capitalism. Autonomy can be found only in play, because the modern work world is so terribly regimented. In his *Lonely Crowd*, David Riesman (1950: 63–73) links other-directedness to the idea that even the act of learning must be 'fun', and that everyone must always be 'nice'. Indeed, the world-wide popularity of Sesame Street, that postmodernist television programme that glorifies the alleged 'fun' of learning, bespeaks the continuing relevance of Riesman's classic. Other-directedness *is* a postmodern value orientation, despite the fact that Riesman never uses the word postmodern. Like the postmodernist, the other-directed type is more concerned with morale than old-fashioned morality, yearns for experience and spectacle, and is socialized to behave as a consumer of imagery.

But Riesman shows the dark side of other-directedness. If everyone is always portrayed in the media as friendly, tolerant, and happy, that leaves no room for justified indignation or anger. And contrary to Sesame Street dogma, learning is *not* always 'fun'. Learning demands attention and concentration, and these things are typically painful (see Ribot's 1896 classic on this subject). Postmodernism tries to make everything seem like play, even work and learning. It thereby leaves no room for discourse that is able to acknowledge the painful aspects of work and learning. How is this postmodern strategy different from old-fashioned repression and obfuscation?

Rojek (1985) takes up leisure as an important aspect of modernity, and makes the point that leisure is more than just free time, because someone's leisure time is another's work time. Rather, leisure mirrors modernity intimately through its privatization, individuation, commercialization (leisure is run on business lines), and above all, civilizing process of restraint and 'pacification'. Contrary to both Bell and Riesman, Rojek's analysis leads to the conclusion that autonomy and freedom from the drudgery of work can no longer be achieved in postmodernist play. Rather, play becomes a kind of work: one *must* have fun in postmodernist culture, and 'fun' becomes increasingly expensive. Rojek invokes a host of *fin de siècle* thinkers for his theoretical scaffolding, from Marx to Foucault, and shows that even when we moderns engage in leisure, we do *not* escape modernity. Rather, we become further embroiled in it. Indeed, any tourist will testify to the veracity of Rojek's observations. Postmodernist vacations are usually stressful; there are few exotic places left in the world; and most vacation spots promise to deliver the same, bland product – fun. Postmodernism has levelled and homogenized what used to be exotic hot spots such that one could just as well spend one's 'leisure' time in a shopping mall. In fact, shopping frequently becomes the primary activity in postmodernist vacations.

Elias's (1982) *The Civilizing Process*, invoked by Rojek and many others engaged in discourse of this sort, deserves additional mention, yet its essential message is vintage *fin de siècle*. That message is that civilization necessitates restraint of human passion, and this restraint leads to discontent, something that Freud (1930) had claimed long ago, and – more importantly – many of Freud's colleagues had expressed independently of him. Moreover, like

Durkheim (1893), Elias depicts civilization not as the result of rational planning or utilitarian calculation, but as the outcome of a 'force' whose end-result is 'reason' (a perfectly German Romantic idea). An important aspect of this 'force' is differentiation under the process of competition (another unwitting refraction of Durkheim 1893). Civilization's need for the constraint of self-constraint dovetails nicely into Durkheim's overwhelming emphasis on the notion of constraint. In sum, Elias's (1982) work allows one to point to the contemporary relevance of Durkheim's *Division of Labor* (1893) to discussions of modernity and postmodernity.

Elias offers empirical evidence to support his contention by tracing the development of Western manners through the centuries. He demonstrates that compared to our ancestors, we moderns live with far more restrictions on bodily functions; for example, passing gas, belching, sweating, sneezing, slurping, and using the toilet. Sex, nudity, and violence are also more closely regulated. Postmodern advertisements make one feel guilty about perspiration, the slightest lapse in personal hygiene, pimples, wrinkles, age spots, and all sorts of other natural processes that our ancestors accepted as the natural order of things. Contrary to the rhetoric of rebellion and liberation, the postmodern body is tightly regulated, and in some ways, postmodern persons are more inhibited than the Victorians. Consider the ever-increasing aisle and shelf space in postmodern stores devoted to 'personal care products'. Were postmodernism a genuine rebellion against modernity, this should not be the case. Here is one more bit of evidence that despite the rhetoric of rebellion, postmodernism is merely an extension of the modern civilizing process.

THE AMBIGUITIES OF POSTMODERNISM

Calinescu (1987) offers a most comprehensive treatment of modernity in that he explores its meanings among diverse intellectuals, from artists to sociologists. Like Frisby (1984, 1989), Rojek (1989) and so many other commentators, Calinescu isolates Baudelaire as *the* writer on modernity. He notes that the term 'modern' has been used typically in a pejorative sense from Shakespeare, through Baudelaire, up to the present. Calinescu notes that Alexis de Tocqueville touched on modernity when he was amazed by and criticized American superficiality and excessive

reliance on ever-changing public opinion. Closer to us, the sociologists David Riesman (1950), Daniel Bell (1976), and Robert
Bellah (1985) have all touched in one way or another on the transitoriness, superficiality, and vacuous intellectualism of modern
life. In fact, one of the best definitions of modernity is contained
in the title of Marshall Berman's (1982) book *All That Is Solid Melts
into Air: The Experience of Modernity*.

Frisby (1986: 12) refers to postmodernism as the end of modernism in its nascent state, and this nascent state is constant.
Habermas (1987: 3) captures postmodernism well with the formula, 'The premisses of the Enlightenment are dead; only their consequences continue on.' Other authors already discussed refer to
postmodernism similarly as the extreme end-points of the negative aspects of modernist subjectivism, narcissism, and relativism
(Bauman 1987; Frisby 1989; Rutler 1987; Vattimo 1988). These
extreme products of postmodernism include nihilism, kitsch, bad
taste, and a delight in decadence. In postmodern kitsch, anything
and everything is cheaply imitated (without the remotest regard
for Benjamin's aura), endlessly repeated, and made banal – to the
delight of audiences and consumers. Not just the media, but intellectuals also produce and cater to kitsch. Allan Bloom's (1987)
forceful message is that most of what passes for intellectualism
since the last century has been poorly understood vulgarization of
fin de siècle intellectual life.

But here we arrive at another fundamental ambiguity. Some
writers derive postmodernism from the abstractionism of modernity, while others derive it from its opposite, cheap sentimentality. Thus, the USA has been referred to by some writers as the
Disneyland culture (this is intended to be pejorative). These same
writers cite pure, good feelings found in old comedies (Groucho
Marx and Jimmy Durante, for example) as the antithesis to postmodernist Disney kitsch, referred to pejoratively as the 'AIDS of
culture' (Rochberg 1988). The obvious problem with this line of
reasoning is that Disneyland can be a source of pure, non-kitsch
joy for scores of people. One person's kitsch *can be* another person's naïve aura. Foreigners frequently display delight when a
cliché is explained to them. The cynic might respond, is the 'heart'
always right? Might sentimentalism be pejorative, and have something to do with emotional excesses of the 'heart'?

The present book is a long reply to this ambiguity concerning the role of the heart in postmodernism. The short answer that gets to the point is this. Along Schopenhauerian (1818) lines, I believe that postmodernist bad taste originates with the mind, not the heart nor its sentimental derivatives. What is often referred to as bad taste, kitsch, cliché, and cheap sentimentality bespeaks a dominance of abstractionism that fails to find a genuine emotional component in phenomena. Postmodernist, cheap sentimentality betrays itself by its commercialism. Emotion and nostalgia are typically used to sell something, or for some other rational, instrumental purpose. In the context of Schopenhauer's philosophy, genuine, sublime emotion is essentially 'will-less', non-calculating, non-instrumental, and without rational or conscious purpose and plan. Such 'will-lessness' is becoming increasingly rare in the postmodernist world.

Cahoone (1988) locates modernity in the same subjectivism that other authors emphasize, only he begins his analysis with Descartes as the father of modernity, a strategy shared by Judovitz (1988). Again, this is balanced by emphases on the German influence, such that Barnouw (1988) locates the origins of modernity in Weimar culture, while Rundell (1987) begins with Kant. One will find Saint Augustine, Milton, Darwin, Freud, Marx, the Talmud, the Renaissance, and Hegel, of course, as well as a host of other thinkers, philosophies, and eras invoked by writers as originators of modernity (see Bowler 1988; Kallen 1932; Larson 1927; Love 1986; McSwain 1988; Marcus 1984; Nelson 1981; Rose 1965). Most writers usually end their analyses with Habermas. His work is typically understood as a desire to 'finish' the project of the Enlightenment, and if this is true, it seems to be a strange goal given the fact that the Enlightenment and modernity are typically used in a pejorative sense by many students of modernity (a fact acknowledged by Habermas, his students, and critics).

The essential point is that most of these works and authors give us a 'collective representation', in Durkheim's sense, of *fin de siècle* pessimism, cynicism, and disenchantment that essentially repeats the previous *fin de siècle* spirit. Postmodernism is not really new, original, or genuine. It pretends to rebel at modernity, whereas it merely extends it. By contrast, the previous *fin de siècle* sought truly to rebel against modernity's vicious abstractionism, its overemphasis on the mind – and it largely failed in this attempt at rebellion.

In sum, modernity in its broadest sense represents the many dimensions of that massive social change from Tönnies's (1887) *Gemeinschaft* (community) to *Gesellschaft* (society); traditional economics to industrialization and capitalism (Riba 1985); Durkheim's (1893) mechanical solidarity to organic solidarity; Riesman's (1950) traditional-directed societies to inner-directed to other-directed societies; along with numerous other refractions of this same theme of a movement from 'heart' to 'mind' (see Bailey 1958). Modernity is represented by 'the dandy' as a social type for Baudelaire (1863), as the blasé urbanite for Simmel, and the anomic egoist for Durkheim. It finds its energy in 'the metropolis' for Simmel and in 'civilization' for a host of other *fin de siècle* writers. Literary giants from Rimbaud to Tolstoi mirrored these sociological theories of decadent 'progress'. Modernity is the permanent end to humankind's innocence, and despite acknowledgement of the obvious benefits of modernity (mainly technological gadgetry), for most writers, it represents something pejorative, negative, decadent, or otherwise abhorrent. Postmodernism seems to be an extension and exacerbation of *Gesellschaft* values, other-directedness, anomie, and other elements of modernity already dealt with by *fin de siècle* sociologists, not a genuine rebellion nor reaction against modernity.

In contrast to postmodernist philosophy, as it is called by Murphy (1989), Durkheim's stand on modernity – and by extension, postmodernity, even though he never used this word – is complex. He embraced its positive aspects of cosmopolitanism, high regard for the dignity of the individual, and sense of progress. At the same time, he condemned egoism, anomie, and its other negative aspects. Chapter 3 is devoted to Durkheim's stand on the *fin de siècle*, which is an indirect way of getting at his stand on the process of modernity. For the purposes of this discussion, it is essential that one does not react to modernity in a uni-dimensional manner, whether that reaction is cynicism, postmodernist surrender to bad taste, or some other conservative, fundamentalist reaction in the name of the nation, or of an idealized and idolized working class or religion. The hallmark of the Durkheimian tradition is a serious, non-sentimental, optimism in the face of sobering and honest pessimism about things that one should consider alarming and decadent.

THE DURKHEIMIANS ON MODERNITY

In this final section, I intend to summarize the works of two of Durkheim's most prolific disciples, Célestin Bouglé and Maurice Halbwachs, as their works pertain to modernity, postmodernism, and the related themes of this book (even though they did not use these precise words). Surprisingly, these works have preserved a freshness that speaks to us today, as we approach the next *fin de siècle*, and they orient one in approaching Durkheim's legacy as it pertains to modernity in a manner that his followers might have intended.

In an essay entitled 'Darwinism and Sociology' (1909), Célestin Bouglé notes that in his time, one found the traces of Darwinism almost everywhere as a reaction against the persistent dualism of the Cartesian tradition. (Note that postmodernists frequently claim to be making a similar rebellion against Cartesianism.) In line with Simmel's definition of modernity (and it must be recalled that Bouglé admired Simmel as well as Durkheim), Bouglé isolates the sociological import of Darwinism as a 'philosophy of Becoming'. This is an open-ended Becoming, with no final, predetermined goal, no transcendent design. In contradistinction to his version of modernist Darwinism, Bouglé (1909: 468) faults Comte and Spencer for their teleological evolutionary schemes, in which final goals are abstractly preconceived through deduction, and Bouglé declares that Durkheim followed in the wake of Darwin. How many fruitless debates and attacks on Durkheim's alleged functionalist teleology might have been avoided had someone read and taken seriously Bouglé's essay!

For Bouglé, the important question raised by Darwinism is whether it leads to democracy or the 'aristocratic theories of Nietzsche' (470). If one's answer falls with Nietzsche – as so many contemporary answers have – then Nature as well as society become arenas in which we are all reduced to gladiators. (Benjamin's 1973 description of how Baudelaire arrives at the notion of the modern hero is similar to this image, even though Baudelaire pre-dates Nietzsche.) This view leads to pessimism. Bouglé adds that like Nietzsche, Marx sees struggle and only struggle in this version of Darwinism, so that Marx, too, is a *fin de siècle* pessimist despite his utopian visions (this is a hotly debated sore point among neo-Marxists, of course).

But according to Bouglé, Darwinism should lead to a democratic response, and cites the works of Espinas (one of Durkheim's teachers) and Kropotkin for the interpretation that side by side with the struggle for existence, we find 'association for existence' (473). Most important, for the purposes of this book, Bouglé cites Durkheim as a democratic neo-Darwinian. Because this context for apprehending Durkheim has never been used by subsequent scholars, I should like to quote generously from Bouglé's insightful remarks (475–6):

> Let us take for example Durkheim's theory in *Division of Labor*. The conclusions he derives from it are that whenever professional specialisation causes multiplication of distinct branches of activity, we get organic solidarity – implying differences – substituted for mechanical solidarity, based upon likenesses. The umbilical cord, as Marx said, which connects the individual consciousness with the collective consciousness is cut. The personality becomes more and more emancipated.... Here one sees that the writer [Durkheim] borrows directly from Darwin. Competition is at its maximum between similars, Darwin had declared; different species, not laying claim to the same food, could more easily coexist. Here lay the explanation of the fact that upon the same oak hundreds of different insects might be found. *Other things being equal, the same applies to society*. He who finds some unadopted speciality possesses a means of his own for getting a living. It is by this division of their manifold tasks that men contrive not to crush each other. Here we obviously have a Darwinian law serving as intermediary in the explanation of that progress of division of labour which itself explains so much in the social evolution. (Emphasis added.)

The interested reader may wish to verify that Durkheim ([1893] 1933: 266–69) does, indeed, cite Darwin in precisely the manner suggested by Bouglé. The more important point is that the Durkheimians did not romanticize primitive forms of social association, as many postmodernists do in their emphasis on nostalgia, because the Durkheimians recognized that competition is most fierce under conditions of minimal differentiation. At the same time, they avoided Nietzsche's and Baudelaire's cynical conclusions regarding modernity by noting that open-ended Becoming *can* lead to democracy, co-operation, and other desirable

31

traits. Thus, Durkheim criticizes severely 'those retrospective reveries of the philosophy of the eighteenth-century' that posit a 'paradise lost' (269). On the contrary, Durkheim writes, 'there is in our past nothing to regret', and adds that

> If the hypotheses of Darwin have a moral use, it is [to show] the moderating influence that society exercises over its members, which tempers and neutralizes the brutal action of the struggle for existence and selection (197).

In another neglected work, *The Evolution of Values* (1926), Bouglé takes up a topic subsumed under the rubric of modernity that is still hotly debated, cultural and moral relativism. Bouglé again castigates 'Nietzsche [who] seeks to revise the system of values by preaching the Gospel of aristocratic hardness' (1926: 8). The consequence of adhering to Nietzsche seems to be the nihilism of adhering to no moral values, a condition in which 'values are engulfed in the night of indifference' (12). But Bouglé points to a neglected alternative that is full of hope (16):

> Here again, we recognize the fundamental thought of the sociological work of Émile Durkheim. His last writings are full of this idea that society is essentially the creator of ideals. By its properties, by the peculiar forces which emerge from the assembling of men, are to be explained the characteristic of those great magnets which we call values.

Bouglé (27) observes that *both* Simmel and Durkheim regard values as *habits* – a crucial *fin de siècle* concept dropped from the modern vocabulary according to Camic (1986) – facts, realities, things. In other words, even if some values seem to vary from culture to culture and person to person, other values are also fairly constant. For example, democracy seems to be a modern value that has surived and continues to break through totalitarian regimes. Consider the demise of communism in the late 1980s in Eastern Europe!

Bouglé stresses that for Durkheim, society is not a 'super policeman' that merely constrains individuals (34). Rather, society is a 'fiery furnace', a magnet that surrounds values with the quality of desire, in contradistinction to the Marxist overly rationalist understanding of values (21). Thus, 'values are not so many dead weights which oppress us, burdening our breasts; far rather are they magnets which draw out, and are worthy to draw out, our convergent effort' (37). Because of this soberingly optimistic, neglected aspect of values, Bouglé argues, values resist the iconoclasts like Nietzsche who seek to turn all values on their heads (16).

Bouglé takes a similar jab at Marx (p. 43): 'Indeed, if economic organization tends, as Marx said, to transform a whole class of men into appendages of the machine, humanity will raise a protest.' This has occurred to *some* extent since Bouglé's writings. Further support for Bouglé's claims can be found in the fact that humanity has raised protests in the latter portion of the twentieth century against apartheid in South Africa and the brutal suppression of democratic movements in China, Romania, Czechoslovakia, and elsewhere. (Of course, one must still explain humanity's silence with regard to many other brutalities in this century.)

Maurice Halbwachs opens a similarly interesting window on the previous *fin de siècle* in his obscure *Psychology of Social Class* (1958). Halbwachs begins with the opposition between the peasant and civilized classes of the urban bourgeoisie, an analogue to Durkheim's (1893) distinction between mechanical and organic solidarity, respectively. He notes that peasants become attached to the soil, even to poor, dry, and dismal regions. Halbwachs contrasts this loyalty to the soil with the urban, and specifically American (in his book) habit of going into debt to buy land as an investment. 'Land' and 'house' take on entirely different meanings in pre-modern versus modern and postmodern contexts. In postmodern culture, 'land' and 'house' tend to become decidedly *kitsch*.

Like Bouglé and Durkheim, however, Halbwachs refuses to romanticize pre-modernity. Thus, without a trace of contemporary, postmodernist nostalgia for the past, Halbwachs writes with regard to the peasant (1958: 35):

> The houses may be close together, but the inhabitants are separate in their interests and preoccupations, which are not concerned with the same pieces of the land and are rarely corporate. Of course, the peasants gather together for evenings during the winter, and again on holidays and market days. They work together at harvest time and during the vintage; but for the rest of the year the families live quite separately. Nobody considers anything but himself or his own kin. Just as a

village sometimes ignores, envies and detests a neighbouring village, so it happens only too often that families envy each other from one house to the next, without ever a thought of helping each other. Sourness, egoism, and individualism are found at every social level. These people are thrifty and live sparely. They are keen to extend their land. But they do not worry about their fellows. There is no natural tendency, even amongst the members of the same village or the same district, to work together for the common good.

Durkheim (1893) named primitive solidarity 'mechanical' precisely because it does not really bind people together, but is brittle and breaks apart under times of stress. As illustration, consider the fact that one of the most distressing problems in developing nations today, still characterized in large measure by mechanical solidarity, is that governments are often unable to unify a plethora of competing villages, districts, and nationalities, and that these subgroups often go to war with one another. On a more concrete and palpable level, I would like to disclose the fact that in visiting the 'primitive' village in Yugoslavia that my ancestors inhabited, I found ample confirmation of Halbwachs's and Durkheim's observations. I invite the reader to compare peasant versus 'civilized' settings that he or she knows with regard to these Durkheimian observations, because they constitute a crucial aspect of the present discussion. Postmodernist nostalgia for the 'good old days' distorts the real harshness of the past.

But Halbwachs does not romanticize modernity either. He cites a preoccupation with an unlimited profit as the major characteristic of the bourgeoisie, and adds that 'once such a desire is conceived it can only increase indefinitely' (45). Halbwachs devotes many pages to Max Weber's *Protestant Ethic and the Spirit of Capitalism* (1904) in order to find common ground between Weber's and Durkheim's depictions of the modern bourgeoisie. This common ground is Durkheim's (1893) concept of economic anomie, mirrored in Weber's (1904) depiction of the irrational desire for unlimited gain – and Halbwachs also footnotes Thorstein Veblen's notion of limitless consumption in this regard. Halbwachs describes modernity in terms of the mind: 'measurement and calculation, scientifically organized factories, standardized needs, accountancy, administration, bureaucracy' (1958:

48). All this stands in opposition to the 'natural inertia' of the past: 'custom, tradition, instinct, and habit' – the heart.

The feverish pace of modern societies promotes immoral egoism, according to Halbwachs, although he does not spell out how this modern egoism differs from the egoism of the primitive peasant. 'In other words', Halbwachs sums up, 'rationalization and scientific methods have slowly substituted an abstract intelligence for a personal spirit in business firms, dehumanizing them' (62). Halbwachs cites Henri Bergson (his master prior to his becoming Durkheim's disciple) to make the point that consumption does not automatically lead to happiness, that it can be destructive as well constructive (137):

> Men are well aware of this; hence the passionate interest now taken in every form of association and every institution inspired by community feeling. They have understood that collective effort is necessary to organize the pursuit of happiness socially in something so complex as modern civilization. Happiness, in fact, is not in these circumstances the automatic result of increasing wealth and productivity. Perhaps even, as Bergson suggested, austerity, restrictions and even a certain asceticism is a necessary element in material satisfaction.

Halbwachs adds to this dense paragraph the optimistic hope that sociology can contribute to the scientific study of this new collective effort, and ends his study abruptly. The ray of hope that emerges from Halbwachs's *fin de siècle*, pessimistic appraisal of modernity is that unlike the primitive, the modern (and postmodern) human has the potential for association and co-operation in the face of the dark side of modernity – along the lines of Bouglé's analysis of the import of Darwinism. In fact, happiness can be achieved only through collective co-operation, not according to the law of the jungle.

Thus, Durkheim, Bouglé, Halbwachs, and Durkheim's other disciples alert us to the fact that much of the contemporary literature on modernity and postmodernity may suffer from a misplaced romanticism and nostalgia concerning the past, excessive use of the paradise-lost theme, and undue cynicism concerning the present and future. The Durkheimians do not sugar-coat the very real dehumanization that has resulted from 'civilization', yet they manage to find real grounds for hope. The core of their version of sociology suggests that a genuine critique of modernity and postmodernity can lead to constructive, positive, even soberly optimistic consequences.

Chapter Three

DURKHEIM'S ERA

The cult of feeling versus the cult of reason

To anyone who is familiar with a diverse sampling of literature from the *fin de siècle*, it is curious if not shocking that in most current textbooks, secondary sources, as well as treatises, sociologists usually posit something like a straight line from the optimistic, rationalist philosophies that informed the works of the Enlightenment precursors of sociology, among them Saint-Simon, Comte, and Kant, to present-day sociology. This applies to Parsons (1937), Habermas (1987), and most sociologists who fall between them. As a rule, sociologists simply fail to acknowledge the long intellectual detour from the optimistic Enlightenment to our cynical age through what Ellenberger (1970) calls the *fin de siècle* spirit exemplified by Schopenhauer's philosophy, the Romantic and pre-Romantic forces that led up to it, and Schopenhauer's many disciples, especially Nietzsche. They casually ignore an era that Nietzsche described as one in which 'the whole great tendency of the Germans ran counter to the Enlightenment', and in which 'the cult of feeling was erected in place of the cult of reason' (Nietzsche 1968: 84). Similarly, Durkheim commented in 1914 that 'in our time we are witnessing an attack on reason; actually it is an all-out assault' (Durkheim [1913] 1960: 386).

I have suggested in the previous chapters that postmodernism is more an extension of modernity than a genuine reaction against it. By contrast, the previous *fin de siècle* spirit attempted a genuine rebellion against modernity's excessive abstractionism. The crucial distinction between postmodernist pseudo-rebellion and the *fin de siècle* spirit is that the latter glorified feeling and passion even as it noted the benefits of reason. By contrast, postmodernist overemphasis on impulse, play, and feelings are a shallow imitation of the *fin de siècle* spirit. The purpose of the present chapter is to elaborate on this theme.

Compare the first sociology textbook printed in the USA, *Introduction to the Science of Sociology* (1921) by Park and Burgess, with any contemporary sociology textbook. Park and Burgess were educated during the *fin de siècle*, and exemplified the *fin de siècle* spirit in their choice of style, themes, topics, and authors. Thus, they acknowledge the vital importance of irrational forces in social explanations; they address the issue of human nature and how it changes in relation to the social milieu; and they question whether 'progress' really exists and how it can be measured. By contrast, contemporary, postmodernist texts (short on actual text and long on images, of course) hardly mention irrationality, human nature, or the possibility that progress may cause as many problems as it seems to solve. An excellent illustration of this contrast is the treatment of the topic of collective behaviour (riots, fads, crazes, social movements, revolutions, and so on) by Park and Burgess versus postmodern textbook authors. Park and Burgess acknowledge Le Bon's importance in explaining why individuals in crowds sometimes succumb to irrationality, that the individual loses his or her rational restraints to the powers of the 'group mind'. In stark contrast, postmodern authors argue that Le Bon is irrelevant, and that seemingly irrational, wanton, even brutal collective acts (lynchings, riots, executions, and the like) can be explained 'rationally'. For the purposes of the present discussion, one is not interested in which explanation is more adequate. Rather, the important point is that postmodern authors do not even consider explanations that involve the irrational, even though these same authors often purport to rebel at modernist narratives (which are excessively rational), and to be open to alternative narratives.

Or consider how thoroughly the work of Talcott Parsons (1937) eclipsed Pitirim Sorokin's (1957) inductive, empirical theory of social change. Parsons was the supreme postmodern abstractionist, while Sorokin continually emphasized the power of irrational forces. Sorokin (1963) notes in his autobiography that early in his career he had predicted correctly that the present century would be one of wars, revolutions, and much bloodshed as humanity undergoes the death pangs of sensate culture. Despite the obvious validity of many of his predictions, Sorokin has sunk into almost complete obscurity while Parsons's hyper-optimistic theories of rational social action are currently being revived. Again, the essential point is that from a sociology of knowledge perspective applied to sociology itself, Parsons represents the victory of modernity's vicious abstractionism – transformed into postmodernist culture – over Sorokin's typically *fin de siècle* style and content.

One could explain this remarkable obfuscation by noting, again, that an important element of modernity is that it is ruled almost exclusively by the mind at the cost of suppressing, repressing, and otherwise denying the heart. In contradistinction to this modern scenario, it must be remembered that sociology was born in the age of Romanticism and that it paralleled the Romantic movement in literature (see Clark 1975). Even Henri Saint-Simon and Comte, despite their avowed positivism and faith in reason, argued that love was to be the basis of social solidarity in their utopian dream-societies, a point argued convincingly by Robert Carlisle (1988). Sorokin attempted to revive this Romantic emphasis on feeling when he established the Harvard Center for Creative Altruism, and argued that modern societies ought to adopt Christ's teachings from the Sermon on the Mount (see Sorokin 1947). Contemporary sociologists write in the modern vein that has reversed this rule: the mind is more important than the heart, and futuristic visions of societies resemble Orwell's excessively rationalist society more than the Romantic visions.

In their controversial *Primitive Classification*, Durkheim and Mauss ([1902] 1975: 88) concluded that social evolution essentially entails the dissolution of heart into cold-blooded intellectualism (again, a sentiment shared by scores of other *fin de siècle* thinkers):

> Thus the history of scientific classification is, in the last analysis, the history of the stages by which this element of social affectivity has progressively weakened, leaving more and more room for the reflective thought of individuals. But it is not the case that these remote influences which we have just studied have ceased to be felt today. They have left behind them an effect which survives and which is always present; it is the very cadre of all classification, it is the ensemble of mental *habits* by virtue of which we conceive things and facts in the form of co-ordinated or hierarchized groups. (Emphasis added.)

39

Again, Durkheim and Mauss manage to find hope despite their *fin de siècle* pessimism. I have underscored the word 'habits' above, because the concept of habit has been deliberately and systematically eliminated from social scientific discourse since the previous *fin de siècle* (see Camic 1986). The Durkheimians have a point when they insist that our social habits maintain some amount of heart in our modern lives, especially in the form of social rituals. Whether these contemporary rituals involve sporting events, religious services, rock concerts, or even the most mundane rituals involved in following the social norms that rule dining, bathing, socializing, and the like – they tie us to the social affectivity of our ancestors that gave rise to these rituals in the first place.

Here I disagree again with Zijderveld (1979), who understands clichés and routine behaviour as nothing but postmodernist kitsch. On the contrary, habits and rituals are among the few things left in the postmodern world that link us with tradition and non-abstractionist reality. Witness Robert Hertz's (1909) fascinating study of right- and left-handedness in the Durkheimian context of collective representations. Hertz shows that right and left symbolize the sacred and the profane, respectively, in language, politics, gestures, and diverse aspects of behaviour. Each time we extend the right hand in greeting, for example, we are engaged in a habit that binds us to our ancestors, even if we are not aware of it.

T.S. Eliot was one of Durkheim's more important contemporaries who also grasped the importance of ritual in a modern world that was heading ever-faster into abstractionism. Eliot reviewed Durkheim's *Elementary Forms* (an elaboration of the earlier 1902 work on primitive classification with his nephew Marcel Mauss), and may have been influenced by its thesis in writing his famous poem, 'The Wasteland'. In this review, Eliot notes something that has escaped the attention of most of Durkheim's sociological commentators, that 'the savage lives in two worlds, the one commonplace, practical, a world of drudgery, the other sacred, intense, a world into which he escapes at regular intervals, a world in which he is released' (in Menand and Schwartz 1982: 314). Alas, modern persons have the same need to escape into this world of social affect, but according to Durkheim and Eliot, less opportunity, and less awareness of what little opportunity exists. This need may explain the fanaticism exhibited by fans of sporting, music and other events that capture what Durkheim called 'collective effervescence' in postmodern life. There can be no doubt that despite modernity, we have our totems and totemic systems – witness any football game, British or American.

One does not like to belabour the point that Durkheim's commentators have missed this humanistic aspect in Durkheim's works, but it must be stressed, because it is integral to the argument being made here. The bias of modernity has blinded us to the pre-modern forms, rituals, and norms that have survived despite modernity, that can offer us solace, release, and relief. Nietzsche, Durkheim, and their contemporaries were among the last intellectuals to write on the 'cult of feeling' without embarrassment. Today, what Unamuno (1913) calls the new Inquisition of Science would label their concerns and modes of expression as unscientific. Yet, even by today's scientific standards, historical evidence abounds to suggest that Nietzsche and Durkheim were correct in their depictions of the era in which they lived and wrote (see Bailey 1958, Bailey 1988; Baillot 1927; Bloom 1987; Ellenberger 1970; Janik and Toulmin 1973; Lukács 1980; Magee 1983; Meštrović 1988a and b). *Fin de Siècle* writers in diverse fields were expressing various aspects of Romanticism, and they were expressing it with pathos. Consider the works of Tolstoi, Yeats, Hardy, Melville, Mann, Conrad, T.S. Eliot, Proust, and D.H. Lawrence among the artists; Wittgenstein, James, Bergson, Guyau, Lalande, and Nietzsche among the philosophers; and even the precursors of the social sciences, Simmel, Wundt, Ribot, Tönnies, Jung, Pareto, Mosca, Le Bon, and Tarde. Most of them lamented the loss of heart that accompanied so-called progress, and most of them may be considered as Schopenhauer's disciples in some fashion (Magee 1983; Meštrović 1989a).

According to Magee (1983: 284), 'by the turn of the century ... Schopenhauer was an all-pervading cultural influence'. Even those who would argue that Magee's assessment is extreme would find it difficult to deny that Schopenhauer's influence was at least noteworthy, or that it is supported by other notable authors. Thus, Ellenberger (1970: 281) writes: 'It is difficult for us today to imagine the fascination that Schopenhauer's philosophy exerted upon the intellectual elite of that time.' In his neglected *Schopenhauer and Nietzsche*, Georg Simmel ([1907] 1986: 23) supports these assessments when he asserts that 'the absolute preponderance of suffering over happiness in life is the definitive portrait of life's value that gave Schopenhauer's philosophy its general significance and signature'. The important point is that Schopenhauer was a philosopher of the heart who attacked Kant and excessive intellectualism in general. He was Nietzsche's self-acknowledged 'master' until Nietzsche's madness and cynicism became extreme, and Nietzsche turned even on Schopenhauer. Schopenhauer may be considered a symbol of the *fin de siècle* more than Hegel or any other philosopher from the Romantic era (see Durant 1961).

THE RELATIONSHIP BETWEEN DURKHEIM'S SOCIOLOGY AND SCHOPENHAUER'S PHILOSOPHY

Durkheim described well the true reasons for the origins of sociology in his neglected *Socialism and Saint-Simon* (1958: 239):

> What does the development of sociology signify? How does it happen that we experience the need to reflect on social matters, if not because our social state is abnormal, because the unsettled collective organization no longer functions with the authority of instinct?

His comment still applies to the malaise, disorganization, and *anomie* in contemporary, postmodernist social life, despite the fact that, incredibly, some contemporary sociologists would like to drop entirely the concept of anomie and its synonyms from the sociological vocabulary. And what Durkheim wrote about the need to reflect on social matters applies equally to the need to reflect on the status of his thought today. The reaction to him is also abnormal, in that he is criticized severely at the same time that he continues to function as a sort of totem for contemporary sociologists.

Durkheim's sociology is informed, at least indirectly, by Schopenhauer's philosophy, and Schopenhauer's pessimistic philosophy had supplanted the vulgar version of Comte's optimistic positivism at the turn of the century. There is no need to 'prove' any 'direct' influence in this regard, nor would it be possible to offer such 'proof'. Too many authors have noted the significance of Schopenhauer's philosophy for the *fin de siècle* for one to assume that Durkheim could have been immune. John Stuart Mill, who

42

was considered one of Comte's disciples in England for a time, severely criticized Comte and his excessively rationalistic philosophy, and concluded that Comte's writings bore the imprint of his madness (see Mill 1968). Deploige (1911) notes that by the time Durkheim arrived on the scene, Comte's followers had dispersed (even Littre), and sociology had been dormant for thirty years, unable to inspire followers. Bouglé (1896) and Lévy-Bruhl (1903b) concede grudgingly that Comte never had the influence within France nor outside its borders that German Romantic philosophers enjoyed. The current totemic worship of Comte is an ideological invention that betrays more about postmodernity's need for an abstractionist caricature than anything historically accurate about Comte's influence (see also Gouldner 1958).

By contrast, the essence of Schopenhauer's (1818) philosophy, set forth most eloquently in his *World as Will and Representation*, is that the 'will to life' (to which he also referred as the 'heart') is more powerful and more important than the mind or rationality. Humans rationalize, after the fact, what they desired in the first place. Durkheim subscribed to this Schopenhauerian belief – also found independently in Saint-Simon, and later refracted in Nietzsche's writings – in all his major writings, and made it explicit: 'Human deliberations, in fact, so far as reflective consciousness affects them are often only purely formal, with no object but confirmation of a resolve previously formed for reasons unknown to consciousness' (Durkheim [1897] 1951: 297).

Moreover, Durkheim was a dialectician, not a straight-line positivist. The evolution from mechanical to organic solidarity is not a complete, all-or-nothing process. Rather, it involves a tension such that even as we get more modern and more individualistic, there will always remain some remnants of the collective conscience. The fact that some collective affect always remains even within and despite modernity offers hope in the face of gloomy assessments of the sort made by T.S. Eliot. We will always have some things in common, from language to habits that are common to a particular people.

It is interesting that like Nietzsche, Durkheim frequently uses the anti-Enlightenment word 'cult'. A cult carries overtones of religion, sacredness, metaphysics, and above all, feelings. For Durkheim, the sacred appeals to feelings and desires in a spontaneous fashion. Thus, he refers to individualism as a cult of the

43

individual, a new socially instituted 'religion' that will replace traditional religions, and that will break through totalitarian regimes. The many political revolutions against communist regimes that began occurring in the late 1980s seem to vindicate Durkheim's prediction. It seems that an unconscious narrative of individual freedom and democracy is an integral part of modernization. Ironically, postmodernist authors rebel at all Western narratives, presumably even against this democractic one, under the guise that all narratives must be oppressive.

But Durkheim contrasts sharply this cult of the individual with mere egoism, anomie, narcissism, and other varieties of 'lower' individualism (see Meštrović 1988a). For Durkheim as for Schopenhauer, egoism is a state in which the unfettered, modern will tramples on the 'will to life' of other persons due to a lack of compassion. Durkheim felt that the process of modernization would lead to increased individualism conceived of as this benign, 'higher', irrational 'cult of the individual' *as well as* the cancerous egoism and anomie. This complexity in Durkheim's thought has been missed completely by writers who start with the premiss that he was a 'pure mind' positivist. It is high time one appreciates the fact that Durkheim was a Romantic who wrote in the *fin de siècle* spirit of his times.

Still another level of depth and complexity that Durkheim brings to these issues, a level that leads to comparing him with the literary giants of his era, is that he does not condemn egoism or anomie completely. In *Suicide* especially, but also throughout his writings, Durkheim refers to anomie as an indispensable aspect of the 'spirit of progress'. Without anomie, one would not question tradition, and progress would be stifled. A little anomie is good for a person and a person's society, although it is not clear at what point anomie becomes excessive in Durkheim's scheme of things. Anomie is an integral aspect of modernity, because it signifies change.

Finally, it is fascinating that regarding his use of both the terms 'cult of the individual' and anomie, Durkheim was refracting traditional religious beliefs at the same time that he was being highly innovative. The obviously religious overtones of the term 'cult' have been mentioned, but it is also important to note that the term *anomie* is similar to the word *anomia* which was used to translate various words for 'sin' by St Jerome and others (see

Meštrović 1985). Thus, neither individualism nor anomie are something bland and rational for Durkheim. In using the concept of anomie, Durkheim did not intend Merton's (1957) meaning of 'normlessness' – a word that Durkheim never used in any case, and that is loaded with Enlightenment assumptions of rational social order and control (see Meštrović and Brown 1985). Rather, the concepts anomie and 'higher' individualism, as used by Durkheim, immediately invoke the 'cult of feeling', because both resonate with collective representations that humankind has constructed to express some of its most basic and essential needs.

To phrase the matter differently, Durkheim was echoing Baudelaire's influential thesis that evil (anomie) is seductive, and in this regard, Baudelaire himself was following in the wake of Schopenhauer's discourse on evil as a state of the unfettered will. (The most current extension of Baudelaire's thesis is Katz's 1988 *Seductions of Crime*.) One does not turn to crime out of Merton's (1957) bland 'normlessness', but because one derives some degree of satisfaction and pleasure from crime. It is not enough to formulate hypotheses and test them empirically (with the aim of 'falsifying' them) to be faithful to the *fin de siècle* spirit that gave birth to sociology. It is also important to be sensitive to the continuities between sociology and the irrational aspects of Western culture as a whole. This is evident especially in Schopenhauer's philosophy, which he explicitly aligned with the pessimism and passion he believed was inherent in Christian religions and Western culture in general. (Of course, Schopenhauer also made conceptual linkages between Christianity and Hinduism, Buddhism, and other religious, philosophical systems as well, but that is beyond the scope of the present discussion.)

THE CONTRAST BETWEEN THE CULTURAL CONTEXT IN WHICH DURKHEIM LIVED AND POSTMODERN CULTURE

Consider, however briefly, the other great intellectuals and artists who wrote in Durkheim's time, from Baudelaire to Jung. If Durkheim's sociology does not fit easily into the spirit of modern positivism, it certainly dovetails nicely into the *fin de siècle* concerns of his contemporaries. The concept of anomie and its equivalents fascinated *fin de siècle* intellectuals and artists because anomie is an inevitable byproduct of modernization, and because it is exacerbated by so-called rational progress. Consider, for example, the extraordinary similarities to Durkheim's observations concerning anomie found in the following passage from Ralph Waldo Emerson, despite the fact that Emerson never used the word anomie explicitly:

> In our large cities, the population is godless, materialized – no bond, no fellow-feeling, no enthusiasm. These are not men, but hungers, thirsts, fevers, and appetites walking. How is it people manage to live on – so aimless as they are?.... It seems as if the lime in their bones alone held them together, and not any worthy purpose. There is no faith in the intellectual, none in the moral universe. There is faith in chemistry, in meat, and wine, in wealth, in machinery, in the steam engine, galvanic battery, turbine wheels, sewing machines, and in public opinion, but not in divine causes.
>
> (Emerson 1960: 204).

It is a mistake to conclude that because Durkheim's contemporaries did not use the word anomie explicitly, they were not concerned with the perceptions that gave rise to the concept of anomie in the first place. The *fin de siècle* stands out in the history of humankind as the era in which anomie was perceived more powerfully than in any other.

Thus, in his *France, Fin de Siècle*, Eugen Weber (1987) explains that intellectuals in that era thought that their civilization was decadent, and just like the Roman Empire folded, many thought that Western civilization was about to collapse. (Of course, Pitirim Sorokin formalized this sentiment, shared by Spengler.) The problems that the French and other Europeans perceived in the *fin de siècle* are remarkably similar to our own. Syphilis, wars, political scandals, economic catastrophes, the increase in rates of mental illness, suicide, smoking, and drug abuse concerned them. They read in their newspapers about satanism, devil worship, and the spread of the occult, and of course, our media is saturated with similar reports. They started talking about the rise of homosexuality – lesbianism became almost a fad. Sado-masochism was much discussed, and they wrote much about the rise of immorality in the family, in sexual relations, and the general style of life. The

46

fin de siècle was not a docile, sterile, Victorian era as it is sometimes depicted. Rather, it was an era of perceived explosions in the amount of sexual licence, vice, and crime – in a word, phenomena that Durkheim discussed under the rubric of anomie – and people were troubled by these developments. The concern with immorality became so widespread that Durkheim's efforts to establish a science of morality seemed to be a natural response, well in keeping with similar efforts on the part of his distinguished colleagues, Bergson (1932), Lévy-Bruhl (1905), Simmel (1893), Wundt (1907), and others.

In his *Two Sources of Morality and Religion* (1932), Henri Bergson, who was Durkheim's colleague at the Sorbonne, picked up where Durkheim left off in relation to these *fin de siècle* concerns. Bergson's central thesis, all but forgotten today, was that morality based on rationality is inadequate, because it was rationality that brought on the immorality of the *fin de siècle* in the first place. The other and more adequate source for morality, for Bergson, was to be the heart: passion, feeling, and irrationalism. Lucien Lévy-Bruhl, also Durkheim's colleague at the Sorbonne and eventual disciple, preceded Bergson's thesis by many years in his *Ethics and Moral Science* (1905). Along the lines of Schopenhauer (1841), Durkheim, Lévy-Bruhl, and Bergson were seeking the sources for a new morality *not* in positivism, but in irrationalism – the very opposite of today's efforts to place morality in the context of cognitive and rational development, exemplified by Kohlberg, Piaget, and Habermas.

Consider Charles Dickens's classic *A Christmas Carol*, representative of his many novels that focused on the theme of compassion in the midst of a seemingly heartless, anomic world. The essential message of Dickens's classic is that Scrooge has to learn compassion. To appreciate how removed our postmodern age has become from the *fin de siècle* concerns that gave rise to this character, simply compare the original black and white version of the film based on this book with the 1988 film version entitled 'Scrooged'. The 1988 Scrooge is not portrayed as having a problem with the fact that he lacks compassion. Rather, his problem is merely that he is rude to everyone – a typically postmodern problem, right out of Riesman's (1950) descriptions of other-directedness. In other words, the postmodernist Scrooge is 'not nice', and he has to learn how to 'have fun'. Gone is the heart-wrenching agony of the original Scrooge who had to arrive at the insight that he had lost his heart for the sake of success. No such serious, moral message marks the modern version of this nor most other postmodernist re-makes of *fin de siècle* works. To repeat, postmodernism perpetuates modernity's vicious abstractionism, and does not really rebel against it.

Along these lines, Victor Hugo's *Les Misérables* (revived in 1989 as a popular Broadway play) takes up the Schopenhauerian theme of compassion from a Romantic perspective. Baillot (1927) is probably correct that Hugo was one of many artists who prepared French consciousness to be receptive to Schopenhauer's philosophy, which was immensely popular among French intellectuals from 1880 to the turn of the century. (And Baudelaire discusses Hugo and Delacroix in the context of modernity as well.) Again, the immense popularity of Hugo's classic bespeaks the receptivity of the popular consciousness at that time to the idea that a compassionate heart was to be valued over rationality or success, an idea that would draw cynical snickers today if portrayed in the same way.

Among the precursors of the social sciences, one finds many intellectuals taking sides with the 'heart' side of the heart–mind dualism, at the same time that they criticized the anomic, heartless aspects of modernization. The most striking example is Tönnies's *Community and Society* (1887) in which he romanticizes the past and condemns the future that he felt would be characterized by the 'rational will' of *Gesellschaft*. Without using the word anomie, Tönnies portrays modern *Gesellschaft* in a manner that is commensurate with Durkheim's (1893) explicit linkage between anomie and the progress of the division of labour.

Across the Atlantic, William James distinguished between the 'once born' and the 'twice born' in his *Varieties of Religious Experience* (1902). The 'once born' are the rationalist, bourgeois, modern optimists who live a life of superficial decadence without ever realizing it. James's portrait of the 'once born' resonates with Durkheim's portrait of the anomie egoist, Baudelaire's dandy, and Riesman's superficial, other-directed type. By contrast, the 'twice born' see through the hypocrisy and emptiness of modern life, and must pass through an 'abyss' of emotional anguish that sometimes takes up a good portion of their lives, a period of intense pessimism, irrationality, and neurosis. But once they emerge, the 'twice born', while not necessarily less pessimistic than before, are motivated by a spirit of genuine compassion for the suffering of others.

Nietzsche's attack on rationality is well-known, although Bloom (1987) is correct that even Nietzsche has been bastardized by modernity into a kind of rationalist. According to Nietzsche, who was Schopenhauer's most famous disciple, (1968: 42):

> In the great whirlpool of forces man stands with the conceit that this whirlpool is rational and has a rational aim: an error! The only rational thing we know is what little reason man has.... One might invent such a fable [of rationalism] and still not have illustrated sufficiently how wretched, how shadowy and flighty, how aimless and arbitrary, the human intellect appears in nature. There have been eternities when it did not exist; and when it is done for again, nothing will have happened. For this intellect has no further mission that would lead beyond human life. It is human, rather, and only its owner and producer gives it such importance, as if the world pivoted around it. But if we could communicate with the mosquito, then we would learn that it floats through the air with the same self-importance, feeling within itself the flying center of the world.

Nietzsche is essentially correct: irrationality has been with humanity far longer than rationality, and governs far more of its behaviour. His message is typical of the *fin de siècle*, but it is still subject to great controversy and disagreement in interpretation. For example, Sloterdijk (1987) and Habermas (1987) read Nietzsche as a cynic, whereas Durkheim (1950) read him as a German Romantic who allowed for the pure perception of truth through artistic visions even if not through rationalilty. I shall have more to say on this in chapter 3.

Tolstoi was also a great admirer of Schopenhauer, according to Magee (1983). Tolstoi's *Anna Karenina* is a novel about a rich, conceited, aristocratic lady who ends up committing suicide after not being able to find satisfaction in her rational, bourgeois life. In fact, Anna is another excellent illustration of Durkheim's anomic type of person, whose decadence leads to suicide, as well as a female version of Baudelaire's decadent dandy. Again, contrast Tolstoi's depiction with the postmodernist film about suicide entitled *Ordinary People*. The family portrayed in this film seems to suffer more from the stigma of not being as 'nice' as the other middle-class families than from the suicidogenetic forces that are operating within it. Similarly, the mark of Schopenhauer on Herman Melville is found in works as seemingly diverse as *Moby Dick*, 'Bartleby the Scrivener', 'Billy Budd', and *The Confidence Man*, among others. In these works Melville displays a Schopenhauerian pessimism and concern with the irrational that finally spills over into a deep-seated cynicism in his last great novel, *The Confidence Man*. Rochberg-Halton (1986) offers an interesting interpretation of *Moby Dick* as a condemnation of modernity: Ahab represents the anomic, modern egoist who is obsessed in his quest to kill the great white whale, and who loses all traces of compassion and humanity as a result of this obsession.

Thomas Mann (1939) wrote plainly about his high admiration for Schopenhauer, as well as Schopenhauer's far-reaching influence on other *fin de siècle* artists. Consider Mann's 'Death in Venice' as an illustration of this *fin de siècle* spirit. It is about an artist who is famous and old, on vacation in Venice. All his life he had been the modern artist – abstract, rational, cold and calculating, not to mention comfortable. But Mann portrays this old artist in Venice as falling in love suddenly and uncontrollably with a boy in a homosexual manner and dying from the plague. Mann's story is a severe and not so subtle indictment of the modern artist, but most of Mann's novels harp on a similar theme.

Joseph Conrad's *Heart of Darkness*, which was incidentally the model for the popular movie *Apocalypse Now*, is also an expression of Schopenhauerian pessimism. T.S. Eliot's 'The Wasteland', D.H. Lawrence's many novels, Hermann Hesse's *Steppenwolf* and *Siddartha*, among many others, are all excellent illustrations of the *fin de siècle* disenchantment with and severe indictment of modern, rational, bourgeois morality (discussed in Magee 1983). It is interesting that the essential traits of Hesse's *Steppenwolf*, a rootlessness and alienation from others characteristic of the wolf of the steppes, have been reproduced unwittingly in many cartoon characters used for the entertainment and indoctrination of contemporary children into modernity. Does not *Steppenwolf* fit accurately the portraits of Bugs Bunny, Daffy Duck, Porky Pig, and other rootless, asocial cartoon heroes? The cynicism expressed by these cartoon characters is actually quite severe, as illustrated by the popular 1988 film *Who Framed Roger Rabbit?*, a film that pushed the decadent aspects of Bugs Bunny and his friends to their extremes.

I have by no means exhausted the list of examples, but such an undertaking would take me too far astray from my aims in this book. Nevertheless, if we examine the truly dominant themes for intellectuals and artists in Durkheim's time, historical and primary source evidence abounds to suggest that they revolved around a Romantic, Schopenhauerian, *fin de siècle* spirit of pessimism and disenchantment with the beginnings of modernity (see Baillot 1927; Ellenberger 1970; Janik and Toulmin 1973; Magee 1983). This does not mean that the *fin de siècle* was immune to optimism, only that the 'great works' from that era are decidedly pessimistic.

In sum, Schopenhauer's 1818 thesis that the 'will to life' (passion, feeling, and desire) is exacerbated by enlightenment, progress, and modernity finally took root in Western consciousness starting in the 1860s, and reached its zenith in the 1880s. Durkheim's concept of anomie as a state of 'infinite desires' seems to be a refraction of this Schopenhauerian depiction of the infinitely striving will. For Durkheim, anomie is an inevitable aspect of modernization, and despite the fact that he acknowledged some of its benefits (all questioning of tradition involves some degree of anomie), he condemned it overall as a state of immoral *dérèglement* (see Meštrović 1988a). Other intellectual and literary giants from the *fin de siècle* seem to have mirrored Schopenhauer's and Durkheim's concerns despite the fact that they did not use the word anomie explicitly. Finally, the postmodernist narrative of rebellion against narrative has distorted the import of these *fin de siècle* intellectuals. Along with Durkheim and Schopenhauer, the works of Tolstoi, Dickens, Melville, and other *fin de siècle* geniuses, when confronted at all, are distorted into a bland, 'fun' version of the serious messages they were proposing.

REDISCOVERING DURKHEIM IN HIS PROPER HISTORICAL AND SOCIAL CONTEXT

Like his contemporaries, Durkheim took sides with the 'heart' side of the heart–mind dualism. Indeed, it would be difficult to explain his meteoric rise to fame had he clung to Comte's, Kant's, or other decaying rationalisms in his milieu. (By the same token,

Durkheim would probably remain an obscure failure had he used that same *fin de siècle* style in today's postmodernist milieu.) The problem is that our postmodernist age has repressed and denied the reality of the *fin de siècle*, and has conceitedly falsified history. This does not stem from dishonest intentions on the part of individual authors, but from the tendency of postmodernity to use history without context or regard for truth (Calinescu 1987). Thus, really to understand Durkheim, one has to start with the premiss that he was writing in the *fin de siècle* spirit that drew its sustenance from the cult of feeling.

This new starting point in apprehending Durkheim in no way negates his scientific bent, nor his penchant for empiricism. It is a commonplace error to align empiricism with positivism when, in fact, as Thomas Mann (1939) has argued, Schopenhauer was the real father of empirical social science. In a word, empiricism is really far more irrational than rational. Schopenhauer criticized Kant's apriorism as being incompatible with empiricism because it deduces propositions from the 'mind' instead of starting with inductive, perceptual data. Even Comte's positivism is more rationalistic than empirical, more philosophy than fact. Empiricism holds affinities with irrationalism and the 'heart', *not* rationalism, as Lalande ([1926] 1980) and many other *fin de siècle* philosophers have argued.

Harry Alpert (1960: 972) captures this complex facet of Durkheim's influence when he writes that

> Even Madison Avenue would have had difficulty projecting the proper image of Émile Durkheim. For Durkheim's complex personality was, in fact, a blending of at least two different images. One is the image of the serious, austere, forbidding, unsmiling scientist and professor who insists on rigorous application of logical reasoning and on strict methodological procedures. The other image, equally valid, is that of the fervent prophet and social critic, the passionate moralist, the intense patriot, and the ardent philosopher seeking truth with reason and clarity.

The *fin de siècle* spirit can be used to explain this apparent paradox about Durkheim. Turn of the century intellectuals, from Schopenhauer to Thomas Mann, regarded the intellect as the product of the 'heart', not the other way around. Thus, Durkheim's austere rationalism was fuelled by a passion and pathos that he betrays in his writings again and again. Were Madison Avenue to sell Durkheim today, they would have to depict his respect for science as a derivative of the cult of feeling. Madison Avenue wouldn't touch such a project.

Chapter Four

SIMMEL AND DURKHEIM AS THE FIRST SOCIOLOGISTS OF MODERNITY

Throughout this book, we are seeking the *fin de siècle* alternatives to Enlightenment versus postmodernist cynicism and nihilism. The sociologies of Georg Simmel and Émile Durkheim constitute important instances of these alternatives.

As mentioned previously, Frisby (1986) labels Simmel as the first sociologist of modernity because of Simmel's emphasis on constant change, flux, and the infinite restlessness of 'life' as the hallmarks of what has come to be called modernity. But if Simmel was the first, then Durkheim was certainly the second sociologist of modernity. These conceptual linkages between and among Durkheim, Simmel, and modernity are not common knowledge, yet they can be substantiated, and they lead to important consequences in apprehending the origins of the concept of modernity. Out of all of Durkheim's contemporaries, Simmel is the most important for the purposes of the present discussion. And French Romanticism, which gave birth to French sociology from Saint-Simon to Durkheim, was derived from German Romanticism, beginning with Goethe (see Clark 1975). Thus, by emphasizing the affinities between Durkheim's French, philosophically informed sociology and Simmel's German, philosophically informed sociology, one may hope to arrive at a clearer, or at least newer, understanding of the antecedents, nature, and consequences of modernity (and by implication, of postmodernity as well).

Simon Deploige (1911) argued long ago that Durkheim's sociology is more essentially German and Romantic than French and rationalist, but his argument is marred by his overall aim to demonstrate that Durkheim's thought is inferior to the Catholic dogma of St Thomas Aquinas. And Deploige (1911) has been

54

ignored in any event. Nevertheless, Deploige preceded Bloom (1987) in arguing for the importance of *fin de siècle* German culture. Indeed, it is important to appreciate that the Germans began the revolt against 'pure mind' sooner than any other group of European intellectuals.

Bloom (1987) could be accused of closing prematurely the very discussion he thus opens because he, like the professors he criticizes, does not dig deeply enough into the philosophical underpinnings of the thinkers he treats, and omits a host of others. For example, Bloom focuses on Schopenhauer's disciple Nietzsche without paying sufficient attention to Schopenhauer, and he does not even mention Georg Simmel, Émile Durkheim, William James, or Ferdinand Tönnies! This is shocking. Bloom goes so far as to claim that 'with the possible exception of Weber and Freud, there are no social science books that can be said to be classic' (1987: 345). This is clearly a false and unfair conclusion.

Out of the many thinkers that Bloom omits, Simmel and Durkheim deserve special attention. David Frisby (1984, 1986) and Michael Kaern (1985) have already delineated several areas of convergence between Simmel and the Durkheimians. Durkheim's disciple, Célestin Bouglé, carried on an extensive correspondence with Simmel. Also, in his neglected *Les Sciences sociales en Allemagne* (1896) Bouglé devotes a chapter to Simmel's attempt to establish the scientific study of morality, a project that Durkheim imitated in France. In the concluding chapter of this obscure 1896 book, Bouglé suggests parallels between Durkheim's and Simmel's efforts in the field of ethics that stop short of suggesting that Durkheim stole his ideas from Simmel. It should be noted that Deploige (1911) accuses Durkheim bluntly of stealing Simmel's ideas in this regard.

Michael Kaern (1985) links Simmel and Durkheim with Vaihinger's (1924) 'as if' philosophy as well as the founders of *Volkerpsychologie*, Lazarus, Steinthal, and Wundt. These constitute important conceptual linkages between these two sociological giants. When Durkheim visited Germany in 1885, it is known that he travelled to Berlin, but it has not been documented whether he met Simmel. Durkheim certainly knew of Simmel's works, because he reviewed him in *L'Année sociologique* – usually negatively – but Simmel simply ignored Durkheim (a situation somewhat analogous to the 'mutual unawareness' of Durkheim and Max

55

Weber as discussed by Tiryakian 1966).

As one traces the intellectual affinities between Simmel and Durkheim back through succeeding waves of German Romanticism, Baudelaire's influence on both sociologists, and the 'folk psychology' of Lazarus, Steinthal, and Wundt, one finally arrives at Schopenhauer and Nietzsche – in a sense, the two end-points of German Romanticism. Simmel wrote a book in 1907 entitled *Schopenhauer and Nietzsche*, in which he pinpoints the importance of *fin de siècle* philosophy – especially the divergence between Schopenhauer and Nietzsche, despite their overall affinity – to the origins of the social sciences, but this work has been almost completely ignored until very recently. It was not translated into English until 1986. In a 1987 review of this translation, Frisby finally notes the need to examine further the linkages between Simmel's philosophical sociology and Schopenhauer's philosophy. The same need exists with regard to Durkheim.

Simmel ([1907] 1986: 22) wrote that humans are simultaneously citizens of two worlds, the phenomenal world and the world of the thing-in-itself, but that the latter is the stronger and more important force – a clear refraction of Schopenhauer, Nietzsche, and the many German Romanticists who fall between them. Durkheim made much the same assertion in his review (1889) of Tönnies's *Community and Society* (1887).

I will continue to place more emphasis on Schopenhauer than Nietzsche, for the simple reason that Nietzsche is widely regarded as Schopenhauer's disciple (see Magee 1983) despite their differences, and because Nietzsche represents the cynicism that marked the end of an era that Schopenhauer launched (Sloterdijk 1987). Furthermore, Simmel ([1907] 1986: 13) asserted that Schopenhauer 'is without a doubt a greater philosopher than Nietzsche'.

Simmel captures the general significance of Schopenhauer's philosophy for the intellectual climate as well as the social state of his times when he writes in his *Schopenhauer and Nietzsche* that (53):

> With some few exceptions, which amount really to a *quantité négligeable*, all philosophers prior to Schopenhauer conceived of man as a rational being.... During the past several dozen years, the absolute preponderance of suffering over happiness in life is the definitive portrait of life's value that gave Schopenhauer's

philosophy its general significance and signature, with respect to the *culture of emotion*. Schopenhauer made suffering into the absolute substance of emotionally experienced existence and did so against a manifold of pessimistic interpretations which declared the world to be a vale of tears, life not to be worth living, and happiness a passing dream: he made suffering into an a priori definition that grows out of the central roots of our existence, and made sure that none of its fruits could be of a different essence. (Emphasis added.)

Clearly, Simmel treats Schopenhauer's philosophy as a kind of symbol for and concentrated expression of this extensive *fin de siècle* pessimism. In *Suicide*, Durkheim ([1897] 1951: 370) also refers to Schopenhauer's philosophy as a symbol for the *fin de siècle* in which he lived. Good reasons exist for pessimism, according to Schopenhauer's philosophy, and both Simmel and Durkheim are aware of them. Schopenhauer's 'will to life' is an entity of 'boundlessness', and it is 'infinity within us' (Simmel [1907] 1986: 26). It is 'like a fuel that energizes the most different kinds of machines', but that never runs out of energy (25). Moreover, heightened rationality is like throwing more fuel on to the raging fire of the will, because Schopenhauer felt that knowledge and consciousness also stem from the will. Thus, Simmel (43) is quite correct to conclude that for Schopenhauer, 'humanity, which is the locus of the highest consciousness, is the arena for the maximum increase of a self-devouring will whose unity excludes the possibility that it could ever achieve satisfaction'. In fact, 'all being is sentenced by the oneness of will to finding always only itself and never satisfaction' (45). The parallels with Durkheim's notion of anomie as the 'infinity of desires' are obvious and have already been documented (see Meštrović 1988a).

In sum, Simmel betrays his own complex attitude towards heightened rationality that produces, paradoxically, heightened irrationality as a symptom of modernity ([1907] 1986: 29):

Rejecting eighteenth-century rationalism and its esteem for consciousness, the nineteenth century values being as our immediate reality and considers consciousness one of its accidental and sporadic powers, a flickering light that does not even symbolize a continuity with being that would make being accountable to it. This shift in accent is as pronounced in some of the romantic and mystical tendencies of the century as it is in the materialistic and historicizing trends. In Schopenhauer's metaphysics of the will, there is an irrepressible feeling that we are assured of being in a manner diverse from conscious recognition. Thus, rationalism – which was dethroned by Kant in the special area of epistemology and was replaced by experience as the sole bearer of the possibility of cognizing reality – loses with Schopenhauer its hold on a total view of man.

In these regards, one should note Durkheim's own efforts to 'renovate' rationalism in the face of a similar recognition that traditional rationalism had been forever dethroned by pragmatism and other modern irrationalisms.

Without a doubt, the concept of 'life' is central to all of Simmel's works. It is a remarkably faithful reflection of Schopenhauer's 'will to life' as well as Nietzsche's 'cult of feeling'. Thus, Simmel (1971: 379) writes that 'Life cannot obtain any meaning and purpose from beyond itself. It will always grasp its own will though it be disguised in a thousand forms.' He adds that 'it is the essence of life to generate its guidance, salvation, opposition, victories, and victims'. In some instances he seems to echo Nietzsche's philosophy, which posits a Dionysian force that breaks through Apollonian forms, as when Simmel (391) writes: 'Life can express itself and realize its freedom only through forms; yet forms must also necessarily suffocate life and obstruct freedom.' But ultimately, Simmel sides more with Schopenhauer's version, as when he concludes that 'whenever life expresses itself, it desires to express only itself; thus it breaks through any form which would be superimposed on it by some other reality' (382). Like Durkheim and Schopenhauer, Simmel seems to believe that society is the ultimate 'objectification' of 'life' in modern times: 'Mankind has created association as its general form of life' (Simmel 1971: 36).

The importance of these moves by Simmel and Durkheim is that they betray a German, Romantic understanding of society as a force *sui generis* that exists independently of the human agent. This understanding rests on the social realism cited by Bouglé (1896) and Deploige (1911), and criticized by Lukes (1985). This conceptualization of society is thoroughly non-modern, poorly understood, and still largely ignored in contemporary sociology.

Contemporary sociology prefers the postmodern version of society as something that can be reduced to the subjective views of its individual members.

For Schopenhauer, the 'will to life' is portrayed as existing prior to and independently of human conceptions and representations, what Simmel called 'forms' and Durkheim called 'representations'. The 'will to life' wills itself into a myriad of 'ideas', but always without rational aim or purpose on the part of human agents. The 'will to life' wills itself *through* human agents and their subsequent rationalizations. But for Schopenhauer, the will is fundamentally free of utilitarian calculation and rational goals. Simmel's and Schopenhauer's characterizations of 'life' are essentially similar to Freud's notion that we are all 'lived' at the same time that we live, as well as Durkheim's fundamental thesis that society acts through individuals, sometimes without their full, conscious awareness of this influence.

In his essay, 'Eros, Platonic and Modern', Simmel (1971: 235) makes explicit his anti-Enlightenment focus on the passions as a force stronger and more important than the rational mind:

> The history of philosophy reveals the peculiar and not particularly praiseworthy fact that its claim to provide a deeper estimation of life has been left unfulfilled with respect to a number of the most important and problematic elements of life. Apart from occasional observations, philosophy has nothing to tell us about the concept of fate; nothing on the enigmatic structure of what we call 'experience'; nothing, before Schopenhauer, about the deep meaning which happiness and suffering have for life insofar as this meaning is morally significant. Perhaps the most neglected of all the great vital issues has been love – as though this were an incidental matter, a mere adventure of the subjective soul, unworthy of the seriousness and rigorous objectivity of philosophical endeavor.... Were they [philosophers] actually to do their job properly – something for which there is still no better description than the somewhat old-fashioned expression, wisdom about life – and thus rank their labours according to the potency of life's elements, the preponderance of these labours would most surprisingly have to shift to the question of the meaning which love has for the soul, for fate, and for being.

So many years after Simmel wrote the lines above, it is still true that any attempt to bring the concept of love into sociological discourse is bound to be met with the cynicism so aptly described by Sloterdijk, as if one is going to say something 'silly' and non-scholarly, as in love songs. In everyday modern culture, if one is overcome with tears from love or compassion, one is told 'to get a grip', and this still applies especially to males. If the topic of love is to be admitted into social scientific discourse, it must be subsumed under a rubric like the current 'sociology of emotions', which still ignores Simmel's anti-Enlightenment sentiments, and suffers from excessive positivism. Meanwhile, even though the open expression of sentimental love is suppressed in abstractionist modernity, it finds continuous expression in 'love songs', which, in keeping with the commercial tendency of postmodernism, change week to week. Moreover, Simmel posits a dualistic quality to 'love' as being simultaneously virtuous and destructive, 'higher' and 'lower' much like Freud's dualistic Eros and Durkheim's dualistic *homo duplex* (discussed in Meštrović 1982). According to Simmel (1971: 16), 'we must conceive of all these polar differentiations as of *one* life'. By contrast, postmodernist culture paints a blandly happy face on all love.

A Schopenhauerian scholar will spot immediately the similarity between Simmel's sentiments and choice of words in the long passage quoted above concerning the modern suppression of Eros, and Schopenhauer's admonishment to philosophers concerning love in his famous 'Metaphysics of Sexual Love' (an essay that influenced Freud and the novels of D.H. Lawrence especially, discussed in Magee 1983). Thus, Schopenhauer writes ([1818] 1969b: 531):

We are accustomed to see the poets mainly concerned with describing sexual love. As a rule, this is the principal theme of all dramatic works, tragedies as well as comedies, romantic as well as classical, Indian as well as European.... Therefore, after what has here been recalled, we cannot doubt either the reality or the importance of the matter [of love], and so ... we should be surprised that a matter that generally plays so important a part in the life of man has hitherto been almost entirely disregarded by philosophers, and lies before us as a raw and untreated material.

Schopenhauer goes on to argue that the deepest and most lasting love is not the love of like for like, but the love between complementary opposites – a self-conscious and clear echo of Plato's famous parable.

Similarly, Durkheim takes as his starting point in his *Division of Labor* (1893) this German idea found in Schopenhauer and Simmel that the complementary love of opposites between the sexes serves as the model for the deeply unifying forces of organic solidarity that bind together diverse individuals in contemporary societies! Durkheim's apparently paradoxical view stands in stark contradistinction to the Parsonian notion of 'normative consensus'. For Durkheim, the more primitive mechanical solidarity is based on kinship and affection of like for like, on similarities (akin to the Parsonian normative consensus), yet it falls apart easily (see also Halbwachs 1958). But organic solidarity is the more powerful 'glue' that holds societies together, because it is based on diversity, complementarity, and individualism – the erotic attraction of dissimilar individuals.

Similarly, Simmel claims that society is unified even by antagonism, opposition, and heterogeneity, the 'other' sides of 'love'. He is expressing something that bears more resemblance to Schopenhauer's dualistic 'will' and Durkheim's enigmatic pronouncements on organic solidarity than anything like functionalism or other current teleologies. To repeat, the 'will to life' is far removed from utilitarianism, rational goals, and teleologies (see Simmel 1986: 49–51). Simmel's notion of 'life constantly moves between these two tendencies (the positive and negative).... It makes the unity, which after all comprises both contrasts, alive in each of these contrasts and in their juncture' (Simmel 1971: 16). This is another important intellectual affinity shared by Simmel and Durkheim.

Simmel's 'life' behaves like an agent within the human agent, much like Freud's 'instincts' and Durkheim's 'representations'. As objectifications of the will (an idea that began with Hegel), these phenomena are not subject to utilitarian calculation on the part of the mind. Rather, Simmel's 'life' seems to rule the mind even if the mind believes in the illusion that it is the superintendent of motives. For Simmel, especially, 'life' acts with disregard not only for the rationally chosen ends of human agents, but towards its own forms, its own products: 'Every goal or end of the will that actually is achieved can only be a point of transition and never a final destination, because the will is self-identical in all things and in all moments of life: when one reaches a goal one is received by oneself' (Simmel 1986: 49). In terms of life and forms, according to Simmel, 'life, as we have said, can manifest itself only in particular forms; yet, owing to its essential restlessness, life constantly struggles against its own products, which have become fixed and do not move along with it' (Simmel 1971: 376).

Contemporary theorists have not incorporated Simmel's dualistic version of modernity (and by extension, postmodernity), in which the surface restlessness of life opposes permanent and fixed forms. In many versions of modernity – including postmodernism – there is nothing 'underneath' the appearances of life. This applies especially to vulgar versions of pragmatism, which Durkheim criticized.

Moreover, Simmel believed that this chronic conflict between form and life – seemingly a refraction of Schopenhauer's conflict between will and idea – even though it has become acute in many historical epochs, is the most basic theme of modern culture (Simmel 1971: 393). Here is another version of 'civilization and its discontents', and it is founded on the same Schopenhauerian basis that informs Freud's (1930), Tönnies's (1887), Durkheim's (1893), Masaryk's (1883), and a host of other versions of the same theme. The basic Schopenhauerian principle is this: Enlightenment does not abate the power of the 'will to life', but instead expands its horizon of desires. Knowledge unleashes the previously somewhat restrained or at least primitive and complacent will. Schopenhauer was fond of quoting Ecclesiastes I, 18 in this regard, that 'He who increaseth knowledge, increaseth sorrow', and of pointing out that contrary to the Enlightenment, the history of Western culture has always been characterized by an ambivalence towards progress. To repeat, Durkheim's characterization of anomie as a state of unlimited desires exacerbated by enlightenment also rests on this Schopenhauerian, Western understanding of human nature.

SIMMEL'S AND DURKHEIM'S EPISTEMOLOGIES BASED ON THE CULT OF FEELING

Simmel's *Philosophy of Money* (1978) – which, incidentally, Durkheim had reviewed and criticized – begins with an epistemological critique of naive realism that parallels Durkheim's own critique in *Sociology and Philosophy* ([1924] 1974), and especially the opening moves of Schopenhauer's (1818) *World as Will and Representation*. Thus, Simmel (1978: 103) writes that science 'has abandoned the search for the essence of things and is reconciled to stating the relationships that exist between objects and the human mind from the viewpoint of the human mind'. Compare Simmel's claim with Schopenhauer's ([1818] 1969a: 1) dramatic opening lines to his *World as Will and Representation*:

'The world is my idea': This is a truth which holds good for everything that lives and knows, though man alone can bring it into reflective and abstract consciousness. If he really does this, he has attained to philosophical wisdom. It then becomes clear and certain to him that what he knows is not a sun and an earth; that the world which surrounds him is there only as idea, i.e., only in relation to something else, the consciousness, which is himself.... No truth therefore is more certain, more independent of all others, and less in need of proof than this, that all that exists of knowledge, and therefore this whole world, is only object in relation to subject, perception of a perceiver, in a word, idea.

Clearly, for both Schopenhauer and Simmel, the notion that an 'objective' reality can exist completely independently of the passionate human subject is a contradiction, an impossibility. The same is true for Durkheim ([1895] 1982: 34), who had insisted that he 'had expressly stated and reiterated in every way possible that social life was made up entirely of representations'.

Thus, for Simmel, Durkheim, and many of their contemporaries, 'reality' can be known only as a representation. Nevertheless, unlike William James and some pragmatists, modernists, and postmodernists (for this complex discussion, see Rochberg-Halton 1986), Simmel does not opt for the extreme cultural relativism position characteristic of modernity in which the 'reality', Kant's thing-in-itself or noumenon, is completely abandoned.

63

Neither Simmel nor Durkheim opt for epistemological nihilism. Instead, Simmel believes that 'all this, even if carried to its conclusion, would still allow, or even require, a fixed point, an absolute truth' (Simmel 1978: 103). In a way, this is like Schopenhauer's claim that the 'will' is the 'other side' of the representation, hence simultaneously permanent and relative, object *and* subject. Simmel believed that any other stance with regard to the relativity of truth leads to a 'vicious circle' whereby psychologically derived truths are derived psychologically. This is precisely the state in which many contemporary social sciences are found. Thus, Simmel writes (103), 'This is not only a point of the greatest importance for the general view of things on which the following discussion is based, but ... it deserves closer scrutiny.' Similarly, many scholars have already argued that Durkheim's representationalism is nevertheless a stance against relativism (see Joas 1984; Meštrović 1988a; Rojek 1985).

Schopenhauer insists that his starting point in philosophy is neither the object nor the subject, but both. Object and subject are an antagonistic unity. Similarly, Simmel (1977: 91) writes that 'Objectivity cannot be detached from its subjective foundation, nor can these elements of subjectivity be eliminated.' In contradistinction to the contemporary epistemological crises that stem from an extreme polarization of object and subject (resulting in a polemic between sociology's quantifiers versus its qualifiers), Simmel's sociology seems to aim for integration, totality, and comprehensiveness in explanation. Like Freud and Durkheim, Simmel will apparently entertain psychological explanations within sociological ones, and in this regard too he parts with disciples of Comte (see Alpert 1939a; Meštrović 1982; 1987).

For Simmel, knowledge is in constant flux, knowable only through representations that are nevertheless always changing. This is remarkably similar to William James's notion of the 'stream of consciousness', Bergson's extreme intuitionism set forth in *Creative Evolution* (1944) and elsewhere, and of course, Durkheim's (1912) equally extreme position that both science and religion are crystallizations of the infinite flux of representations – all of these being derivatives of Schopenhauer's (1818) philosophy. Elsewhere Simmel (1980: 99) elaborates that 'the observable is only a bridge and a symbol', not anything like a given, 'hard' fact, such that 'in principle, no explanation is ever ultimate or exhaustive' (1980: 130). Almost exactly as Schopenhauer dismisses both idealism and realism in the opening pages of his *World as Will and Representation*, Simmel dismisses both philosophical doctrines with the claim that 'both theses represent a one-dimensional distortion of the substance of this problem' (1980: 144). According to Simmel (146), the 'remarkable result' of this assumption that truth is simultaneously relative and absolute is that 'a phenomenon is assimilated and fashioned by life' such that 'as an object of knowledge, this phenomenon acquires the status of an autonomous representation'. This is again similar to Schopenhauer's basic claim that the representation is the objectification of the will. Thus, for Simmel, Durkheim, Freud, and many of their contemporaries, when the human agent confronts 'truth', it is a matter of an individual will grasping a more generalized will that is in constant flux, fixed by the individual's mental categories, which are eventually dissolved by life. Although constant change is the hallmark of modernity, these *fin de siècle* thinkers managed to retain social realism and some absolutes in the modern sea of relativism.

In *Problems of the Philosophy of History* (1977), Simmel attacks the thesis implied by the doctrine of historical realism that truth can be a copy of reality: 'There is no sense in which historical knowledge can ever qualify as a copy of the events as they actually occurred' (1977: 87). It is interesting that Durkheim makes a similar argument in his *Pragmatism and Sociology* ([1955] 1983), and that in this regard, both thinkers again reflect Schopenhauer's philosophy. Pragmatism and sociology were both born in an era that rebelled against Kant's strict formalism, his unquestionable and permanent categories. In fact, Simmel (1977: 76) writes that 'it is most essential to dispose of historical realism'. The realism of the Enlightenment is old-fashioned and naive, yet both Simmel and Durkheim sought to maintain some sort of sophisticated realism in their epistemologies (see Deploige 1911).

Given Simmel's non-positivistic epistemology, it is obvious that like Durkheim, Weber, and Freud, Simmel would not hold to any version of what passes for empirical verification today, Popper's (1934) version of repeated hypothesis testing that aims not at truth, but falsification, finding an error. Instead, for Simmel and his contemporaries 'life' *cannot* repeat itself because it is in constant flux. Hence, all reality is subject to 'error' at all times, because it is never exactly the same from one moment to the next. Nietzsche (1968: 46) illustrates this point in a deceptively banal discussion of leaves by noting that 'no leaf ever wholly equals another, and the concept of "leaf" is formed through an arbitrary abstraction from these individual differences, through forgetting the distinctions' which occur from one object (leaf) to the next, among human observers, and the passage of time (for a related discussion, see also Vaihinger 1924). Durkheim (1912) refracts Nietzsche's and Simmel's arguments in the concluding chapter of his *Elementary Forms*, wherein he argues that all representations are immediately re-touched, modified, and changed by the individual human agent's *private* representations of the more 'objective' collective representations. Replication of 'findings' is a complete impossibility for most turn of the century philosophers.

Thus, Durkheim (1908) believed that one, well-designed experiment is sufficient to establish a law, even if it is not replicated by subsequent experiments (because it cannot be replicated in the *fin de siècle* sense), a sentiment shared also to some extent by many of his distinguished colleagues, including Max Weber (see Meštrović 1982; Turner 1986). Similarly, Simmel holds that 'a law is "valid" – it holds or functions – regardless of whether the case it describes occurs one time or a million times' (Simmel 1977: 129). Compare this claim by Simmel with Schopenhauer's ([1813] 1899) elaborate argument in *The Fourfold Root of the Principle of Sufficient Reason* that the will manifests itself in one well-grasped case as well as in a million cases. Simmel and his contemporaries are not holding to any version of positivistic experimentation, but to the notion that science and art both aim at 'pictures' of reality that can be superseded at any time, but are nevertheless 'valid', fixed, and 'objective', despite the many epistemological caveats discussed above.

Simmel adds that 'laws, of course, are timelessly valid. Therefore they are valid for every event' (1977: 129). It is striking how similar this claim is to Schopenhauer's thesis that the 'will' and its manifestations are independent of the Kantian categories of time and space, a claim also echoed explicitly by Durkheim (1908), that if one could prove A is the cause of B, the relation would hold independently of the categories of time and space. Undoubtedly, Simmel and Durkheim seem to have followed Schopenhauer's lead and tried to break out of Kant's formalism. How far they were successful in this aim is a separate matter, beyond the scope of the present discussion. My aim in this section is to suggest that cogent alternatives to postmodernist epistemological relativism and nihilism can be found in *fin de siècle* writings, and that these alternatives have been forgotten or obfuscated.

Thus, Simmel (1977: 133), like others writing in the *fin de siècle* spirit, believed that 'it is impossible to establish whether any given law really is absolutely valid' at the same time that he believed in the objectivity of truth! This complicated and apparently paradoxical position also shows some similarity to Durkheim's complicated critique of pragmatism in his *Pragmatism and Sociology* ([1955] 1983). Simmel (1977: 82) concludes: 'The difference between art and science is only a matter of degree.... There is no knowledge as such: knowledge is possible only in so far as it is produced and structured by constitutive concepts that are qualitatively determined.'

Just as any artistic interpretation can be superseded by subsequent interpretation, there is no last and lasting scientific truth. Yet, it is not necessary to succumb to the cynicism of extreme cultural relativism which abandons the notion of truth completely. This is the complex and disturbing (from a positivistic point of view) epistemology that Simmel, Durkheim, and many of their contemporaries bring to sociology. And in this regard, Bloom (1987) is especially correct: turn of the century thinkers in general and German thinkers in particular did not hold to anything like our contemporary faith in science as we know it. But in a more fundamental sense, Bloom is incorrect to align the *fin de siècle* thinkers only with nihilism, cynicism, and extreme relativism. Here he follows the mistaken path established by many writers on modernity, a path that leads to a conceptual dead-end. It should be clear from the above discussion that Simmel and Durkheim maintained hope, faith in science, and a belief in some sort of objectivity *despite* their thoroughly *fin de siècle* critiques of Kantian formalism and other Enlightenment doctrines.

SIMMEL'S AND DURKHEIM'S CONCEPTS OF THE UNCONSCIOUS

Thomas Mann (1939) credits Schopenhauer for being the father of modern psychology because of his focus on the concept of the unconscious – itself a refraction of the passionate will – and his active focus on studying the manifestations of the unconscious empirically. Ellenberger (1970), in particular, has traced the origins and extent of the concept of the unconscious for the *fin de siècle* spirit beyond Freud's well-known usage. Simmel and Durkheim were no exceptions to this *fin de siècle* spirit. Durkheim (1908) held an elaborate conceptualization of the unconscious, even though this aspect of his sociology has been almost completely ignored (discussed in Meštrović 1982, 1986, 1988a). Bergson's (1944) own concept of the unconscious, and its possible influence on Durkheim, should also be investigated in future discussions of this sort.

The idea of the unconscious expresses modernity at the same time that it undercuts the project of modernity. On the one hand, the existence of the unconscious allows for cynical unmasking of traditions and bourgeois rationalizations. The unconscious, according to Freud, does not recognize the limitations of space, time, or logic. On the other, the unconscious can defy rational social action, and resembles Schopenhauer's 'will to life' as well as Nietzsche's 'cult of feeling'. It is tyrannical and absolute, and for some *fin de siècle* thinkers, the complete antithesis of cultural relativism (consider Jung's archetypes, for example). Despite its ambiguous qualities and the impossibility of defining the unconscious (as Freud admitted), it is striking that from Merton to Habermas, the concept of the unconscious has been virtually dropped from social scientific discourse. Postmodernist discourse, in particular, ignores the concept of the unconscious, despite the fact that it pretends to rebel at the narrative of modernity.

In line with the 'cult of feeling' characteristic of the *fin de siècle*, Simmel believed that the individual unconsciously completes fragmentary impressions of objects in a manner that conforms to previous experience (1977: 46). The human agent is not and cannot be fully aware of all the 'forms' within nor without, and all of these 'forms' are fuelled by a 'life' that is in perpetual flux. Thus, Simmel (169) concludes that 'reality might be compared to an elixir which flows through the mere contents of ideas. When it evaporates, they [forms] are left behind as uninteresting and insubstantial shells, all that remains of the identifiable or expressible logical content of such an idea.'

These rational forms are subject not only to perception, but also to what Simmel calls apperception (98). Apperception is the

ability to grasp unconsciously and intuitively – on the basis of feelings – the unity, coherence, and order in the multiplicity and heterogeneity of sense perceptions. (This is essentially similar to
Bergson's emphasis on intuition, as well as William James's own
writings of apperception.) Simmel even seems to be implying
something like Jung's notion of the 'collective unconscious' (a
phrase also used by Durkheim) when he claims that these apper-
ceptions are 'stored in [one's] organism as genetically transmitted
recollections' (96). Most surprising is Simmel's Platonic assertion
that because of the unconscious, 'the process of learning really
would be only a form of recollection or recognition' (ibid.). Of
course, Nietzsche went on to develop this idea into his well-known
concept of the eternal recurrence of the same, itself a refraction
of Schopenhauer's claim that the will is eternally the same
throughout history despite the myriad of representations through
which it is objectified when it combines with human consciousness. This eternal, fixed Idea is part of the 'other side' in Baudelaire's famous definition of modernity, ignored by postmodernist
culture.

The similarity between Simmel's conception of knowledge as
recollection and other similar Western notions, especially Plato's,
are obvious. Schopenhauer, too, felt that our character is 'set' in
early childhood and we spend the rest of our lives coming to know
what was, in a sense, predestined. Freud went on to refract this
idea into the notion that psychoanalysis can never really change
the character pattern that was established in childhood, but may
help establish some insight. Schopenhauer, like Simmel, cites
Plato in this regard. Similarly, Durkheim and many of his colleagues emphasized the importance of habits established in childhood as the affective and most important determinants of
behaviour (see Camic 1986).

When Simmel writes that 'objects of knowledge are not
presented to us as things in themselves, but only as phenomena'
(1977: 66), he almost seems to have plagiarized Schopenhauer.
But these phenomena are never known fully and rationally. A
part of them is always engulfed in the unconscious, the will. Thus,
the subject matter of history and sociology, according to Simmel,
presupposes an 'unconscious mental basis or foundation' (63) and
an 'unconscious purposiveness' (56).

69

SIMMEL'S OWN CIVILIZATION AND ITS DISCONTENTS

Scores of writers have observed that *fin de siècle* intellectuals and artists were obsessed with the theme of decadence in civilization. Again, Freud (1930) seems to have been given all the credit and notoriety for this move, when, in fact, it was shared by many of his colleagues. For the purposes of this chapter, it is important to note that the general explanation for the pessimistic stances of *fin de siècle* precursors of sociology is that the 'will' (or passion and desire) is stronger than the rational mind, and that with the simultaneous enlightenment of the will conjoined with the disintegration of modern society, the will is no longer contained and regulated. Passion is unleashed in the modern world even as modernity and postmodernity try to repress this fact. The result is Durkheim's anomie as the immoral infinity of desires that pour tumultuously through previous barriers that held them in check; Freud's id that is fuelled by Eros which in turn leads to civilization at the price of unhappiness; Nietzsche's Dionysian forces that break through Apollonian forms; Tönnies's 'rational will' of *Gesellschaft* that replaces the 'natural will' of *Gemeinschaft*, and many other versions of this conflict, including Simmel's own set forth in his 'Conflict in Modern Culture' (1971).

However, it is in the opening pages of his *Schopenhauer and Nietzsche* that Simmel really explains the philosophical underpinnings for his version of civilization and its discontents. In contradistinction to the typically modern, highly abstract, Parsonian theory of social action, which emphasizes goal-oriented behaviour and rational social action, Simmel (1986: 3) argues that:

It is a paradox that all higher cultures of our type are structured so that the more they evolve the more we are forced, in order to reach our goals, to proceed along increasingly long and difficult paths, filled with stops and curves.... The will of animals and of uncultured humans reaches its goal, if that will is successful, in, so to speak, a straight line, that is, by simply reaching out or by using a small number of simple devices: the order of means and ends is easily observable. This simple triad of desire–means–end is excluded by the increasing multiplicity and complexity of higher life.... Thus, our consciousness is bound up with the means, whereas the final goals which import sense and meaning into the intermediate steps are pushed toward our inner horizon and finally beyond it.

For Simmel, modern persons struggle with the question of the meaning of life precisely because the connection between ends and means eludes them. This is *not* a rational connection any more. Rather, this connection is veiled, obscured, and sometimes seems to be entirely lost or severed. The culprits for this state of affairs, according to Simmel, seem to be enlightenment, progress, and the complexity of the division of labour. Bureaucracy, technology, the endless steps to achieving goals that humans set for themselves – these are the realities of modern living. Thus, human 'will' and passion become disconnected from the idea. The two sometimes function separately. For Simmel, as for Durkheim, Freud, Tönnies, Nietzsche, and some of his other contemporaries, the resultant tension, confusion, and other components of malaise seem to be inescapable and are bound to increase with the development of modernity (and by extension, postmodernity).

Like Durkheim and Freud, Simmel recognizes that eras other than ours have had to deal with this disconnectedness between the will and idea, but believes that our situation is worse. This is a debatable point, of course. Nevertheless, Simmel insists that the meaning of life became a problem with Christianity, which could give a solution only by positing an afterlife, a transcendent goal that would make sense of the lack of connection between means and goals in this life. But in the *fin de siècle*, 'Christianity lost its appeal.... The need, however, for a final goal in life has not been lost' (Simmel 1986: 5). Simmel's connection of this problem with Schopenhauer's philosophy is intriguing:

> Schopenhauer's philosophy is the absolute philosophical expression for this inner condition of *modern* man.... As the exhaustive reason of all things, [the will] condemns to eternal dissatisfaction. Inasmuch as the will can no longer find anything outside itself for its satisfaction, and because it can only grasp itself in a thousand disguises, it is pushed forward from every point of rest on an endless path. Thus, *the tendency of existence toward a final goal and the simultaneous denial of this goal are projected into a total interpretation of reality....* Contemporary culture is also aptly described through its desire for a final goal in life, a goal which is felt to have disappeared and is gone forever. (Emphasis added.)

The Schopenhauerian will to life (refracted into Simmel's 'life' and Freud's use of Eros), which is a striving without aim or end, resulted in culture at the same time that it rid culture of final goals, ends, forms, and rules. All that is left is the naked will, and this is the penultimate characteristic of postmodernity. Yet the will is by nature painful and insatiable, as Schopenhauer ([1818] 1969a: 254) explains:

> The desire lasts long, the demands are infinite; the satisfaction is short and scantily measured out. But even the final satisfaction is itself only apparent; every satisfied wish at once makes room for a new one ... no attained object of desire can give lasting satisfaction, but merely a fleeting gratification.

Simmel seems to have grasped the full import of Schopenhauer's philosophy, that as the will objectifies itself through history, it destroys its restraints, unleashes itself, and thereby condemns persons to perpetual unhappiness.

IMPLICATIONS AND CONCLUSIONS

By restoring Durkheim and Simmel to the *fin de siècle* spirit that informed the works of many of their contemporaries, and by pointing to the affinities between them, the potential exists that one may appreciate better the contributions of both sociologists to the study of modernity and postmodernity. The works of neither Simmel nor Durkheim fit anything like Parsons's (1937) non-contextual, idiosyncratic, and heartless paradigm of 'rational social action' nor Habermas's (1987) equally heartless efforts to complete the project of the Enlightenment. Rather, an examination of the 'climate of opinion' extant at the turn of the century – which Parsons ignores and Habermas obfuscates – exposes something that might be called the paradigm of 'irrational social action'. In this *fin de siècle* view, humans are ruled by feelings, desires, and irrational forces of which they are scarcely or imperfectly aware, that lead them to behaviours and motives which they rationalize afterwards. Hardly an essay written by Durkheim or Simmel could not be re-appreciated in this new context.

Consider, for example, Simmel's famous yet still misunderstood essay 'The Metropolis and Mental Life'. Simmel echoes Schopenhauer's famous distinction between the heart and mind when he claims in this essay that 'the essentially intellectualistic character of the mental life of the metropolis becomes intelligible as over against that of the small town which rests more on feelings and emotional relationships' (1971: 325). We have seen that the Durkheimians emphasized a similar trend. In no uncertain terms, Simmel is accusing the process of urbanization of leading to a modern 'heartlessness' and lack of compassion that Tönnies (1887) had already exposed in his depiction of the heartless 'rational will' of *Gesellschaft*. This is a severe indictment of modernity, but despite Simmel's pathos and similar trends found in Durkheimian writings, as well as the works of many of their contemporaries, both modernization and urbanization are depicted in contemporary sociology textbooks as essentially rational and benign phenomena.

Simmel's philosophically informed sociology leads to the problem of how the irrational is to be integrated with enlightened, rational social progress in modern times. To repeat, for Schopenhauer, Durkheim, Simmel, and many *fin de siècle* thinkers, it is not the irrational 'will' nor 'life' that leads to destructiveness, malaise, and decadence, but the enlightened, unintegrated 'will to life' that is unleashed by excessive, unintegrated, rationalism. Yet, with few exceptions, already noted in chapter 1, the problem of modernity is not depicted in such terms in contemporary social scientific textbooks. Consequently, the paradoxical and contradictory nature of postmodernism as an anti-narrative narrative fits well Simmel's descriptions of an all-devouring will that creates culture at the same time that it destroys culture.

Simmel's (1971: 248) conclusion in his essay 'Eros, Platonic and Modern' is another severe indictment of modernity:

> But what mankind grown old, differentiated, and sophisticated can no longer support is this: to transform the world in its reality, its love, its meaning, and its spiritual values into a logical structure of abstract concepts and analogous metaphysical essences and to perceive this as the deepest happiness of the spirit.

Simmel's indictment applies especially to neo-Parsonian sociology, which has transformed the 'heart' of its precursors into a dry, abstract, and cold-hearted system of 'rational social action' that pretends that the irrational is irrelevant, trivial, or otherwise inconsequential in explaining social behaviour. Finally, Simmel's indictment applies to postmodernist philosophies, which are as cold and heartless as modernity ever was or will be.

Chapter Five

DURKHEIM'S STAND ON THE *FIN DE SIÈCLE*

How did Durkheim feel about the times in which he lived? The answer to this important question cannot be found in a form as concise as, let us say, Simmel's, *Schopenhauer and Nietzsche* (1907), yet an answer can be found scattered throughout Durkheim's writings. Over and over again, Durkheim comments on the uneasiness, anxiety, malaise, disenchantment, pessimism, and other negative characteristics of his age. His comments on the leading proponents of the *fin de siècle* spirit – among them, Bergson, James, Nietzsche, and Guyau – are mixed with sympathy as well as outrage. But his remarks on the Enlightenment philosophers, Hobbes, Montesquieu, Rousseau, Comte, Kant, Saint-Simon, and others, are unequivocally critical with regard to their *naiveté*, optimism, and simplicity.

It has been noted that Baudelaire is the most frequently cited 'totem' in discussions of modernity and postmodernity. Consider the intriguing similarities between Baudelaire's descriptions of 'The Dandy' in his 1863 *Painter of Modern Life* and Durkheim's descriptions of the anomic egoist. Baudelaire refers to the dandy as the ideal type of the modern person who is idle, rich, blasé, and involved in a 'cult of self', engaged in the perpetual pursuit of happiness who nevertheless suffers. Moreover, Baudelaire regards dandyism as a social institution, even a religion, with its own rules. The primary rule is the maintenance of an 'air of coldness which comes from an unshakeable determination not to be moved' (Baudelaire [1863] 1965: 29). The 'dandy is a sunset; like the declining daystar, it is glorious, without heat and full of melancholy' (ibid.). Walter Benjamin's (1973) observation that for Baudelaire, modernism exists under the sign of suicide, resonates with Durkheim's (1897) claim that suicide is the 'ransom money' of civilization. Finally, like Durkheim, Baudelaire suggested that 'dandyism appears above all in periods of transition' ([1863] 1965: 28), and given the many revolutions that occurred in nineteenth-century France, this view is credible.

To the best of my knowledge, Durkheim never referred to Baudelaire directly in his writings. One is free to speculate on this omission by Durkheim. But I would venture the observation that Baudelaire is more famous today than he was in his or Durkheim's lifetime. Nevertheless, Baudelaire intended his essay on the mod-ernist dandy to serve as an introduction to a proposed yet never completed work entitled *Famille des Dandies*. In this work, he wanted to include Chateaubriand's *René* as the representation *par excellence* of the decadent dandy. By coincidence, Durkheim cited this same work by Chateaubriand as an illustration of the anomic type.

In contrast to the reception that Baudelaire received in his life-time, Chateaubriand became an overnight success with the publi-cation of his *Atala* and *René* in 1805. These works constituted the first step by French artists to emulate the spirit of German Romanticism that had been unleashed by Goethe's *Werther* (see Clark 1975). Chateaubriand exerted an influence on Lamartine, Hugo, George Sand, Flaubert, and Rimbaud, among other literary giants who were fascinated with the modernist theme of decadence. And Durkheim (1897) commented on the works of Chateaubriand, Lamartine, and Goethe in the context of a discus-sion on egoism and anomie, phenomena that he regarded as decadent. In other words, it is possible to draw an indirect connec-tion between Baudelaire's 'dandy' and Durkheim's modern, anomic, egoist via these works.

For example, in his discussion of Chateaubriand's *René*, Durk-heim ([1897] 1951: 286–7) comments on a quotation taken from page 112 of the 1849 French edition of this literary classic:

> In our own day one of the types which perhaps best incarnate this sort of spirit [disgust with life] is Chateaubriand's René [who] is the insatiate type. 'I am accused,' he exclaims unhap-pily, 'of being inconstant in my desires, of never long enjoying the same fancy, of being prey to an imagination eager to sound the depth of my pleasures as though it were overwhelmed by

their persistence; I am accused of always missing the goal I might attain. Alas! I only seek an unknown good, the instinct for which pursues me. *Is it my fault if I everywhere find limits, if everything once experienced has no value for me?*' (Durkheim's emphasis.)

Durkheim associates René with Goethe's

Werther, the turbulent heart as he calls himself, enamoured of infinity, killing himself from disappointed love, and the case of all artists who, after having drunk deeply of success, commit suicide because of a chance hiss, a somewhat severe criticism, or because their popularity has begun to wane (286).

In keeping with the connection among Chateaubriand, Goethe, and Lamartine espoused by contemporary literary critics and writers on modernity, Durkheim (278–81) discusses Lamartine's *Raphaël* in this same context:

One form of suicide, certainly known to antiquity, has widely developed in our day: Lamartine's *Raphaël* offers us its ideal type. Its characteristic is a condition of melancholic languor which relaxes all the springs of action. Business, public affairs, useful work, even domestic duties inspire the person only with indifference and aversion.... It becomes [a] kind of morbid joy which Lamartine, himself familiar with it, describes so well in the words of his hero: 'The languor of all my surroundings was in marvelous harmony with my own languor. It increased this languor by its charm. I plunged into the depths of melancholy. But it was a lively melancholy, full enough of thoughts, impressions, communings with the infinite, half-obscurity of my own soul, so that I had no wish to abandon it. A human disease, but one the experience of which attracts rather than pains, where death resembles a voluptuous lapse into the infinite. I resolved to abandon myself to it wholly, henceforth; to avoid all distracting society and to wrap myself in silence, solitude and frigidity in the midst of whatever company I should encounter; my spiritual isolation was a shroud, through which I desired no longer to see men, but only nature and God.'

Durkheim takes this quotation from page 6 of an undated French edition of Lamartine's *Raphaël*. I should add that much has been lost in the English translation of these passages, and the interested reader may wish to consult the French originals.

My own reading of these works by Chateaubriand, Goethe, and Lamartine leads me to the conclusion that Durkheim did not pick isolated quotations to fit a preconceived conclusion, but grasped the essentially decadent, even morbid, qualities of the literature by these famous authors. There can be no doubt that these authors harp on the melancholy, egoism, and essential solitude of their heroes over and over again. Moreover, the French edition of Durkheim's (315–23) quotations indicates that the words used by Chateaubriand and Lamartine to describe their dandyist 'heroes' include *tristesse*, *maladie*, and *douleur*, words that Durkheim used elsewhere in his descriptions of anomie (Meštrović 1988a). Thus, good reasons exist to suppose that Durkheim was indirectly mirroring Baudelaire's indictment of the modern dandy in his own comments on French Romanticism. In these passages, neglected by Durkheim's contemporary commentators, Durkheim is essentially applying what passes today as the sociology of knowledge perspective to literature. Durkheim concludes his literary analysis as follows:

> This description conclusively illustrates the relations and differences between egoistic and anomic suicide, which our sociological analysis had already led us to glimpse. Suicides of both types suffer from what has been called the disease of the infinite.... The former is lost in the infinity of dreams, the second in the infinity of desires.
>
> ([1897] 1951: 287)

The notion of 'infinity' is found in many pre-Romantic, Romantic, and *fin de siècle* writings, especially Schopenhauer and von Hartmann. It stands in sharp contrast to the static schemata of goals and means found in contemporary sociologists from Parsons to Habermas.

The essential point is that like Baudelaire, Durkheim is passing judgement on the Romantic hero as decadent. Baudelaire's and Durkheim's sentiments reverberate in the massive psychiatric literature of the late nineteenth century that dealt with hypochondriasis, neurasthenia, hysteria, suicide, and other 'moral' diseases. More important, archetypes of these Romantic heroes may be found in our *fin de siècle*, not just in the cheap novels sold at

78

grocery check-out counters, but as the staple of 'soap operas' as well as the cartoon characters that entertain modern as well as postmodern children on Saturday mornings. The uncommitted egoist who lives an erratic life of decadence is such a common symbol in modern times that he or she hardly draws the attention that they did in the Romantic era. Decadence is taken for granted today, from Bugs Bunny to J.R. Ewing. And soap operas made in the USA, which glorify decadence, are broadcast all over the world as we approach the next *fin de siècle*, even into communist countries.

THE DECADENCE OF PRAGMATISM

The most important indicator of Durkheim's attitude towards the *fin de siècle* is to be found in a series of lectures he delivered in 1914–15 entitled, 'Pragmatism and Sociology'. There exist many reasons why these lectures should be reappreciated in the context of discourses on modernity and postmodernism. Modernity and pragmatism share a penchant for what is in flux as opposed to the permanent and static; they rebel at traditional modes of knowing the world; and they are both highly abstract. Both postmodernism and pragmatism merely pretend to rebel at Enlightenment narratives. Both doctrines take a casual, even playful attitude towards truth, and both place a premium on the practical, tangible, and immediate as opposed to the hidden, the unconscious, and the difficult-to-grasp that characterize traditional metaphysics. In a word, pragmatism shares with postmodernist philosophies an ambiguous, contradictory, and superficial stance towards truth. As such, Durkheim's analysis of pragmatism is indirectly relevant to many current discussions of postmodernism.

In the opening lines of his first lecture, Durkheim declares, 'We are currently witnessing an attack on reason which is truly militant and determined.' While Durkheim sympathized with pragmatism's effort to transcend the limitations of naive rationalism, he also regarded it as a 'public danger'. Note that much postmodernist discourse takes a similarly militant tone towards traditional epistemologies (see Murphy 1989).

For the sake of context, it is important to realize that William James, who even in Durkheim's time was regarded as an important promulgator of pragmatism, was famous in France at the turn of the century. James gained this foothold in France through his

79

friendships with Renouvier and Boutroux – Durkheim's teachers at the École Normale – and Bergson, Durkheim's acquaintance from his student days at the École Normale, as well as Durkheim's colleague at the Sorbonne. Out of all these majestic figures, Bergson was the most popular and the most powerful, a public figure by today's standards. William James was identified with Bergsonism in the public consciousness in France as well as by Durkheim in these lectures. And Bergsonism stood for the revolt against reason, for intuitionism, *l'élan vital*, and other essential aspects of the *fin de siècle* spirit.

In his 1983 introduction to these lectures on pragmatism, Allcock has already noted that Durkheim regarded pragmatism as an example of intellectual anomie (see also Meštrović 1988a). In addition, one could make the case that pragmatism, as understood by Durkheim, resembles what Baudelaire termed dandyism. The tone of Durkheim's attack indicates that he regarded pragmatism as superficial, decadent, and frivolous. It is the intellectual component of the social institution of dandyism depicted by Baudelaire.

At the time these lectures were delivered, there existed a remarkably widespread decline of the prestige associated with the intellect and reason. The most popular philosophers of the day included James, Bergson, Croce, Nietzsche and Spengler. It can be conjectured that Durkheim organized his lectures on pragmatism as a way of 'getting back' at Bergson through an attack on William James, himself popular in France. As Durkheim puts the matter, 'In Bergson, whom he considered the destroyer of intellectualism, James believed that he found his best argument' ([1955] 1983: 27). Durkheim charges that James 'borrows certain arguments' from Bergson (9); that James's pragmatism is really based on Bergson's arguments (28); and that 'to a very great extent, James's whole argument closely follows developments in Bergson' (32).

Thus, these lectures constitute a juxtaposition of rivals, Bergson and Durkheim. Bergson is the anti-intellectualist who stands for spontaneity and intuition – an important component of Baudelaire's ambiguous definition of modernity. But Durkheim accounts for the 'other side' of Baudelaire's famous definition. Durkheim admits that there exists an excessively simplistic element in Cartesian rationalism, but he wants to reform rather than abandon rationalism to nihilism and subjectivism. According to

Durkheim, 'The problem is to find a formula which will both preserve what is essential in rationalism and answer the valid criticism that pragmatism makes of it' (2).

The complicated structure of Durkheim's argument must be appreciated. Durkheim distances pragmatism from Nietzsche, German Romanticism, and German philosophy in general. Rather, he aligns pragmatism with Anglo-Saxon philosophy, Bergson, and James. In essence, Durkheim is defending aspects of *fin de siècle* German Romantic philosophy which had been influencing him at least since 1887 and his relationship with Wundt (see Deploige 1911). Contrary to many contemporary accounts, including Habermas (1987), one cannot derive pragmatism from German Romantic philosophy, because this philosophy, following as it did in the wake of Schopenhauer and Hegel, accounts for an underlying, 'objective' reality that pragmatism simply wants to dismiss. This is an extremely important point given the efforts by Habermas (1987) to depict Hegel as the first important modern subjectivist.

For example, Durkheim credits Berthelot with the erroneous claim that the first form of pragmatism is to be found in Nietzsche (2). Durkheim disagrees: There is no link between pragmatism and German Romanticism, nor is it of 'German inspiration'. He adds, 'We, however, see it [pragmatism] rather as belonging to the Anglo-Saxon tradition of thought' (2). Moreover, according to Durkheim, there exist 'some profound differences between Nietzsche's thought and pragmatism', and

> It should be noted that what Nietzsche does not say is that what is useful is true. What he does say is that what *seems* true has been established as a result of its utility.... [Yet] there is a truth which only liberated spirits can attain. The artist is the very type of this spirit, freed from all rules and capable of adapting himself to all the forms of reality and of understanding *intuitively* what is hidden beneath appearances and fiction. There are no such ideas in pragmatism, for which there is no 'surface of things' quite separate from the basis on which they rest (3).

Without mentioning Schopenhauer directly, Durkheim has isolated the Schopenhauerian element in Nietzsche's complex philosophy: Nietzsche maintains the notion of a veiled yet objective reality that lies beneath our surface impressions of that reality.

(See Nietzsche's 1874 neglected tribute to Schopenhauer in this regard.) To phrase the matter differently, Durkheim credits Nietzsche for maintaining Baudelaire's 'other side' of the transitory and contingent that constitute modernity. By contrast, for James and pragmatism, 'everything takes place on the plane of phenomena, which is very far from Nietzschian thought' (4). Here again, both pragmatism and postmodern philosophies intersect on the issue of disdain for essences, and a penchant for surface explanations. By contrast, Durkheim, like Nietzsche, Schopenhauer, and Baudelaire, also understands 'objective' social reality to lie hidden beneath a veil of representations and symbols. Moreover, the pragmatist, unlike Nietzsche, is optimistic, and 'knows neither anguish nor uneasiness' (4).

While these remarks by Durkheim concerning Nietzsche are brief, taken in their proper context, they constitute an important interpretation of the impact of Nietzsche's philosophy. Durkheim clearly finds common ground between his sociology and Nietzsche's philosophy, and distances both from decadent versions of pragmatism. Durkheim's interpretation of Nietzsche stands in sharp opposition to the many glib understandings of Nietzsche as a cynical irrationalist and precursor of postmodernist philosophies.

Even more interesting is the fact that Durkheim refuses to align pragmatism with Peirce! Granted, the first person to use the word pragmatism was Peirce, but, Durkheim notes, 'Peirce refused to ally himself with James' and 'Peirce did not repudiate rationalism' (6). This is remarkably similar to Rochberg-Halton's (1986) more recent defence of Peirce against the modernist attitude. Thus, Durkheim concludes, 'It would be more accurate to see William James as the true father of pragmatism' (1983: 7).

Durkheim's attack on James is far-ranging, and I have summarized it elsewhere (Meštrović 1988a). In general, Durkheim depicts pragmatism as a happy-go-lucky philosophy (again, a trait shared with postmodernist philosophies), incompatible with the fact that truth is often painful (74). Durkheim objects to the fact that for James, there is no need to look beneath concepts. Moreover, despite his avowed rationalism, Durkheim does not believe that all truth is rational: 'Scientific thought cannot rule alone. There is, and there always will be, room in social life for a form of truth which will perhaps be expressed in a very secular way, but will nevertheless have a mythological and religious basis' (91). Durkheim is clearly expressing a non-positivistic belief in the power, efficacy, and usefulness of myths and religion that seems to align him with pre-modernity. Yet, he is an advocate of science and rationalism!

In truth, Durkheim's stance on the *fin de siècle* is extremely complex: he admits that sociology and pragmatism are 'children of the same period', and therefore share some common themes. But he seems to imply that sociology is the more serious child in the rivalry with pragmatism. By extension, one could argue that postmodernist philosophies are descendants of pragmatism, and that Durkheim's serious 'child' (his version of sociology) clearly lost the popularity contest.

THE ROLE OF RELIGION IN MODERNITY

Durkheim had been criticizing William James at least since 1898, when he refers to him in his discussion entitled, 'Individual and Collective Representations'. James is mentioned again, along with pragmatism, in the opening and concluding sections of Durkheim's *The Elementary Forms of the Religious Life* (1912). It is important to see the essential continuity between Durkheim's lectures on pragmatism and his works on religion: for Durkheim, there exists an objective reality behind and beneath religion and religious symbols and practices, and that reality is society. Even in his 1912 work on religion, Durkheim was expressing an anti-pragmatist, anti-modernist argument that is commensurate with Schopenhauer's belief that religion expresses in allegorical form truths that are not essentially different from scientific truths.

Hence, the religious and the sacred are superimposed on empirical, physical reality ([1912] 1965: 261); the reality which is the foundation of religion does not necessarily conform objectively to the subjective ideas which believers have of it (465); and above all, one must go *beneath* the symbol to the reality it signifes: 'But one must know how to go underneath the symbol to the reality which it represents and which gives it its meaning' (14). It is important to appreciate that in all these ways, Durkheim is essentially following in the footsteps of Schopenhauer, Wundt, and Nietzsche while distancing himself from Anglo-Saxon utilitarianism, Bergson, and the decadent varieties of modernity and postmodernism.

To be sure, there exist similarities between Durkheim and Bergson's (1932) open or dynamic religion with its source in mysticism and intuition, as well as James's (1902) pessimistic conclusion that the all-suffering twice-born are the more genuinely religious compared to the once-born. Like Bergson and James, Durkheim conceives 'religion to be like the womb from which come all the leading germs of human civilization' ([1912] 1965: 255). In keeping with both Bergson's and Schopenhauer's philosophies, Durkheim felt that religion even contributed to the forming of the intellect itself (21)! Myths weave connections between humans and animals as well as other humans in society, and cause persons and things to exist in 'mystic sympathy' with one another (174). Without using the phrases will to life or *élan vital*, Durkheim depicts totemism as the symbolism for a religion of an impersonal god without a name or history, immanent in the world and diffused in many things and persons: 'In other words, totemism is the religion, not of such and such animals or men or images, but of an anonymous and impersonal force, found in each of these beings, but not to be confounded with any of them. No one possesses it entirely and all participate in it' (216). It should be noted also that Bergson (1932) refers favourably to Durkheim when he comes to discussions of this sort in his own works. Clearly, these majestic figures from the *fin de siècle* found common ground.

Nevertheless, Durkheim regarded Bergson, James, and even Guyau as too 'happy go lucky' and cheerful in their rebellion against the rigid formalism of previous rationalisms. For Durkheim, despite change, religious representations nevertheless consistently represent sorrow and suffering, and more importantly, these representations correspond to the objective 'nature of things' (see Meštrović 1989c). Thus, Durkheim refers to the 'state of incertitude and confused agitation' ([1912] 1965: 475) in his day, and asserted that,

> The old gods are growing old or are already dead, and others are not yet born. This is what rendered vain the attempt of Comte with the old historic souvenirs artificially revived: it is life itself, and not a dead past which can produce a living cult (475).

(Note that Comte has been revived as a totemic figure in sociological discourse in this century.) He felt that his *fin de siècle* exhibited more than its normal share of agitation and pessimism, but that essentially these are inescapable facts of life that religion reflects. Thus, Durkheim concludes the *Elementary Forms* with the claim that asceticism is an essential element of religion (351); that pain and suffering are necessary conditions of social life as well as religion (351); and that sorrow and suffering have the power to bind people together as joy and happiness never can (354).

These conclusions are essentially similar to Schopenhauer's and von Hartmann's basic theme that religion teaches that life is a cross to bear, and that the essence of life is suffering. It is extremely intriguing that Durkheim finds a linkage between the pessimism of modern Christian religions with the hazing ceremonies of primitive aborigines! More importantly, Durkheim again challenges the postmodernist tendency to paint life with a happy face, a trait shared by 'happy go lucky' pragmatism.

SUICIDE: THE MOST OBVIOUS *FIN DE SIÈCLE* THEME

Because Durkheim's works have been misread from the bias of the Enlightenment, the continuities among his works on pragmatism, religion, the division of labour, and suicide have been obscured. Durkheim's *Suicide* (1897) has been the subject of seemingly ceaseless criticisms due to the fact that it does not and cannot fit optimistic, Enlightenment perspectives that have been used to apprehend it. However, when read in the context of Durkheim's stand on the *fin de siècle*, his *Suicide* offers a fascinating and unique sociology of knowledge interpretation of the pessimistic philosophies of Schopenhauer and von Hartmann. Thus, Durkheim writes ([1897] 1951: 366):

> Indeed, it is wrong to believe that unmixed joy is the normal state of sensibility. Man could not live if he were entirely impervious to sadness.... So melancholy is morbid only when it occupies too much place in a life; but it is equally morbid for it to be wholly excluded from life.

The popular 1980s song, 'Don't Worry, Be Happy', seems to represent the postmodern version of the attempt to exclude pessimism completely from social consciousness. Durkheim would have one consider that such hyper-optimism is morbid. But how much melancholy is too much? This is the crucial question that Durkheim never answered. What emerges from a careful reading of *Suicide* is that he felt that excessive optimism was as decadent as excessive pessimism, and that the amount of pessimism extant in his day was excessive: 'Too cheerful a morality is a loose morality; it is appropriate only to *decadent* peoples and is found only among them. Life is often harsh, treacherous or empty. Collective sensibility must reflect this side of existence, too' (366, emphasis added). Durkheim's conclusion is consistent with his attack on the overly optimistic aspect of pragmatism, and is relevant to critiques of the overly optimistic aspects of postmodernism.

Referring to the pessimistic doctrines of life found in ancient Rome, Greece, as well as in Buddhism and Jainism, Durkheim concludes that (370):

> The formation of such great systems [of pessimism] is therefore an indication that the current of pessimism has reached a degree of abnormal intensity which is due to some disturbance of the social organism. *We well know how these systems have recently multiplied.* To form a true idea of their number and importance it is not enough to consider the philosophies avowedly of this nature, such as those of *Schopenhauer, Hartmann,* etc. We must also consider all the others which derive from the same spirit under different names. (Emphasis added.)

To treat the philosophies of Schopenhauer, von Hartmann, and other pessimists of his day as symbols or representations of an underlying reality is a unique achievement possible only in Durkheim's sociology (although there exists some overlap with Simmel's treatment of Schopenhauer and Nietzsche). Unlike the vulgar pragmatists and postmodernists, Durkheim is not willing to accept the import of these pessimistic philosophies merely on their face value, without passing moral judgement on them. On the other hand, Durkheim does not condemn these philosophies from the modernist perspective of the Enlightenment. Rather, he regards pessimistic philosophies and representations as symbols of malaise and decadence. Yet, he is unsure how much of this malaise is normal and how much is excessive!

Durkheim's next move is to extrapolate from Schopenhauer and von Hartmann to other representations of this same underlying, objective problem of social decadence, and he does so in a manner that is relevant and easily accessible to empirical verification (370):

We must also consider all the others which derive from the same [pessimistic] spirit under different names. The anarchist, the aesthete, the mystic, the socialist revolutionary, even if they do not despair of the future, have in common with the pessimist a single sentiment of hatred and disgust for the existing order, a single craving to destroy or to escape from reality. Collective melancholy would not have penetrated consciousness so far, if it had not undergone a morbid development; and so the development of suicide resulting from it is of the same nature.

It should not be difficult to find social indicators for the types that Durkheim lists above, and compare their prevalence from Durkheim's *fin de siècle* through the years up to the coming *fin de siècle*. Are increases in suicide rates related to relative increases in these social types? This is an empirical question that has never been posed by sociologists.

Durkheim is severe in his judgement of his times. He refers to the 'objective causes of suffering' and 'an alarming poverty of morality' (387) in his day. He refers also to the 'state of deep disturbance from which civilized societies are suffering' and 'the current of collective sadness' (391) characteristic of the times in which he lived. It is intriguing that Durkheim treats suicide as the symbol of *fin de siècle* suffering (to repeat, a connection cited by Benjamin in his analysis of Baudelaire). This may seem to be an obvious connection at first blush, and is certainly to be found in Schopenhauer's philosophy. But close examination of most of the suicide research since Durkheim's day indicates that the connection between suicide and suffering has been almost completely obscured in the positivistic correlations used by postmodernist social scientists. Here is another important foreshadowing of Durkheim's attack on pragmatism as well as an indicator of his implicit allegiance to Schopenhauer's philosophy.

Durkheim claims that civilization in his day existed in 'a state of crisis and perturbation' (369). Moreover, he referred to suicide as the 'ransom money' of civilization (367). This is an arresting phrase reminiscent of Schopenhauer's claim that death and suffering are the 'debt' humans pay to life (discussed in Cartwright 1988a), as well as Freud's (1930) conclusion that guilt (which in German can be translated literally as debt) is the price humans pay for civilization.

When evaluating Durkheim's stand on the *fin de siècle*, it is important to note that he never resolved completely the question of how much sadness and pessimism is normal to development and progress. Schopenhauer's and other pessimistic philosophies of his day taught that Enlightenment always brings increased suffering. This message is the essence of what Ellenberger (1970) calls the *fin de siècle* spirit. Durkheim certainly shared this spirit at least in part, as when he writes that (366):

> From certain indications it even seems that the tendency to a sort of melancholy develops as we rise in the scale of social types. As we have said in another work [*The Division of Labor*], it is a quite remarkable fact that the great religions of the most civilized peoples are more deeply fraught with sadness than the simpler beliefs of earlier societies. This certainly does not mean that the current of pessimism is eventually to submerge the other [optimism], but it proves that it does not lose ground, that it does not seem destined to disappear.

Durkheim's reference to the other work in this passage is to page 266 of the 1893 French edition of the *Division of Labor*. We have seen that Durkheim repeated this claim in the conclusion of his *Elementary Forms* and even his lectures on pragmatism, wherein he concluded that truth is sometimes painful. Again, essential to understanding Durkheim's intentions is the fact that he, like Schopenhauer, regarded religion as a system of representations or symbols that reflect objective, underlying social realities. Religion is concerned with pain and suffering, and increasingly concerned with these pessimistic phenomena as civilization progresses, because civilization leads to discontent. Postmodernist philosophies tend to obscure and repress pessimism in favour of a boosterish optimism.

According to Durkheim, 'The entire morality of progress and perfection is thus inseparable from a certain amount of anomie' (364). Durkheim characterized anomie as a state of 'infinite desires' that resulted from enlightenment, a condition reminiscent of Schopenhauer's notion of the unleashed will (see Meštrović 1988a). Increased desires lead to unhappiness for the simple reason that the attainment of one object of desire immediately widens the horizon for other objects to be desired, attained, and desired again, to infinity. While Durkheim lamented this increase in anomie in his day, he also clearly recognized that it was an inevitable accompaniment to progress, at least in part. Durkheim adds in a footnote on page 365 that, 'Neurasthenia is a sickness from the point of view of individual physiology; but what would a society be without neurasthenics? They really have a social role to play.' The social role referred to is that of innovation and progress. In long but scattered sections of *Suicide*, Durkheim argues that the anomic neurasthenics are an inevitable, somewhat essential, yet regrettable aspect of modernization.

In addition to religion, art and literature also symbolize the underlying state of society in Durkheim's scheme of things. He explains in an important passage (213):

> One of the constitutive elements of every national temperament consists of a certain way of estimating the value of existence. There is a collective as well as an individual humor inclining peoples to sadness or cheerfulness.... Then metaphysical and religious systems spring up which, by reducing these obscure sentiments to formulae, attempt to prove to men the senselessness of life and that it is self-deception to believe that it has purpose.... They merely symbolize in abstract language and systematic form the physiological distress of the body social.

Religious and other symbols are merely the 'echo of the moral state of society' (300).

One may wonder why Durkheim did not evoke the many other literary giants of his time as illustration of this theme, among them Baudelaire, Flaubert, and Zola. One will never know the answer to this question for certain. But it is worth repeating that Durkheim does refer to several pieces of 'great' literature as symbolic expressions of the anomic type of person he describes in *Suicide*. These include Lamartine's *Raphaël* (278–80); Chateaubriand's *René* (282); and Goethe's Werther (286). These characters are all depicted by Durkheim as anomic types who are 'enamoured of infinity' (286).

Durkheim even makes an important sociological analysis of the import of von Hartmann's philosophy in this regard (280):

> [There is an] element of truth in the parallelism Hartmann claims to observe between the development of consciousness

and the weakening of the will to live.... To think, it is said, is to abstain from action; in the same degree, therefore, it is to abstain from living.... But this does not mean, as Hartmann believes, that reality itself is intolerable unless veiled by illusion. Sadness does not inhere in things; it does not reach us from the world and through mere contemplation of the world. It is a product of our own thought.

In other words, Nature and Reality are *not* objectively decadent, according to Durkheim. Rather, humankind has created decadence. It is also interesting in this regard that Theodule Ribot (1874, 1896), the founding father of French psychology and one of Durkheim's masters according to Mauss ([1950] 1979a) and Bouglé (1938), incorporates this pessimistic conclusion concerning the relationship between the development of consciousness (achieved presumably through education and other aspects of Elias's civilizing process) and the decline of the will to live in his psychology. For example, in his work on attention, Ribot (1896) argues that every time one pays attention to anything, the rest of the organism and the entire will to live languishes, at least momentarily. This is probably why attention and study in particular are so exhausting for humans. It should be noted also that Ribot (1874) wrote an influential treatise on Schopenhauer, and that his psychology incorporated metaphysics (see Lévy-Bruhl 1899). In sum, Durkheim agrees with von Hartmann, Ribot, and others from the previous turn of the century that an increase in 'consciousness', knowledge, and enlightenment automatically brings about a dimunition of the desire to live. This is a horrifying conclusion.

METHODOLOGY FOR WHAT?

It would be a mistake to conclude from Durkheim's critique of pragmatism that he was against practicality. On the contrary, he continually stressed that sociology must address and remedy the social problems of its age. But that is the point: the need for sociology is an expression of the unconscious perception of decadence and malaise. Far from the armchair, deductive approach to science stressed by Merton (1957) and neo-positivist postmodernists within the social sciences, Durkheim's sociology carries an inductive tone of urgency that stems from wanting to respond to the crises caused by modernity and its attendant anomie, pessimism, and disenchantment.

Even in his terse *Rules of Sociological Method* (1895), Durkheim makes an important allusion to the times in which he lived in the context of a controversial discussion of how one should distinguish the normal from the abnormal. It should be noted that this distinction is the most controversial and least understood aspect of his sociology, and that the controversy stems from the postmodernist relativity of all values as well as Durkheim's ambivalence in his stand towards the *fin de siècle*. He simply could not decide how much decadence was appropriate to 'civilization' and how much was excessive – and Baudelaire was just as ambivalent on the same issue. Thus, Durkheim writes in his *Rules* ([1895] 1982: 95):

> For instance, to know whether the present economic state of the peoples of Europe, with the lack of organization that characterizes it, is normal or not, we must investigate what in the past gave rise to it. If the conditions are still those appertaining to our societies, it is because the situation is normal, despite the protest that it stirs up. If, on the other hand, it is linked to that old social structure which elsewhere we have termed segmentary [mechanical solidarity] and which, after providing the essential skeletal framework of societies, is now increasingly dying out, we shall be forced to conclude that this now constitutes a morbid state, however universal it may be.

Alongside religion, the economic infrastructure was one of Durkheim's favourite targets of discourse, and he attacked it as a fertile source of anomie. Again, he regarded the economic crises of his day as a symbol of a deeper underlying disorder.

Durkheim's *Rules of Sociological Method* deals, as everyone knows, with 'social facts'. What is often not appreciated sufficiently is that social facts express the collective aspects of the beliefs, tendencies, and practices of the group ([1895] 1938: 7). In other words, social facts are collective representations, objective symbols of underlying realities. They are *not* the subjective viewpoints of individuals, as Lukes (1985) mistakenly insists. Rather, they are expressions of an underlying reality that eventually 'objectify' themselves through individual consciousness – a German Romantic idea difficult to comprehend in English contexts as well as postmodern philosophies.

Even the French term that Durkheim uses, *fait social*, does not really translate neatly into the supposed English equivalent of 'social fact'. *Fait* is a derivative of *faire*, a term that denotes all sorts of 'doing' in society (see Durkheim 1895: 14). Thus, Durkheim could treat phenomena as diverse as socialism, religious rites, and suicide rates as 'social facts': all of these can be interpreted as indicators of a fixed reality, an anchor in the sea of postmodernity. The important point is that even Durkheim's 1895 methodological classic expresses the *fin de siècle* spirit of unmasking the surface, illusory aspects of reality in order to redress social decadence. Or at least, it can be read in this manner.

PROGRESS AND HAPPINESS

Durkheim's first major classic, *The Division of Labor in Society* (1893) is chock-full of Durkheim's opinions on the times in which he lived, and is entirely consistent with the classics mentioned and analysed thus far. Durkheim argues that the moral state of a society or its degree of immorality can be measured by suicide and crimes (1893: 13). Economic activity is the most decadent social institution in modern societies, and deprived of all moral character, it exacerbates the normal amount of anomie that accompanies modernity (13). Yet new institutions 'flow' in the mould of ancient institutions (165), so that one can always hope to find some remedy for this pessimistic state of affairs. According to Durkheim, there exist limits to the power of happiness: pleasure occurs between too intense and too weak states of consciousness (213). He asks, can happiness be measured by the preference of life over death? He answers in the affirmative, and then points out that the more civilized humans become, the more they commit suicide (226), indicating increasing unhappiness as civilization progresses. In fact, Durkheim ([1893] 1933: 50) argues:

> The average number of suicides, of crimes of all sorts, can effectively serve to mark the intensity of immorality in a given society. If we make this experiment, it does not turn out creditably for civilization, for the number of these morbid phenomena seems to increase as the arts, sciences, and industry progress.

Elsewhere in this classic Durkheim argues that, 'The true suicide, the sad suicide is in the endemic state with civilized peoples' (247), and 'is even distributed geographically like civilization' (247). According to Durkheim, 'Civilization is concentrated in the great cities, suicide likewise' (247). Clearly, Durkheim is using suicide as a symbol for underlying, hidden, masked, malaise, and decadence. Like Simmel and other *fin de siècle* thinkers, Durkheim locates the 'metropolis' as the source of modernity and decadence. He is acting towards society like a psychoanalyst would act towards his or her patient.

Even though this aspect of Durkheim's thought had been missed in contemporary, postmodernist, overly optimistic readings of his work, Durkheim could not be more blunt: 'What the mounting tide of voluntary deaths proves [is] that the general happiness of society is decreasing' (249). Referring to the ambiguity concerning the dividing line between too much and too little unhappiness that I have already uncovered, Durkheim adds (219):

We have not lived under present conditions long enough to know if this state is normal and definitive or simply accidental and morbid. *Even the uneasiness which is felt during this [Durkheim's] epoch in this [economic] sphere of social life does not seem to prejudge a favourable reply.* (Emphasis added.)

Durkheim lists the following as indicators of anomie drawn from the times in which he lived: industrial and commercial crises, especially bankruptcies (1893: 344); class struggle and the antagonism between capital and labour (345); the absence of regulation in labour–capital relations (359); the movement of economic activity from the family to the factory (362); the extreme rapidity of change (362); conditions in which a sense of collaboration among workers is missing (363); and excessive routine that reduces the worker to a cog in the machine (363). It is interesting that every one of the observations that Durkheim makes continues to be a significant problem as we approach the next *fin de siècle*. Pragmatist, neo-positivistic, and postmodernist readings of Durkheim tend to ignore the issues that Durkheim raises above. If invoked at all, some of them are invoked, typically, in the context of Marxist social theory.

In keeping with Durkheim's ambiguous stand on unhappiness, he concludes that it is neither necessary nor possible for social life to be without struggles. Rather, the role of solidarity is not to suppress competition but to moderate it (357). This is another of many indicators of Durkheim's fundamental ambivalence towards the *fin de siècle*.

Chapter Six

THE GERMAN ROOTS OF DURKHEIM'S SOCIOLOGY

Prior to the publication of Durkheim's classic *Division of Labor* in 1893, one can trace a long period of gestation for Durkheim's ideas. I have indicated that the major theme in Durkheim's works is that the object of sociology is to get not at the subjectively perceived symbol, but what it hides and expresses, the underlying reality. This Durkheimian aim is entirely in keeping with Ellenberger's (1970) characterization of the *fin de siècle* spirit of unmasking the surface reality to get at the underlying reality, and just as entirely at odds with neo-positivism, pragmatism, modernity, and postmodernist philosophies. One finds Durkheim both commenting upon and expressing this major theme in his reviews of Spencer's (1886) *Ecclesiastical Institutions*; Guyau's (1887) *Non-Religion of the Future*; Tönnies's (1887) *Community and Society*; and other works that he reviewed prior to the publication of his *Division of Labor* (1893).

Given that Durkheim was so critical of the French cultural milieu in which he lived, the obvious question arises, where did he obtain his philosophical assumptions? I believe that a likely answer is German *fin de siècle* philosophy. This is evident from ruling out the influence of Comte's philosophy, which was not as influential in Durkheim's time as is purported today; from the affinities between Durkheim's sociology and Simmel's sociology already discussed; from the affinities between Durkheim's philosophical assumptions and Schopenhauer's philosophy, also already discussed; and from thinkers as diverse as Deploige (1911) and Bloom (1987) who suggest that German *fin de siècle* philosophy dominated European culture during the era in which sociology was born. This is a connection worth pursuing.

Thus, great emphasis must be placed on Durkheim's visit to Germany in 1885–6 to study with Wilhelm Wundt. Wundt's *Ethics* was published in 1886, and Durkheim, along with his followers, reviewed Wundt's major works in *L'Année Sociologique* and elsewhere. Wundt, a disciple of Schopenhauer, Steinthal, and Lazarus, was among the first precursors of the social sciences to treat symbols in this *fin de siècle* manner. This is the essence of Wundt's *Volkerpsychologie* or 'folk psychology', co-founded by Lazarus and Steinthal in Germany, the immediate precursor of Durkheim's and Simmel's sociologies, still poorly understood today (Kaern et al. 1990). In fact, in the two 1887 essays that Durkheim wrote as reports of his study trip to Germany, he has nothing but praise for the German moralists and economists of his time, while he heaps severe criticisms on the utilitarianists, Kantians, and the French economists of his day (discussed in Hall 1988).

In 1907 Durkheim had occasion to publish two letters as replies to the criticisms of Simon Deploige, who accused Durkheim of stealing his ideas from Wundt and other Germans. Durkheim's replies are interesting in the context of his defence of Nietzsche and German philosophy in general as well as his attack on Bergson and William James, invoked earlier. Durkheim wrote in response to Deploige:

> As for all these German works of which Monsieur Deploige speaks, it was I who made them known in France; it was I who showed how, although they were not the work of sociologists, they could nonetheless serve the advancement of sociology. Indeed, I rather exaggerated than played down the importance of their contribution. Thus I provided the public with all the elements needed to evaluate it.... I certainly owe a great deal to the Germans ... but the real influence that Germany has exerted upon me is very different from what he asserts.
>
> (Lukes 1982: 258)

Durkheim never indicates what this real influence was. Durkheim also responded that 'when I read the *Ethik* of Wundt I had been tending in that direction for a long time already' (259). These defensive remarks by Durkheim only serve to tantalize, not to lessen the import of Deploige's charge. Is Deploige ([1911] 1938) correct that Durkheim's sociology is more German than French in inspiration?

Despite Deploige's fascinating thesis, nothing substantive has been written by Durkheimian scholars about his visit to Germany. What did he study? Who or what else influenced him in Germany? Did he attend Simmel's lectures while in Berlin? Short of indicating the need for research to answer these and related questions, a number of points concerning the intellectual debt of Durkheim to Wundt and Wundt's German precursors are obvious.

First, given Durkheim's highly polemical style, it is noteworthy that Durkheim never criticized Wundt publicly, and always referred to his works with respect. This is frankly shocking, if not courageous, given Durkheim's criticisms of fellow Frenchmen and French culture, and given France's humiliating defeat by Germany in 1871, which Durkheim witnessed during the German occupation of Epinal. This respect for Wundt seems to spill over into a general tone of serious respect for turn of the century German philosophy and culture in general.

Second, the broad outlines of Wundt's concerns with *Volkerpsychologie* and ethics correspond with Durkheim's representationalism and science of morality, respectively. If we want to seek out Durkheim's ultimate stand on the *fin de siècle*, it seems that the answer might still be buried in the Wundt archives in Leipzig. Durkheim would not succumb to excessive optimism nor pessimism, and criticized both. But he embraced the scientific study of these phenomena. In this regard, there can be no doubt that Wundt's folk psychology foreshadowed Durkheim's sociology, just as surely as Schopenhauer and von Hartmann paved the way for Wundt with their own philosophical 'psychologies' (as suggested by Thomas Mann in 1939).

Third, this connection between Durkheim and Wundt, along with Wundt's Schopenhauerian roots, brings one back, full circle, to Bloom's (1987) thesis in *Closing of the American Mind* concerning the neglected importance of turn of the century German philosophy. Bloom hardly mentions most of the figures that have been presented in this chapter, and especially neglects Durkheim. Nevertheless, he may be more correct than he or his critics suppose. As Deploige (1911) as well as Baillot (1927) painstakingly demonstrate, even French literature and philosophy at the turn of the century are essentially German and particularly Schopenhauerian by inspiration.

Thus, it would seem that no discussion of postmodernity is complete without referring to German *fin de siècle* philosophy. Bloom attacks postmodernist cultural relativism using German philosophy as a foil, but his aims are conservative. My aims are to find benign, liberal elements in German *fin de siècle* philosophy as these aided Durkheim in finding alternatives to the repressive rationalist philosophies he was criticizing. However, I do not pretend to offer anything but a thumbnail sketch of what a full version of this proposed project should be like.

THE POLEMIC BETWEEN DURKHEIM AND DEPLOIGE

It is important to elaborate on Deploige's accusation that Durkheim's sociology is essentially German, because Lukes (1985) and other commentators tend simply to dismiss Deploige, and because Deploige's argument is an obscure forerunner of Allan Bloom's (1987) argument. Moreover, Deploige's argument is fascinating in its own right, because of the light it sheds on the origins of French sociology.

Deploige ([1911] 1938: 104) notes that 'Durkheim is both sociologist and moralist', and that Durkheim 'does not remain in the serene regions of cold science [but seeks] to prove that our great modern societies are in a critical state, that they are sick' (99). (This is commensurate with the 'cult of feeling' theme developed in chapter 2.) Deploige observes correctly that Durkheim faults Comte, Spencer, Stuart Mill, and other precursors of sociology for their 'lack of objectivity' (33) precisely because their excessive rationalism blinds them to the sickness of modernity. Deploige, who was a priest, does not seem to regard these nonmodern qualities as faults in Durkheim.

Yet Deploige attacks Durkheim for what he calls his 'social realism', the claim that society is something more than the sum of its individual members, that it is a reality *sui generis*. Curiously, Deploige does not attack Durkheim's argument nor Durkheim the person as much as he is distressed by the German origins of Durkheim's argument. Durkheimian sociology is 'of German origin' according to Deploige, such that 'Wagner and Schmoller, together with Schaeffle, furnished M. Durkheim with his fundamental postulate of social realism' (122).

Deploige notes that Durkheim was not alone in this French borrowing from the Germans. For example, Deploige quotes Renan twice, as saying that 'I owe to Germany what I appreciate most, my philosophy' (125), and again

> The victory of Germany was the victory of science. After Jena, the University of Berlin was the center of the regeneration of Germany. If we wish to rise from our disasters, let us imitate the conduct of Prussia. French intelligence has been weakened; we must strengthen it (122).

Espinas, Bouglé, and a host of other French scholars made trips to Germany to learn from the victors in the war of 1870. It is important to note that Espinas was one of Durkheim's most important mentors, and Bouglé was one of his most important disciples (as claimed by Mauss [1950] 1979a).

In a refreshing break with the typical kitsch depiction of Durkheim as a follower of Comte, Deploige asserts boldly:

> It was not Comte who inspired Durkheim; it was Simmel, a German, sympathetic with the group of Durkheim as critic of morality if not of sociology. In a book hardly known in France outside the followers of Durkheim, Simmel had maintained that ... all the attributes of God can be transferred to society (144).

It is true that Durkheim *did* reproduce Simmel's thesis in his 1912 classic on religion, and Deploige is correct that Simmel paralleled Durkheim's argument in his still untranslated 1893 *Einleitung in die Moralwissenschaft*. One can understand why the idea of reducing the notion of God to society might be offensive to a priest, but Deploige should be given credit for making the linkage between Simmel and Durkheim that has been revived in a different form only recently by Frisby (1984). In any case, Deploige ([1911] 1938: 146) concludes, and again correctly, that 'the ideas and the methods which Durkheim took from the Germans for the most part were new, or at least little known, in France'. When Durkheim presented these essentially German ideas to French intellectuals, he was criticized severely by them – this has been well documented, even by Durkheim's followers (see Lukes 1985).

Deploige is also correct to link the German doctrine of social realism with the notion of the collective soul, spirit, nation, and people *(Volk)* that had existed for some time among writers from Hegel and Lazarus to Neitzsche. Deploige asks the poignant question ([1911] 1938: 151):

> In Germany, Durkheim had heard Schaeffle, Wagner, and Schmoller teach in all serenity the doctrine of social realism. Why did the truth admitted beyond the Rhine become on this side [in France] an error to be driven out? Durkheim had no thought of answering this question. He merely took over his masters' postulate without any concern as to its origin. The fact is that a certain conception of social realism was very widespread in Germany and was already old.

Deploige argues that this German doctrine was offensive to Durkheim's French contemporaries because it represented part of the Romantic structure that the French Revolution had replaced with cosmopolitanism, individualism, and rationalism. (For this reason, I suspect that Durkheim abhorred the French Revolution, despite many efforts to link him as one of its defenders.)

Thus, 'Durkheim's first mistake, when he introduced into France the Germanic theory of social realism, was his failure to suspect the deep and remote roots of the theory' (172) that lead, supposedly, to an anti-French stand. Deploige adds that 'France, on the contrary, continued to pride herself on individualist philosophy, [which] in spite of certain assaults, always succeeded in maintaining its dominance in university teaching' (173).

While one may disagree with Deploige that either German or Durkheim's notions of a living collective entity (society) necessarily opposes individualism (Durkheim explicitly championed individualism, as distinguished from egoism, discussed in Meštrović 1988a), his argument is nevertheless significant. Perhaps Durkheim's sociology was offensive to his French contemporaries also because it opposed the abstractionist modernity that had taken root in France more than in Germany at that time. Social realism is decidedly anti-modern, because it posits a fixed, objective point in the transitoriness of modernity. Durkheim made society the penultimate refraction of this social realism.

According to Deploige ([1911] 1938: 172) 'all things considered, we may conclude that sociology is rather Germanic, since the Germans, without having the word, had the thing itself'. Simmel, Marx, Tönnies, Weber, and Mannheim certainly preferred to call themselves things other than 'sociologist', yet Durkheimian sociology amplifies the best in their theories.

Durkheim continues to be attacked for his social realism, most recently by Lukes (1985). Yet consider that if one removes social realism from sociology, one has opened the portals to all the negative aspects of modernity and postmodernism that have been discussed, including nihilism. A far more fruitful project would be to pursue Deploige's line of reasoning, and analyse further the vicissitudes of German Romanticism and realism. Why, for example, does current linguistics idolize Saussure at the expense of the linguistics put forth by Lazarus, Steinthal, Durkheim, and the German folk psychologists? Why has current political sociology neglected the Hegelian notion of *Volk* in its biased emphasis on Hegel's subjectivism (Habermas 1987)? In general, why has German irrationalism been repressed in contemporary discourses on modernity and postmodernism?

APPLYING THE SOCIOLOGY OF KNOWLEDGE TO THE ISSUE OF SOCIOLOGY'S ORIGINS

Part of the answer to the questions posed above may be extrapolated from Deploige's argument. Following the two World Wars, Germans were depicted and caricatured in extremely negative terms in the rest of Europe and the USA compared to French and British contributions to culture (Eksteins 1989). David Riesman has indicated to me that this negative reaction to German culture was more severe following the First World War compared to the Second. For example, Lukács (1980) and other neo-Marxists delighted in drawing straight lines from German Romanticism to Hitler, even though that is an extremely simplistic and false argument that should not be taken seriously. There are many paths to Hitler's final solution, and it is not at all obvious that German Romanticism and irrationalism had anything to do with it. But this misunderstanding may have been sufficient to create the prejudice against German philosophy that Bloom (1987) finally exposed, but that still persists in academia.

And the true origins of sociology may have been distorted in the shuffle. The false caricature that modern sociology is descended from the French rationalist Auguste Comte rather than the German Wilhelm Wundt may be part of the distortion suggested above. Durkheim's psychologically and philosophically informed sociology withered following his death in 1917, and this may be due, in part, to its German origins as suggested by Deploige. After the First World War, no one was especially interested in either *Volksgeist* or Durkheim's notion of the 'collective conscience', which are admitted by Bouglé (1938) to be equivalent and essential to appreciating Durkheim's sociology. It would appear that these German ideas were simply too offensive to leading intellectuals writing in the beginning of the present century. Yet, without social realism – which is the key idea implied by these German concepts – sociology seems to be succumbing to the forces of modernity and postmodernism that social realism combats (namely, excessive relativism, nihilism, paralysis). Thus, the line of enquiry opened by Deploige in 1911 deserves to be pursued further.

Durkheim's high regard for German *fin de siècle* philosophy contrasts sharply with his unequivocal dismissal of the *naiveté*, felicity, and embarrassing simplicity of the Enlightenment, particularly the French Enlightenment. This is an important point to consider, because it highlights further Durkheim's debt to the German *fin de siècle* spirit, which made it fashionable to criticize rationalism, and because contemporary sociologists continue to misalign Durkheim with the Enlightenment, especially Comte.

Thus, Alvin Gouldner (1958: ix) demonstrates in his neglected introduction to Durkheim's equally neglected *Socialism and Saint-Simon* that in this book Durkheim was engaged 'in a deep-seated polemic against Comte'. Indeed, in this book Durkheim dethrones Comte as the rightful founder of positivism, sociology, and socialism – all of these doctrines are described as being in a state of crisis as humankind approaches the next *fin de siècle* (Filloux 1977; Hayek 1988; Holton 1987; Horowitz 1987). But one will not find this important point noted in any contemporary sociology textbook. Sociology as it is taught in the postmodernist age still pays lip-service to Comte and positivism and simply ignores numerous *fin de siècle* criticisms of Comte and his doctrine (see Deploige 1911).

In any case, Durkheim ascribes the honours of having established sociology, socialism, and positivism to Saint-Simon, but then concludes his treatise with a severe critique of Saint-Simon! He sympathizes with socialism's own sympathy for human suffering, but he considers socialism as nothing more than a representation of another aspect of *fin de siècle* malaise, not its solution. Durkheim applauds Saint-Simon's Romanticism and focus on love as an integrative force, but faults him for his teleology, lack of empiricism, and underlying abstractionism despite his apparent sentimentality (discussed in Meštrović 1988a). Again, it is interesting that Durkheim praises those aspects of Saint-Simon that are closest to German philosophy, and faults him for his rationalism!

In *The Radical Durkheim*, Frank Pearce (1989) finds common ground between Durkheim's and Marx's doctrines. Indeed, it is interesting that both thinkers shared a humanist doctrine of the 'rights of man' and both analysed institutional structures in relation to the development of this doctrine. For the context of the present discussion, it is important to add that at least part of this remarkable convergence may stem from the common influence of German, Romantic philosophy on both thinkers (although Marx was more Hegelian and Durkheim more Schopenhauerian, of course). Moreover, Pearce focuses on Durkheim's socialist leanings and basic sympathy with socialism while noting that Marx and Durkheim diverged on the issue of what the role of the State should be in socialism. Durkheim argued for a strong State government to ensure the functioning of complex societies, whereas Marx felt that the State would 'wither away'.

Now that Marxism itself is withering away, one needs to search out the roots of Marxism's failure as well as the reasons why Durkheim's remarkably similar doctrine was almost completely eclipsed by Marxism. I would venture the reply that despite its Romantic leanings, Marxism was closer temporally and in terms of philosophical assumptions to the Enlightenment. The death of Marxism in the late twentieth century bespeaks the futility of hyper-rationality that led to a monstrous bureaucracy. But the Marxist humanist dream still lives in Eastern Europe and the USSR.

Durkheimianism shares the same humanistic dream, but contrary to the Saint-Simonian, French tradition that Durkheim criticized, it is based on the *fin de siècle* spirit of irrationalism. Marx and Saint-Simon were both overly optimistic about the possibility of reforming human greed and egoism. Durkheim remains starkly pessimistic concerning the power of human egoism, and his version of socialism needs a strong State government to restrain this egoism. At the same time, Durkheim (1950) warned that the

State must not suppress the spontaneous 'will of the people'. A balance must be struck between the irrational will and the rational organ that constitutes the State – these two entities must 'communicate' in Durkheim's political scheme.

DURKHEIM'S STAND ON THE ENLIGHTENMENT

An important aim in this chapter is to contrast sharply Durkheim's high regard for German *fin de siècle* philosophers with his disdain for earlier German or contemporary French, British, and other Enlightenment philosophers and philosophies. The import of Deploige's (1911) fascinating thesis is exposed more fully when one considers Durkheim's criticisms of Enlightenment philosophers.

Durkheim's classics are peppered with explicit, searing criticisms of Kant, especially in his introductory remarks in *Division of Labor, Professional Ethics, Moral Education,* and *Elementary Forms.* Durkheim cannot accept Kant's a priorism, his optimism, categorical imperative, and exclusive focus on duty at the expense of desire. In *Primitive Classification* ([1902] 1975), especially, Durkheim and Mauss argue that society is the empirical, if not metaphysical, origin of Kant's supposedly a priori categories. Despite these obvious facts, Durkheim continues to be misaligned with Kantianism, which was indeed popular in French universities in Durkheim's time. Gouldner may be correct that this error must be regarded as part of the politics and sociology of knowledge within sociology itself. Simply put, Kant and Comte appeal to modernists as well as postmodernists because of their excessive rationalism and abstractionism.

Or consider Durkheim's ([1892] 1965) Latin thesis on Montesquieu and Rousseau, two important French Enlightenment philosophers. To be sure, Rousseau is sometimes invoked today as a precursor of the Romantic movement, but Durkheim makes a strong case for regarding him as an Enlightenment philosopher (see Dent 1989). Durkheim criticizes these two philosophers, along with Hobbes and Comte and Spencer, for treating society as if it were something 'added to nature' rather than a legitimately 'natural' object of scientific study. As Durkheim put the matter: 'If, as assumed by Rousseau, Montesquieu, and nearly all thinkers up to Comte (and even Spencer relapses into the traditional confusion), nature ends with the individual, then everything that goes beyond the individual is bound to be artificial' (66). In other words, Durkheim will not accept that society is only rational, subjective, and artificial. He betrays the social realism that Deploige had isolated, even the Schopenhauerian flavour that society has a 'will' of its own that works despite or outside the domain of human consciousness and reason, a point missed completely by Althusser (1982) and other contemporary commentators.

Along these lines, in all his writings Durkheim is highly critical of utilitarianism and its precursors or promulgators: Rousseau, Condorcet, Stuart-Mill, and Spencer. With regard to Descartes, the very symbol of France's contribution to the Enlightenment, Durkheim does not restrain his criticism. 'We have reasoned so much!', Durkheim lamented in 1887, and despite so much rationality, he observed that there existed more, not less, malaise and uneasiness. His one point of agreement with pragmatists and anti-rationalists is that, indeed, Cartesianism is too simplistic. He makes this especially clear, and calls for a renovation of rationalism, in the conclusions to his *Pragmatism and Sociology*, *Evolution of Educational Thought*, *Moral Education*, and *The Elementary Forms*.

Thus, Durkheim's thought is very much a part of the *fin de siècle* rebellion against the previous Age of Reason, only he tempered this reaction, and did not allow it to spill over into nihilism. Durkheim's fondness for German philosophy never led him over the edge into Nietzsche's cynicism – Durkheim could even find realism and Romanticism in Nietzsche, something that many contemporary commentators have failed to do. In addition to the cynicism uncovered by Bloom (1987), Sloterdijk (1987) and others, there exists a positive, benign, even beautiful aspect to pre-modern German Romanticism, and Durkheim allowed this benign aspect to inform his sociology. And he has been deeply misunderstood in this regard.

IMPLICATIONS

In his *Influence de la philosophie de Schopenhauer en France (1860–1900)* Baillot (1927) devotes considerable attention to Baudelaire, a third-generation Romantic as Baillot calls him. While he cannot prove Schopenhauer's direct influence on Baudelaire textually, Baillot (1927: 209) argues convincingly that Baudelaire's writings are Schopenhauerian in spirit, and that they paved the way for subsequent, direct acceptance of Schopenhauer's philosophy into France. The essential Schopenhauerian claim that 'the world is my idea' found its way into Baudelaire's disgust with modernity as pure subjectivism (163), although it should not be forgotten that Baudelaire admired some aspects of modernity, even some of its ugly aspects. Yet, for Baudelaire, as for Schopenhauer, life is suffering (203). This pessimism and deep critique of modernity found their way into the works of a host of other third-generation French Romantic artists: Delacroix, Vigny, Hugo, Musset, Balzac, Flaubert, Zola, Maupassant, Anatole France, Mallarmé, Verlaine, and Rimbaud, among other lesser known figures.

Thus, the present study points to an intriguing confluence of some French and German Romantic forces as these influenced the origins of Durkheimian sociology. At the present time, I am not able to achieve more than Baillot with regard to the affinities between Durkheim and Baudelaire or Schopenhauer or Wundt. The affinities are striking to one who searches for them, but they hardly constitute 'hard evidence'. But suppose that by some miracle Durkheim could be raised from the dead, and would tell us that either he was or was not influenced directly by reading Baudelaire or Schopenhauer or Wundt. Would this constitute hard evidence? Durkheim would be among the first to reply in the negative, because he insisted – in a typically *fin de siècle* manner – that introspection is an invalid method of enquiry, that no one can ever ascertain with full certainty anything about one's self or society. 'Reality' is always veiled, hidden, and obscured. And collective representations, which come in many guises, are more important than the event of reading or not reading a book. Historians and philosophers agree that Durkheim's age was soaked in collective representations that reflected Baudelaire, Schopenhauer, and other proponents of the *fin de siècle* spirit, especially the German version of this same spirit. They also agree that Comte's positivism had been lying dead and dormant for more than thirty years when Durkheim began teaching sociology.

Thus, the more important point is that once the positivistic approach is cast aside, one is in a position to appreciate the 'landscape' or representations that Baudelaire, Schopenhauer, and Wundt used to apprehend modernity. The *fin de siècle* was an incontestably gloomy period (Ellenberger 1970), with many influences and cross-influences. This, despite the fact that Eugen

Weber (1987) manages to find some optimistic themes in the *fin de siècle*, particularly among the lower classes. Baudelaire and Schopenhauer become symbols or representations of this period. Wilhelm Wundt launched psychology in this same context, drawing on the founders of *Volkerpsychologie*, Lazarus and Steinthal. It seems reasonable to suppose that Durkheim would have noticed the *fin de siècle* spirit, and been influenced by it to some extent.

Earlier, I have suggested that Durkheim's attacks on pragmatism, positivism, and naive rationalism are variations of Baudelaire's attacks on dandyism and modernity as well as Schopenhauer's attacks on Kantianism. Further evidence that these rationalist doctrines lead to the cold, blasé (from Simmel) attitude characteristic of the dandy is evidenced by the fact that as of this writing, Durkheim's concept of anomie has been given up for dead by Besnard (1987) and Orru (1987), the end result of a long and sustained effort to strip anomie of its true meaning at least since the writings of Parsons (1937). The irony is that postmodernity is an age in which only a sleepwalker could deny that contemporary portraits of life resonate with Baudelaire's and Durkheim's portraits that emphasize cynicism, disgust, and decadence. Our age is drowning collectively in cynicism and anomie, yet the positivists tell us that anomie does not exist and cannot be measured. Baudelaire's ([1863] 1965: 27–8) description of dandyism as a 'school of tyrants', an unofficial institution that has formed a 'haughty and exclusive sect', a new aristocracy formed just when everyone else is feeling 'socially, politically and financially ill at ease' seems to fit the rise of positivism in this century.

For example, it must be remembered that Parsons (1937) wrote his treatise on 'rational social action' at a time of great economic, social, and political upheaval. The negative reaction to Hitler's monstrous use of the German concept of *Volk* completely eclipsed Wundt's and Durkheim's benign uses, and propelled Parsons into fame. Similarly, Habermas (1987) frequently cites the negative side of irrationalism while seeking to complete the project of the Enlightenment. Nevertheless, as humankind approaches the next *fin de siècle*, it is experiencing deep economic, social, and political crises again. And it may be that these crises are derived from the Enlightenment, not irrationalism.

Chapter Seven

ETHICS BASED ON THE MIND VERSUS THE HEART, RATIONALITY VERSUS COMPASSION

Suppose, for the sake of argument, that postmodernism were a genuine rebellion against modernity, as so many of its adherents claim (Murphy 1989). If that were true, one would expect post-modern social theorists to rally around someone like Pitirim Sorokin (1947), who was the last, major sociologist to attempt to establish ethics on a non-rational, non-cognitive, and, in a word, anti-modern basis. But in fact, postmodern moral theorists in diverse fields have neglected Sorokin. Modernity presupposes abstractionism and enlightenment, and postmodernists have continued the Enlightenment tradition by linking morality with the mind, not the heart.

It is commonplace for scholars and laypersons alike to use the word 'irrational' to refer to crimes ranging from brutal rapes to Hitler's Final Solution. Individual serial killers must be mad, and Hitler must have ridden on the crest of the collective wave of irrationalism that began with Romanticism (Lukács 1980). In university courses on ethics and moral development, morality is linked solemnly to rationality as well as to cognitive development. Consider, for example, the neo-Kantian overtones found in the moral development theories of Piaget, Kohlberg, Habermas, and their many followers. They never so much as consider the other side of the argument: the common criminal, Hitler, and the many persons who carried out his atrocities, along with other examples of inhuman and brutal actors, may have been overly rational and may not have possessed sufficient amounts of that mysterious, irrational quality called compassion. Postmodernists forget the ancient wisdom that to commit wickedness, one must possess not only cunning, but one must be able to suppress the seemingly natural tendency to empathize.

108

It has been all but forgotten by academics that in his 1841 essay entitled *On the Basis of Morality*, Arthur Schopenhauer offered a severe criticism of Kant's rationalist system of morality. Whereas Kant argued that the basis for morality was duty, Schopenhauer argued that genuine morality must be based on compassion and desire. In short, to use the dualism between the heart and mind that is the basis of much of this book, Schopenhauer aligned morality with the heart and thereby reversed Kant's understanding of morality as a phenomenon of the mind and the Enlightenment. Schopenhauer's argument is compelling, had tremendous influence on *fin de siècle* thinkers, and deserves to be taken seriously. It exposes the hypocrisy of the claim that postmodernism rebels at the grand narrative of modernity.

Schopenhauer's achievement had a lasting impact on turn of the century concerns with the empirical study of morality (see Fox 1980; Lévy-Bruhl 1899, 1905; Logue 1983; Wundt 1907). I will repeat that Simmel (1893) established the scientific study of morality in a Romantic context concurrently with Durkheim's efforts in this same direction, as noted by Bouglé (1896). Durkheim's colleague and collaborator at the Sorbonne, Lucien Lévy-Bruhl (1905: 15), also remarked on the deficiency of 'Kant's teaching [in that] it establishes universal and necessary principles without borrowing anything from experience'. Following Schopenhauer's lead, Wilhelm Wundt's (1907) *Volkerpsychologie* concerned itself in large measure with the scientific study of morality. Similarly, Durkheim and his followers understood their version of sociology as an attempt to establish a science of moral facts (see Durkheim [1920] 1978; Davy 1927; Hall 1988; Lévy-Bruhl 1899, 1905; Mauss [1950] 1979a; Meštrović 1988a; Pickering 1979). Pickering (1979) is correct to cite the works of Landry, Fouillée, Belot, Bayet, and Westermarck as efforts within the programme established by Durkheim. And Durkheim in turn was aware of and reviewed many of the works by these philosophers. The theme that binds all these diverse works together is that they were attempts to find an alternative to Kant's hyper-rational version of morality.

Moreover, the concerns with the scientific, empirical study of morality by the precursors of today's social sciences were part of a larger and more general influence of Schopenhauer's philosophy on what Ellenberger (1970) called the *fin de siècle* spirit that captivated many turn of the century writers in diverse fields.

Although scholars are aware of Durkheim's concerns with the scientific study of morals (see Hall 1987), even if they disagree with how central this concern was for Durkheim's sociology as a whole, the role of Schopenhauer's critique of Kant in general and for understanding Durkheim's writings in particular has been completely neglected in sociological analyses.

For example, Henri Bergson, the philosophical superstar of the *fin de siècle*, betrays Schopenhauer's influence in his own critique of Kantian ethics. In *The Two Sources of Morality and Religion*, Bergson ([1932] 1954: 210) notes that in contradistinction to the Enlightenment belief that intelligence could counsel ethics, 'intelligence ... would more likely counsel egoism' (which is also Schopenhauer's conclusion). Like Schopenhauer, Bergson cites many problems with a purely intellectualist moral philosophy: that such a philosophy can only 'adduce reasons, which we are perfectly free to combat with other reasons' (270); that intelligence is a dissolving power compared to intuition (122); that intelligence can never bring forth moral action, only rationalizations (48); and that 'morality expresses a certain emotional state, that actually we yield not to a pressure [Kant's duty] but to an attraction' (49). In sum, contrary to Kant, Bergson (85) asserts that 'because we have established the rational character of moral conduct, it does not follow that morality has its origin or even its foundation in pure reason'.

Similarly, Lucien Lévy-Bruhl – to whom Hall (1987: 34) refers as 'an independent originator of the sociology of morals' alongside Durkheim – criticizes severely Kant's rationalist system of ethics. In *Ethics and Moral Science* Lévy-Bruhl (1905: 43) refers to Kant's rationalism as 'a strange rationalism' and as 'a theory of a strange kind' (45). This is because for Kant, facts belong to the world of phenomena while the reason that should guide morals is relegated to the unreachable world of noumena: 'The reason to which he [Kant] relates moral order is not the reason that knows, the reason the function of which is to found science: it is the reason that commands and that does so in the name of principles that are not instituted by the reason that knows.' Moreover, with regard to morality, 'Kant demands nothing from the non-intellectual powers of the soul' except obedience, despite the fact that in Lévy-Bruhl's opinion, 'it is not the idea which determines the actions of the greater number of men, but feeling' (44).

In his *Evolution of Values*, Bouglé (1926) echoes the Schopenhauerian tradition when he asserts that moral values cannot be understood apart from human desire. Moral values must be loved, not just obeyed, according to Bouglé, and 'there is no moral education without communication of feelings' (49). Bouglé adds (52): 'In fact one of the clearest lessons of the science of ethics is that, always and everywhere, customs are maintained by a whole system of suggestions, attractions and pressures which act on the feelings.'

Bergson, Lévy-Bruhl, and Bouglé are only three illustrious thinkers among many from Durkheim's intellectual milieu who expressed an awareness of the problems with Kant's rationalist system of ethics along Schopenhauerian lines. (I have dealt sufficiently with Simmel's reliance on the 'cult of feeling' in chapter 2.) And many of these thinkers referred favourably to Durkheim as being in the forefront of efforts to transcend these difficulties with Kant. Even Deploige ([1911] 1938: 94) notes that in Durkheim's science of morality, feelings play a major role, and that Durkheim thought that 'for anyone to construct or logically to deduce ethics is an undertaking that is beside the mark' (12).

Yet, as a rule, Durkheimian scholars, investigators in contemporary moral theory, and postmodernist theorists in general do not acknowledge the polemic between Kant and Schopenhauer and its import for the scientific study of morality. Despite evidence for Schopenhauer's influence on turn of the century intellectuals in general (Ellenberger 1970), and the scientific study of morality in particular, his importance in contemporary studies of morality has been almost completely overlooked. The most dominant forces in modern studies of morality are the works of Kohlberg (1984) and Habermas (1970, 1984), which are informed, explicitly or implicitly, almost entirely by Kant's philosophy or some other variation of the Enlightenment. The contemporary focus in moral theory on the rationalist basis of moral judgement and on duty, along with a neglect of the role of compassion in morality, is a clear indicator of the continued influence of Kant's (1788) problematic influence at the expense of neglecting Schopenhauer's critique.

But the polemic between Kant and Schopenhauer, along with their disciples, is still very relevant to contemporary concerns with morality and to postmodern concerns for a more democratic and tolerant society. Postmodern concerns with being happy, optimistic, and tolerant amount to what Riesman (1950) called morale, not morality. Riesman noted that other-directedness centres on 'being nice' as opposed to the inner-directed need to be certain that one was correct in one's values. The 1980s witnessed an exacerbation of this other-directed trend. The so-called 'me generation' subscribes to the tenet that all moral values are relative so that just about anything goes, so long as one acts 'nice'. In keeping with this boosterish attitude characteristic of the 1980s, contemporary theorists on postmodernism simply neglect the serious topics that concerned moral theorists in the previous century: sympathy, compassion, and the concern of humans for fellow humans. These topics touch on the socialist and communist revolutions that occurred after the previous *fin de siècle*, and the counter-revolutions that are shaking the 1980s and will probably continue into the 1990s. These same topics also touch on the rampant cynicism in capitalist nations, a cynicism that stems from a widespread belief that many corporate and government leaders are routinely immoral and selfish.

I will begin with Schopenhauer's (1841) critique of Kant (1788) regarding morality based on duty versus compassion, and move to a comparison and contrast with Durkheim's philosophical underpinnings for his understanding of the sociological study of morality. The present chapter builds on the insights developed in chapter 3 concerning the importance of the 'cult of feeling', and on the claims of Bouglé (1896), Pickering (1979), and Hall (1987) that the sociology of morals is central to Durkheim's entire sociological thought, and that he was influenced primarily by German moralists of his time in this regard, including Simmel (1893). It is important to be reminded from chapter 6 of Schopenhauer's influence on turn of the century German and French intellectuals in general (see Baillot 1927). Schopenhauer's and Durkheim's emphases on compassion and other components of the heart as the basis for morality will be opposed to Kant's hyper-rational approach to morality and Kant's condemnation of compassion (see Schopenhauer [1841] 1965: 183).

Finally, the claim is being made here that Habermas (1987) and other discussants in the discourse on postmodernity are uncritically perpetuating Kant's errors despite the rhetoric of attempting to account for the shortcomings of the Enlightenment project.

SCHOPENHAUER'S CRITIQUE OF KANT

As stated previously, Schopenhauer's (1818) reputation as a philosopher is based on his strong emphasis on the will to life, what he sometimes called the heart – passion, desire, sexuality, the unconscious, and compassion – as a force stronger and more important than reason, the idea, or the mind. His ethical system is an extension of this basic philosophical position. Thus, in the opening moves of his *Basis of Morality*, Schopenhauer ([1841] 1965: 48) makes clear his aims to criticize Kant's linkage of morality with the mind:

> I allude to the daily writers of compendiums who, with the cool confidence of stupidity, imagine they have established ethics if only they appeal to that *'moral law'* that is supposed to be inherent in our faculty of *reason*..... I therefore confess the particular pleasure with which I set to work to remove the broad cushion from ethics, and frankly express my intention of proving that Kant's practical reason and categorical imperative are wholly unjustified, groundless, and fictitious assumptions, and of showing that even Kant's ethics lacks a solid foundation.

While these opening remarks by Schopenhauer are clearly offensive, the rest of his critique is dispassionate and compelling, and deserves serious consideration.

Thus, Schopenhauer (62) notes that for Kant, ethics 'is to consist of a pure, i.e., a priori knowable part and an empirical one' and that Kant 'rejects the empirical part as inadmissible for the establishment of ethics'. Moreover, Schopenhauer questions how these a priori moral concepts could 'have the power to put bridle and bit on the impulse of strong desires, the storm of passion, and the gigantic stature of egoism' (62). According to Schopenhauer (66), Kant's system of morality is to be based on 'pitiful, miserable duty', *not* anything subjective such as feeling, inclination, impulse, or compassion (70). Indeed, it is a verifiable fact that Kant ([1788] 1956: 75, 91–6) repeatedly rejects any connection between morality and desire, happiness, compassion, or feeling in general (see also Cartwright 1984).

One of Schopenhauer's ([1841] 1965: 90) objections to Kant's system is that, because it is based on duty, and because duty is based on fear of authority – consider Kant's ([1788] 1956: 30) frightful analogy between the law and the gallows – morality based on duty is really egotistical, and therefore immoral: 'All actions that arise from motives of such a kind [the categorial imperative] would always be rooted only in mere egoism' (Schopenhauer [1841] 1965: 137). If we act morally because we feel that we *must*, not because we spontaneously desire to be moral, Schopenhauer argues that this is not really morality: 'To Europeans, the source [of morality] positively must be a command of duty, a moral law, an imperative – in short, an order and decree that is obeyed. From this they will not depart, nor see that such things always have only egoism as their basis' (187).

Note that in both communist and capitalist nations of the 1980s, fear continues to be the basis for most common morality. In communist nations, one fears physical torture or imprisonment for acting on the desire to express one's self freely. But in other-directed USA, one acts out of anxiety and a different sort of fear less one fails to conform to postmodern narratives to look 'cool', be 'nice', and have 'fun'. In both cases, what Riesman (1950) called autonomy and Schopenhauer (1818) referred to as 'spontaneous desire' continue to be exceedingly rare achievements.

Schopenhauer also objects to Kant's linkage between reason and morality (83):

> A man can go to work very rationally and thus thoughtfully, deliberately, consistently, systematically, and methodically, and yet act upon the most selfish, unjust, and even iniquitous maxims. Hence it never occurred to anyone *prior* to Kant to identify just, virtuous, and noble conduct with *reasonable* or *rational*, but the two have been clearly distinguished and kept apart.... Reasonable and vicious are quite consistent with each other, and in fact, only through their union are great and far-reaching crimes possible. In the same way unreasonable and noble-minded can very well coexist.

Thus, in contradistinction to Kant, Schopenhauer (91) writes that one 'can very well will injustice and uncharitableness as a universal maxim'. It is striking that in his own critique of Kant, Durkheim ([1893] 1933: 412) echoes Schopenhauer's line, above, when he writes that 'The egotistical maxim is no more stubborn than the other [charity] in assuming a universal form; it can be practised with all its implied consequences.'

Schopenhauer objects to the fact that animals, as non-rational creatures, are excluded from Kant's system, such that animals 'can therefore be used for vivisection, hunting, coursing, bullfights, and horse racing, and can be whipped to death as they struggle along with heavy carts of stone' ([1841] 1965: 96). Schopenhauer's observations still apply to the lame attempts by animal rights movements to restrict the use of animals in medical experiments, while these other examples of cruelty to animals are allowed to continue. Many postmodern persons still claim their cruel 'right' to wear furs. Slow dogs that are bred for dog racing are still routinely killed in the USA. Long before Darwin, whose importance to sociology Bouglé (1909) made explicit, Schopenhauer argued that humans are bound to animals (as well as plants, indeed all life) on the basis of the will to life that they share, and he concluded that no system of morality that excludes compassion for animals could be truly moral.

Not surprisingly, Schopenhauer praised Hinduism and Buddhism for extending compassion to more of the animal kingdom than the modicum of compassion that Christianity granted to some humans. He allowed for the killing of animals for the purpose of eating food, but not for sport, fashion, or caprice. While one could argue contrary to Schopenhauer that it is not possible or practical for postmodern persons to live like the ancient Hindus, one could just as well argue for Schopenhauer's position: animals may have small brains and therefore undeveloped consciousness compared to humans, but they do feel pain. Even if all cruelty to animals could not be eliminated, a great deal of needless cruelty could be limited.

Schopenhauer also notes that Kant's system does not distinguish between the quantity and quality of an immoral act. For Kant (1788), stealing is stealing, but for Schopenhauer, the act of a dying man who steals bread from starvation is fundamentally different from the act of a rich man who defrauds a poor man of his last possession ([1841] 1965: 155).

But Schopenhauer's most potent criticism of Kant stems from his conviction that compassion and justice – which he regards as a unity, and which I will refer to hereafter as compassion – is the real basis of morality, not duty. Compassion stems from the heart, not the mind. It is *irrational*. Because it is not based on duty and fear, it is a genuine, albeit momentary victory over humankind's

115

innate egoism, and as such is exceedingly rare in the world. It extends to other humans as well as animals.

Schopenhauer argues for the primacy of compassion over duty as follows: he asks the reader to imagine asking someone to evaluate why he should *not* commit an act of murder against someone who has done them wrong. This is an interesting contrast to the *cognitive* moral dilemmas found in modern theorists ranging from Piaget through Kohlberg to Habermas, because Schopenhauer's dilemma focuses on the passionate, irrational desire for revenge. Schopenhauer reviews the many possible *rational* explanations such a person could give, including Kant's, that

> he may say: 'I consider that the maxim for my proceeding in this case would not have been calculated to give a universally valid rule for all possible rational beings, since I should have treated my rival only as a means and not at the same time as an end' (168).

Schopenhauer continues:

> But Titus, whose account I reserve for myself, may say: 'When it came to making the arrangements [for the murder], and so for the moment I had to concern myself not with my passion but with that rival, I clearly saw for the first time what would really happen to him. But I was then seized with compassion and pity; I felt sorry for him; I had not the heart to do it, and could not.'

Now I ask any honest and unbiased reader: Which of the two is the better man? To which of them would he prefer to entrust his own destiny? Which of them has been restrained by the purer motive? Accordingly, where does the foundation of morality lie?

It would be interesting and important to verify empirically whether Schopenhauer (170) is correct to claim that 'Nothing shocks our moral feelings so deeply as cruelty does', and that when confronted with an immoral act, we do *not* ask, as Kant suggested, 'How it is possible to act according to a maxim that is so absolutely unfitted to become a general law for all rational beings?' Rather, Schopenhauer claims that we ask ourselves, 'How could anyone have been so heartless?' At bottom, even the most postmodern cynic does not really ask the Kantian question, and the Schopenhauerian question can touch even the cynic's heart. The important point is that Schopenhauer's critique is cogent, and should not be ignored as it has been in contemporary discussions of this sort. Schopenhauer concludes that 'Boundless compassion for all living beings is the firmest and surest guarantee of pure moral conduct' (172), and this includes compassion for animals.

Even in his time, Schopenhauer pointed to far-reaching implications of his critique with the interesting empirical observation that 'The American penitentiary system is based on this [Kantian system], in which the intention is not to improve the *heart* of the criminal, but merely to put his *head* on the right lines' (194). It seems that his remark still applies to the American prison system, even to some other prison systems, as well as efforts to reform criminals and teach morality via the mind in general. It would be an interesting project to determine how and whether improving the criminal's heart could be made practical.

However, like Plato and Aristotle, Schopenhauer concludes that compassion (like virtue in general) cannot be taught intellectually. It is supposedly an irrational component of human nature that co-exists with egoism, but even Schopenhauer succumbed, in part, to the cynicism that Nietzsche made famous. Durkheim, who was nicknamed 'Schopen' by his students according to Lalande (1960: 23), had to struggle with the problem of how Kant and Schopenhauer could be reconciled in his own version of the science of moral facts. And Durkheim was not a cynic. Even if compassion cannot be taught (and that is debatable), certainly it can be nurtured, and it may even prove to be an important component of socialization.

DURKHEIM'S SCIENCE OF MORAL FACTS

Despite the fact that Durkheim's sociology continues to be misaligned with positivism along with other systems that emphasize the mind rather than the heart, it is easy to recognize the broad outlines of Schopenhauer's influence on Durkheim's system of morality (see Meštrović 1988b). Like Schopenhauer, Durkheim clearly rejects the idea that one is born with a priori systems of morality inscribed in one's consciousness. Rather, for both Schopenhauer and Durkheim, morality is a human invention and is concerned with acts to which persons synthetically attribute praise and blame, what Durkheim (1893) called sanctions (only these inventions are not completely arbitrary). Durkheim and Schopenhauer also share common threads with regard to their condemnation of egoism, their penchant for empiricism, their focus on compassion, and their similar notions of the dualism of human nature. Even if one wants to argue for the alternative that Durkheim's moral thought is *both* Kantian and Schopenhauerian, this argument will not undo Durkheim's disdain for apriorism, for which no middle ground or compromise with empiricism can be found, and it cannot explain why Schopenhauer is generally *not* invoked in discussions of Durkheim's moral thought nor in general discourses on modernity. Habermas (1987), for example, manages to invoke every important German philosopher *except* Schopenhauer.

Indeed, like Schopenhauer, Durkheim was concerned to demonstrate that, contrary to Kantianism and utilitarianism, rationality (in the sense of reflective thought and deliberation) is *not* essential to morality. In a debate held by the French Philosophical Society in 1908 Durkheim asserted that

> As far as the actual facts are concerned, one does not in any circumstances find that reflection has always been and is even today considered a necessary factor in morality. Never at any moment in history has the individual been capable of rethinking the morality of his time as a whole. The philosopher probably does what he can to work it out: but he never succeeds other than in an incomplete, truncated way, and he is well aware of it. In any case, the overwhelming majority of people are content to accept passively the reigning morality as it is, without questioning it and without understanding it. And yet it is incontestable that, in fact, the public *conscience* does not refuse to admit that such non-reflective conduct has some moral character: otherwise scarcely any actions would be considered moral. Conduct which is thoroughly reflective is probably held to be morally superior, but a different form of conduct is judged to be neither immoral nor amoral.
>
> (Pickering 1979: 55)

Durkheim's followers refer to his *Division of Labor in Society* as the opening salvo in his quest to establish within sociology an empirical science of moral facts (see especially Bouglé 1926; Davy 1927; Lévy-Bruhl 1899, 1905; Mauss [1950] 1979a). In his 1893 classic, Durkheim essentially attacks Kantianism, utilitarianism, and other efforts to explain social evolution as the outcome of human calculation and deliberation that leads to predetermined, teleological ends. His followers understood all of Durkheim's subsequent books as part of this same quest to distance the empirical study of morality from purely speculative, abstract, theoretical ethics. According to Durkheim:

> For morality is distinguished by a religious characteristic which places it outside the bounds of truly scientific thought.
>
> (Pickering 1979: 31)

> Morality is not geometry, it is not a system of abstract truths which can be derived from some fundamental notion, posited as self-evident. It is a complexity of quite a different order. It belongs to the realm of life, not to speculation.
>
> (Pickering 1979: 34)

> Even today we do not go so far as to say that for an act to be moral it must be reflective. Otherwise take care lest morality becomes a thing of vanity and luxury. The vast majority of men carry out moral imperatives passively and the more cultivated men only partially reflect upon them. To be sure reflection raises and perfects morality but it is not the necessary condition of it.
>
> (Pickering 1979: 61)

Durkheim's quest to establish within sociology a science of morality culminated in his last, albeit unfinished book, entitled *La Morale* (Durkheim [1920] 1978). As Davy (1927: 55) put the matter, Durkheim's social science is simultaneously a science of morality: the study of social facts was intended to make clear the study of moral facts. In general, throughout his writings Durkheim countered Kant's apriorism, especially in his controversial *Primitive Classification* (Durkheim and Mauss [1902] 1975), in favour of a more Schopenhauerian empiricism.

Consider Durkheim's controversial notion of the 'cult of the individual', that collective form of individualism that he predicted would eventually become the new 'religion of humanity'. Durkheim depicts this higher, collective form of individualism as the outcome of irrational forces, not rational reflection:

119

How is it possible to justify egalitarian ideas by purely logical considerations? The role of logic is to help or oblige us to see things as they are. *But in fact we are unequal.* We have neither the same physical force, nor the same intellectual power, nor the same energy of will. The social services we render are of unequal importance and we are more or less easy to replace in the functions we carry out and we carry them out more or less well, etc. In spite of this, morality demands that to a certain extent we should be treated *as though* we were equal. It ascribes to us an equality which has no empirical foundation. Some powerful cause must therefore intervene which makes us see men other than what they are in tangible experience, which makes us see them in such a way that they appear equal to us, and which consequently transfigures them. (Emphasis added.)

(Pickering 1979: 72)

In general, Durkheim aligns the emergence of new systems of morality with the controversial German Romantic notion of 'moral forces' (see Pickering 1979) that work apart from or despite rational reflection. In this regard, as with the emergence of the division of labour and organic solidarity, Durkheim's descriptions mirror Schopenhauer's depictions of the will as a force that does its work apart from consciousness, that humans rationalize after the fact.

Far from being the conservative he is often misconstrued to have been, Durkheim seems to have been a liberal in a new sense of the term. Whereas liberalism is typically associated with the Enlightenment, utilitarianism, and other rationalist philosophies, Durkheim's liberalism is rooted in irrationalism. Like Schopenhauer, Durkheim apparently believed that rationalism leads to the cynical conclusion that humans are unequal, and that it promotes injustice. It is ironic that the end-point of Enlightenment is Nietzschean, aristocratic hardness, whereas the end-point of an open-ended philosophy of Becoming can be democracy (Bouglé 1909).

DURKHEIM ON THE NOTION OF DUTY

To be sure, pure compassion is as unpractical as pure duty as the basis of moral life. Schopenhauer rejects Kant's notion of duty completely, but Durkheim salvages and keeps some aspects of duty, although not Kant's version. Durkheim denies that duty is the central criterion of morality, and the kinds of duty that he wants to maintain in morality are not deduced from theoretical ethics, but are the result of induction from empirical observations that demonstrate that humans construct rules and associate these rules of conduct with moral conduct. Most importantly, Durkheim regards these rules and values as magnets (Bouglé 1926), as sources of desire, not just the constraints depicted by Elias (1982) and other contemporary writers.

In the original introduction to his *Division of Labor* (Durkheim [1893] 1933: 411–35) – which was dropped in subsequent editions – and elsewhere, Durkheim criticized the a priori basis of Kant's derivation of the notion of duty as well as the establishment of his ethics. Durkheim ([1920] 1978: 195) writes:

> We know that, according to [Kant's] school which has played a considerable role in the history of thought but which today has few representatives, the moral ideal is part of our nature. We find it completely formed within us; it is engraved deep in our consciences. To discover it, we need only look within ourselves, we need only scrutinize and analyse ourselves with care. But even assuming that this fundamental moral notion does have this origin, we can recognize it amid the other ideas which populate our minds only if we already have a representation of what is moral and what is not – that is, if we already have the notion that we are trying to discover. The problem is simply shifted, not resolved.

In other words, *representations* are required to recognize moral rules, even if their origin were presumed to be a priori for the sake of argument, and these representations must have an empirical origin.

While Durkheim kept the seemingly Kantian vocabulary of rules, duty, and obligation in his discussions of morality, he used these terms in the Schopenhauerian context of spontaneous respect for the sacrosanct quality of society's ideal rules, not some dry, abstract, cold, Kantian sense of duty, and not as respect for society's immediately apparent norms. Thus, in an essay entitled 'The Determination of the Moral Fact', Durkheim (1906) attacks further the insufficiency of Kant's argument. According to Durkheim ([1906] 1974: 36),

In opposition to Kant, however, we shall show that the notion of duty does not exhaust the concept of morality. It is impossible for us to carry out an act simply because we are ordered to do so and without consideration of its content. For us to become the agents of an act it must interest our sensibility to a certain extent and appear to us as, in some way, *desirable*. Obligation or duty only expresses one aspect abstracted from morality. A certain degree of desirability is another characteristic no less important than the first.

For Durkheim, desire *does* have a place in morality, even though desire is banished from Kant's (1788) system of morality. For Durkheim, as for Schopenhauer, moral rules must be followed spontaneously, from the heart, not out of passionless duty, which is merely a disguised egoism.

Thus, with regard to the simple obesiance given to moral rules, Durkheim concludes that this is not genuine morality. Rather, Durkheim ([1906] 1974: 48) regards genuine moral rules as being embedded in the notion of the sacred, which inspires respect while 'at the same time it is an object of love and aspiration that we are drawn towards'. Durkheim's many references to the sacredness of the human personality, which he calls variously the 'cult of the human person' and 'cult of the individual' (distinguished sharply from egoism; see the discussion in Meštrović 1988a: 128–41), also include this aspect of respect and compassion. Like Schopenhauer, Durkheim ([1906] 1974: 37) asserts that 'the qualification "moral" has never been given to an act which has individual interests, or the perfection of the individual from a purely egoistic point of view'. Thus, 'morality begins at the same point at which disinterestedness and devotion also begin' (52). From this Durkheimian perspective, one would be forced to conclude that most of what passes for moral theory under the rubric of postmodernism is immoral. (Of course, Durkheim has been criticized for holding this view by Hall 1987, and others.)

Durkheim (53) elaborates on the role of sympathy in morality:

> This explains the moral character which is attributed to feelings of sympathy between individuals and the acts which they inspire.... When one loves one's country or humanity one cannot see one's fellows suffer without suffering oneself and without feeling a desire to help them.

It is worth repeating that Kant was adamantly against such feelings of sympathy as the basis for morality.

Moreover, it is a common mistake to conclude that Durkheim regarded any or all of society's apparent rules as being capable of inspiring respect and promoting compassion (see Bouglé's defence of Durkheim in this regard). Georges Davy (1927: 18–20) also notes that Durkheim distinguished between the collective conscience, which is an ideal, and the 'average conscience', which is frequently vulgar, mediocre, and immoral. To pick one example out of many as support for Davy's claim, Durkheim ([1897] 1951: 317) writes in *Suicide* that 'it is a profound mistake to confuse the collective type of a society, as is so often done, with the average type of its individual members. The morality of the average man is of only moderate intensity'. Thus, to return to Durkheim's 1906 essay on the determination of the moral fact, he argues that 'The society that morality bids us desire is not the society as it *appears* to itself, but the society as it is or is really becoming' ([1906] 1974: 38). Durkheim felt that what he was 'opposing to the collective is the collective itself, but more and better aware of itself' (66). This is another manifestation of the influence of German Romanticism upon Durkheim – modernist philosophies simply cannot account for different layers of societal awareness of itself. Durkheim calls explicitly for a reliance on the faculty of judgement, autonomy, and a higher form of individualism as opposed to blind, passive obedience with regard to society's rules.

Durkheim's condemnation of egoism as the basis for immorality is evident throughout his works, but especially in *Suicide* (see Davy 1927: 58). This includes an intricate discussion of the differences between pre-modern and modern forms of egoism in relation to altruistic and egoistic suicide, respectively (Durkheim [1897] 1951, a theme touched by Halbwachs 1958). Moreover, Durkheim's focus on the affinities between egoism and anomie follows closely Schopenhauer's treatment of the infinitely striving will to life and its relationship to suicide (discussed in Meštrović 1988a, 1988b).

Along these Schopenhauerian lines, it is striking that in his *Socialism and Saint-Simon* ([1928] 1958) Durkheim takes up the theme of socialism understood as a collective representation of compassion and sympathy for the suffering of fellow humans. It is important to link these concerns in this Romantic context with the works of Gouldner (1958), Hayek (1988), and Jay (1988) on socialism. Scholars agree that Schopenhauer's philosophy, as opposed to Nietzsche's cynicism, leads naturally to socialism and concerns with compassion on a societal scale (Cartwright 1984; Hamlyn 1980; Magee 1983). Similarly, in *Moral Education*, and elsewhere, Durkheim ([1925] 1961) argues that altruism is not a mysterious quality rationally induced in humans (as both Comte and Kant maintained), but is a natural, spontaneous quality in persons that co-exists with egoism. Again, this move by Durkheim is strikingly similar to Schopenhauer's conceptionalization of a dualistic antagonism between egoism and compassion as inherent, non-rational qualities.

In sum, as Durkheim ([1906] 1974: 62) explains in the closing paragraph of his essay on the determination of the moral fact, he felt that his system of morality was an escape

> from Kantian *a priorism*, which gives a fairly faithful analysis of the nature of morality but which describes more than it explains. We recognize the notion of duty, but for experimental reasons and without rejecting the valuable aspect of eudemonism.

Like Schopenhauer, Durkheim manages to keep the notions of desire, heart, and empiricism in his system of morality.

THE AGENDA OF PROBLEMS ENGENDERED BY DURKHEIM'S AND SCHOPENHAUER'S CRITIQUES OF KANT

Because Schopenhauer's and Durkheim's critiques of Kant's system of morality have been overlooked in the contemporary social sciences, the idea that morality could be based on compassion as opposed to Kant's transcendental duty does not really exist, and it is not clear how such a morality could be operationalized, subjected to empirical investigations, nor how it fits in with modernity. To be sure, there exist studies on altruistic behaviour, reciprocity, and exchange theory, but these are approached primarily from the philosophical perspectives of utilitarianism and rationalism that are inimical to or otherwise fail to acknowledge the gist of Schopenhauer's critique of Kant. The new problems in moral theory that Durkheim and Schopenhauer bring to the forefront include the following. If ethics is not identical with prevailing opinion, then how will one distinguish the group's real moral values from the illusory ones? If moral values exist in relation to one's group, then how will one address the problem of conflicting values and cultural relativism in relation to different groups? How does one instil in individuals a desire to be compassionate or to be drawn to ethical behaviour from motives other than passive duty? And finally, how does one study compassion as a social fact? Each of these questions confronts some aspect of modernity and postmodernity: subjectivism, relativism, the transitoriness of modern life uncovered by Baudelaire and Simmel, and the nihilism proclaimed by Nietzsche. And my answer to each draws on German Romanticism as opposed to the contemporary replies that draw on the Enlightenment.

It is not clear that either Durkheim or Schopenhauer resolved most of these issues. Pickering (1979) has addressed some of these problems with regard to Durkheim, but Pickering's aims did not include placing Durkheim's efforts in the context of Schopenhauer's philosophy. Deploige (1911) had foreshadowed some of Pickering's concerns, and had aligned all of these problems with German social realism – but his work remains buried in obscurity. With regard to instilling genuinely moral behaviour in individuals, the pessimistic Schopenhauer simply dismissed the possibility that the majority of humankind could be really good in his sense of the term. Virtue is a rarity, and cannot be taught – this is how Schopenhauer ends his 1841 treatise on ethics, a cynical echo of Plato's *Protagoras* that also finds its way to Nietzsche. Nevertheless, Schopenhauer's critique of Kant may provide some fresh avenues in apprehending how the problems raised by Durkheim's moral theory may be resolved eventually.

Piaget, who is regarded by Hall (1987: 70) as 'Durkheim's foremost disciple', found a thorn that continues to trouble Durkheimian scholarship in general and moral theory in particular. According to Piaget's ([1932] 1965: 346) modernist interpretation of Durkheim's troublesome dictum that morality must transcend public opinion,

> One must make one's choice between these two solutions.... For, either society is one, and all social processes, including cooperation, are to be assimilated to pure constraint alone, in

which case right is bound to be determined by public opinion and traditional use; or else, a distinction must be made between actual and ideal society ... [but] how, we would ask, is it possible to distinguish between society as it is and society as it is tending to become?

It is certain that Piaget never resolved this Durkheimian dilemma, and eventually tilted the direction of the scientific study of morality back to the Kantian emphasis on cognitive judgement involved in moral decisions, and on transcendental duty.

If one were to reopen the case that Durkheim was trying to make, then surely one would focus on the concluding pages of his *Sociologie et Philosophie* (1924: 124–41) in the context of German Romanticism established in the previous chapter. In these pages Durkheim argues that contrary to Kant, moral values are not the inherent property of things (132), but refer to society's ideal notions (as suggested in the previous section of this chapter). In fact, Durkheim (1924: 141) makes the arresting remark that sociology is properly the study of values and ideals. The distinction between 'real culture' and 'ideal culture' already exists in the sociological vocabulary (although it is not used frequently and is not typically attributed to Durkheim), so that it may be possible to locate the domain of genuine morality in the realm of 'ideal culture', the ways that a society expresses how individuals ought to behave across generations, even if a particular generation at a particular time period is expressing a different morality in 'reality'. This may constitute part of the solution to the dilemma uncovered by Piaget, although it is by no means obvious in all cases how one should distinguish empirically ideal from real norms.

As for the problem of cultural relativism, one would turn to Durkheim's *Moral Education*, wherein Durkheim ([1925] 1961: 79) admits that there exist 'different degrees of morality if for no other reason than that all human societies are not of equal moral value' at the same time that he alludes to a cosmopolitan 'society of mankind' (81). Durkheim (75) asks the crucial question, 'Ought one to commit himself to one of these groups to the exclusion of others?' He answers in the negative, because there ought not to exist any real antagonisms among one's loyalties to various groups. In Western societies at least, all groups ought to be informed by a general concern for the ideal norms of humanity, what Durkheim often referred to as the cult of the individual. Durkheim explains how this is possible:

> Nations grow upon the foundations of the small tribal groups of former times; then the nations themselves are joined in even greater social organizations. Consequently, the moral objectives of society have been more and more generalized. Morality continuously disengages itself from particular ethnic groups or geographical areas precisely because each society, as it becomes larger, embraces a greater diversity of climatic and geographic conditions, and all these different influences mutually cancel themselves (75).

If this trend continues, Durkheim believes that eventually the ideal at which morality will aim shall be a universal 'society of mankind', not one's immediate group. Thus, according to Durkheim (81), as

> society becomes increasingly big, the social ideal becomes more and more remote from all provincial and ethnic conditions and can be shared by a greater number of men recruited from the most diverse races and places. As a result of this alone, it becomes more abstract, more general, and consequently closer to the *human ideal*. (Emphasis added.)

It is interesting with regard to Deploige's (1911) charge that Durkheim's sociology was exclusively German and anti-French, that Durkheim manages to wed French concerns with the Rights of Man, cosmopolitanism, and some ideals of the French Revolution with his social realism.

In *Socialism and Saint-Simon* (1928), but to some extent even in his *Division of Labor* (1893), Durkheim portrays the internationalization of collective representations as the result of economic trade. Especially in his *Elementary Forms*, Durkheim ([1912] 1965: 474) argues that in addition to economic internationalization, religious ideals and beliefs eventually become internationalized, a fact already treated at length by Pickering (1984). Given the widespread evangelism that has occurred in the world since Durkheim's death, his claims are certainly credible. To update Durkheim, it seems that one should include MTV (Music Television) as another extremely important medium for the internationalization of postmodern values. Moreover, with regard to the ideals of moral individualism that this internationalism is supposed to establish, Durkheim's claims can be defended. For example, democracy and the notion of individual rights seem to be sweeping the world, even the communist nations of the present era. The right to privacy, the rights of various minority groups, the rights demanded by children that children of previous generations could not imagine, and other democratic ideals are taking root in Western and non-Western countries alike. For example, the right to travel, taken for granted in the West, became a burning issue in East Germany's rebellion against communism in 1989. Durkheim's notion of moral individualism as a set of collective ideals that bestow dignity upon the human person seems to be something that most persons in Western societies will probably agree upon, even if public opinion does not always act upon these ideals, and even if the majority of humankind cannot give a rational account of the origin and inception of these ideals. The next century should begin to settle the question of Durkheim's ability as a prognosticator – if anyone still remembers him then.

Durkheim partially resolves the problem of how individuals may desire to be ethical with his notion of the sacred. Pickering (1984: 158) has demonstrated that an important dimension of Durkheim's notion of the sacred is its emotional content: 'The sacred commands respect and is also an object of love and devotion – the sacred is something that is earnestly sought after.' For example, in *Moral Education* Durkheim ([1925] 1961: 96) describes the sacred aura surrounding the ideal notions of what society considers good as follows: 'The good is morality conceived as something pleasing, something that attracts our will, provoking our desire spontaneously ... as a magnificent *ideal* to which our sensitivities aspire spontaneously' (emphasis added). To be sure, the sacred carries other dimensions as well, including an element of fear and duty (Pickering 1984), and these do not escape Durkheim's treatment of morality. But it is certainly possible for Durkheim's sociology to address the Schopenhauerian problem of how the good may be able to attract and motivate individuals by things other than mere duty.

In *Sociology and Philosophy* Durkheim (1924: 132) refers to society as 'le foyer d'une vie morale interne'. Hall (1987: 117) notes that the French term *foyer* was one of Durkheim's favourite images, and that 'the *foyer* was originally the fireplace or hearth, then generally a source of heat and by analogy a center of activity, a focus of interest, or a hotbed of intrigue'. Durkheim consistently refers to society as this 'hotbed' of moral activity, with all of its implications of spontaneous passion and desire (see also Bouglé 1926). While contemporary sociologists have treated his notion of constraint at great length, the notion of society as the *foyer* of moral life has been relatively neglected. Yet this notion holds the potential of resolving some of the difficulties of how Durkheim's morality might be incorporated into modern culture.

Finally, with regard to Durkheim's notion of social facts and studying morals as social facts, it should be noted that the bulk of postmodernist writings in moral theory continue to perpetuate the errors that Schopenhauer and Durkheim attributed to Kant and the Enlightenment. Morality is still studied in relation to cognitive development, deduced notions of moral reasoning, and preconceived notions of what moral behaviour ought to be like, even though some contemporary writers are critical of these modern trends (see Cortese 1984, 1989; Gilligan 1982). In the end, postmodern morality still comes down to the boosterish formula that enhanced ability to reason will lead to being nice and happy. These other-directed values themselves become a duty in postmodern societies. The gist of Schopenhauer's and Durkheim's contribution to Western culture in this regard is that studies of morality ought to begin inductively with a study of how persons actually behave, and the ideal notions of moral behaviour that they actually construct. Such an examination leads to the conclusion that duty and fear are associated with rationalist systems of morality, and that these things can never compare with spontaneous desire and feelings as a method for establishing long-term, genuine morality. To take these two thinkers seriously in this regard is to shift considerably the agenda of topics currently subsumed under the topic of moral development, and to reopen the debate on what Durkheim meant by social facts.

STUDYING MORALS AS SOCIAL FACTS

It has been mentioned previously that Durkheim's follower, Georges Davy (1927), argued that the notions of moral facts and social facts coincide in Durkheim's writings. It follows that the many topics treated by contemporary writers as comprising irreconcilable dualisms (such as the object–subject, fact–value distinctions) are treated dialectically by Durkheim as antagonistic unities, along the lines of Schopenhauer's claim that representations and the will are a unity. Thus, based on the preceding analysis, to study morals as social facts in a Durkheimian fashion, one would study the subjective representations of society's ideal and real norms, as well as the 'thing' aspect of social and moral facts, their objective quality that gives rise to representations in the first place (the German Romantic idea we have been following). In other words, it is possible to unify modern and pre-modern approaches in studying morality, at least for Durkheim.

For example, it would be interesting to consider the sociological aspects of cruelty to animals and the treatment of pets and animals in general, from the perspective of real as well as ideal norms. Philosophically speaking, animals are almost completely exempt from moral responsibility in modern societies, as Durkheim's disciple, Paul Fauconnet argued in his *La Responsabilité* (1920). Does a correlation exist between societies that are generally moral – according to Schopenhauer's and Durkheim's standards of a new and higher form of individualism – and the compassion with which animals in general and pets in particular are treated in such societies? Is cruelty to animals more a modern or a primitive phenomenon?

This question touches on Elias's (1982) theory of the civilizing process. If this process entails ever-increasing restrictions on barbaric practices, does it extend to the humane treatment of animals? At first blush, it would seem that animals are treated somewhat more humanely today than they were in primitive societies. The very idea of domesticating certain animals and treating them as pets, and by extension, as members of a family, seems to bespeak an extension of the civilizing process. And yet contradictions exist in postmodern culture concerning animals, as already illustrated with regard to the fur industry, horse-racing, and other cruel professions that thrive in postmodernist culture. While the complete resolution of this issue is beyond the scope of the present discussion, it is important to introject the issue of animal cruelty into the discourse of postmodernity.

It is interesting in this regard that although social scientists have addressed the issues of prejudice against the aged, women, and adult members of other minority groups, they are relatively silent on the issue of prejudice towards children. The term 'child-ism' or its equivalent is certainly not as recognizable as sexism or racism, for example. Yet consider that children are frequently the victims of many diverse kinds of family and institutional abuse, that juveniles perpetrate the most crime, and that in the West, violent death is among the leading causes of death among young people (discussed in Meštrović and Cook 1988). Even language embodies an unconscious lack of compassion towards children: the terms tot, brat, kid, imp, baby, chap, tyke carry fiendish formal meanings (for example, an imp is a child of the devil or of hell, literally, 'a little devil'). Other terms for children are still more blatantly aggressive: crumb-snatchers, tree climbers, yard-apes, sock-pullers, little monkeys, little monsters, rug-rats, etc. But according to the tenets of Schopenhauer's philosophy, children should be treated with great compassion, because, like animals, they are not really culpable for their acts. Is the fiendish vocabulary used for children a carry-over of collective representations from a primitive era in which, according to Durkheim, a higher form of individualism was not yet firmly established? Are post-modern societies more or less compassionate towards children compared to pre-modern societies? And how do attitudes towards children correlate with Enlightenment? These are among the problems to be included in an agenda based on the present reading of Durkheim and Schopenhauer.

Even in contemporary studies of child abuse, Durkheim's Schopenhauerian observations on this topic are never invoked, and have never been formally tested. Durkheim's essay entitled 'Childhood' is filled with pathos and expressions of compassion for the inherent weakness of children, but is not typically cited by sociologists (in Pickering 1979: 149–54). In *Moral Education* ([1925] 1961: 89) Durkheim argues that cruelty towards children increases with the development of civilization and enlightenment: 'In a word, civilization has necessarily somewhat darkened the child's life.' Focusing on corporal punishment as a social fact, Durkheim (183) claims that 'in beating, in brutality of all kinds, there is something we find repugnant, something that revolts our conscience – in a word, something immoral'. This is a Schopen-hauerian conclusion, and it rests on the Durkheimian argument, explicated above, that the ideal culture of enlightened societies *ought* to lead towards the cult of individualism and respect for the dignity of the child as a person. But in postmodern practice, this does not always seem to be the case. Durkheim continues (184):

> One might think a priori that the harshness of primitive mores, the barbarism of earlier times, must have given rise to this mode of punishment. The facts do not support this hypothesis, however natural it may seem at first glance ... [one comes to] the remarkable conclusion that, in the great majority of cases, discipline [among primitives] is very gentle. Canadian Indians love their children tenderly, never beat them, and do not even reprimand them.... A Sioux chief thought the whites barbarous for striking their children.

Is Durkheim (189) correct that 'the beginnings of culture were signalized by the appearance of corporal punishment'? This hypothesis has never been formally tested. It is interesting that corporal punishment persists in public schools in the USA, and that sadistic imagery and pornography are very popular in Western nations. Here is another instance of postmodern contradiction, a narrative of cruelty that lies beneath the narrative of 'be happy, don't worry'. Schopenhauer's own severe indictment of enlightenment should be noted in this regard, along with his belief that reason and viciousness actually show an affinity for each other. Is this true? Are modernity and postmodernity dangerous for children, because their abstractionism has squelched compassion? If it turns out to be true, then how can one reconcile this finding with Durkheim's claim that the ideal norms of Western societies are supposed to be evolving into a new and higher form of humanism? This problem is intricate, because it is not evident whether the problem lies with Durkheim's theory or the contradictions of postmodern culture.

But the more important point is that both Schopenhauer and Durkheim advocated a genuine empiricism to settle the debates and issues that stem from such discussions. Surely the most important item on the research agenda based on the preceding is to establish whether anything like Durkheim's evolutionary cult of the individual exists. If it does exist, then the postmodernist narratives of rebellion against this narrative ought to be re-evaluated, because one is led to the conclusion that postmodern social philosophy does not promote humane doctrines. If it does not exist, how shall one explain the thirst for freedom, justice, and compassion so openly evident in the latter half of the twentieth century? Other related agendas should include, but not be limited to, the sociological study of collective representations with regard to punishment in general as well as the treatment of criminals, the mentally retarded, the mentally ill, and other stigmatized, weak, members of societies that Schopenhauer and Durkheim felt deserve compassion. It was Durkheim's conviction that empirical studies of this sort would eventually resolve the abstract dilemmas of cultural relativism, the emergence of new values, the role of reason in morality, and other dilemmas engendered by modernity that cannot be resolved in a thoroughly satisfactory manner by purely theoretical considerations.

CONCLUSIONS

Schopenhauer never tried to relate compassion to social factors, and argued that compassion could never be taught. Nevertheless, Schopenhauer's emphasis on compassion as opposed to Kant's duty could be apprehended as part of the previous turn of the century's revolt against the Enlightenment that influenced Durkheim and others in his time. Thus, in his *Two Sources of Morality and Religion*, Henri Bergson (1932) tried to convey the idea of morality as a kind of openness as opposed to Kantian conformity to pre-established rules. Jean-Marie Guyau, in his *Esquisse d'une morale sans obligation ni sanction* ([1885] 1907), which Durkheim reviewed, represents one of the most forceful and, in his time, most popular attacks on morality derived from duty. Pitirim Sorokin's (1947) treatise on love, although published in the middle of the century, is also written in this *fin de siècle* spirit. A host of other now less-known authors turned to the theme of 'openness' as opposed to Kant's formalism in epistemological and moral fields of enquiry. Of course, some elements of this 'openness' dissolved into the various doctrines of modernity, postmodernism, and nihilism. As stated previously, postmodernist discourse seems to be a vulgarization of the *fin de siècle* spirit.

Thus, the previous turn of the century also produced an extreme reaction to the Schopenhauerian critique of Kantian duty, including Nietzsche's ([1901] 1968) 'will to power', and all sorts of ideologies that led to fascism (see Lukács 1980; Mann [1939] 1955) as well as communism. Although Nietzsche began his philosophical career as Schopenhauer's disciple, he eventually turned on his master with a vengeance, precisely on the issue of compassion and pity (Cartwright 1984). Compassion is the morality of the weak, Nietzsche claimed, and with that opened the door to authoritarianism. Subsequent theorists have never clearly resolved whether excessive rationalism or Schopenhauerian irrationalism is to blame for the rise of fascism in the West. This is an extremely important problem, but its full resolution is clearly beyond the scope of this study. The important point is that from the perspective of a sociology of knowledge, the contemporary discourse of postmodernism within the social sciences has closed the door to discussions of this sort, and the entire controversy ought to be re-examined.

It is noteworthy that at present, Schopenhauer has been dropped completely from discussions in moral theory, and that Kantianism and rationalism have been revived in the works of Kohlberg and Habermas. It is as if contemporary sociology is unwittingly overreacting to an excess of 'heart' at the beginning of this century by turning to an excessive preoccupation with the 'mind'. Communism and fascism parallel this movement, because both systems were extremely bureaucratic and non-compassionate, and both depended upon extremely rational techniques of social planning. All this is in keeping with the strong tide of abstractionism found in modernity as well as postmodernism, but it is not an excuse for scholars to ignore the cogent *fin de siècle* critiques of modernist approaches to moral issues.

Schopenhauer's and Durkheim's critiques of Kant, while problematic in their own right, expose the epistemological as well as practical limitations of naive rationalism as applied to moral theory. Epistemologically, social scientists must address the question of whether neo-Kantianism is capable of sustaining empiricism and anything like Durkheim's quest for a science of moral facts. Schopenhauer, Lévy-Bruhl, Durkheim, and many other turn of the century intellectuals argued that deductive, theoretical systems of morality are self-serving abstractions that merely prove what they set out to prove (see Deploige 1911). At present, the postmodernist social sciences are still caught up in the impasse of cultural relativism brought on by Kant, that the noumenon or the thing-in-itself is out of reach, and that humankind must be content with a diversity of subjective representations, but no real truths. But Schopenhauer offered a solution to Kant's impasse, that the thing-in-itself, which he renamed the will, *is* accessible to non-rational and immediate perception, intuition, and imagination. Durkheim followed Schopenhauer's lead in that he felt that morality consisted of moral forces that impose themselves on human consciousness (not the other way around), and that these moral forces could be studied scientifically and empirically. Of course, it is an open question how this can be achieved.

Practically, a resolution must be found to the polemic between Schopenhauer and Kant as to whether morality is to be based on heartfelt compassion versus cold, abstract, rational duty. Durkheim found a *via media* solution in which he kept an empirically based notion of duty in his understanding of morality, but surrounded it with an aura of sacredness that includes heartfelt respect and desire to be ethical. While Durkheim's solution is not without its problems – especially the problem of how it can be implemented – it deserves to be taken seriously enough to be studied and debated. It is high time for social scientists to emerge from the limitations of Kantianism, because Schopenhauer and Durkheim, not Kant, had the last word. Furthermore, postmodernist morality leads straight to extreme moral relativism and nihilism, which are clearly unsatisfactory. Finally, I agree with the philosopher David Cartwright (1984: 92) that 'Kant's insistence that a right-thinking person desires to be free from "even the feelings of sympathy and warmhearted fellow-feeling ... and subject only to law-giving reasons" demonstrates moral pedantry at its worst'.

Chapter Eight

MEDJUGORJE, THE VIRGIN MARY, AND MODERNITY

The cult of the Virgin Mary is the only surviving remnant of primitive female goddesses in modern, Western culture. Scholars in diverse fields agree that female goddesses were the rule, not the exception, the further one travels back into history and pre-history (for a review, see Preston 1982). In a Durkheimian context, the dominance of male gods marks the representationalism appropriate to modern and postmodern values and ideals characteristic of organic solidarity. In the West, male gods took over, so to speak, in recent Judaism and Protestantism. The more ancient, and basic, female goddesses represented the compassion discussed in the previous chapter, fertility, the oneness and totality of Nature and the Universe, and an orientation in which the world was comprehended as one giant womb. The umbilical chord between the individual and any such primal phenomenon has been cut long ago, and the representation of the Virgin Mary is the only symbolic, religious link left between pre-modernity and postmodernity.

Moreoever, at least since 1830 in Paris, she 'appears' only in times of crisis (from this point on, I will drop the quotation marks when I refer to Mary's appearances, but will always treat them from the sociological perspective, not the theological). It is as if her appearances symbolize deep ruptures in the social fabric, a desperate although unconscious and temporary recoil from the abstractionism and bureaucratization of modernity into the past. In *Mother Worship*, James Preston (1982) observes that since the last turn of the century, the study of female icons had been neglected until very recently, and adds (340):

Why this new interest in mother worship, both at the popular level and among scholars? What does the return to a topic that once preoccupied religion specialists tell us about our present world? Could it be we have come to realize the limits of Western science, particularly when it comes to understanding the human imagination?... Is the resurgent interest in female sacred images perhaps an index of our discontent with 'male' iconoclasm, technical progress, bureaucratization, the conquest by reason of all natural vehicles? There is something even more fundamental about our fascination with mother worship. Modern industrialized people are uprooted, lonely, severed from the earth. The mother goddess figure represents a metaphorical image of *primacy*.

Historians agree that the cult of the Virgin Mary reached its height during the Renaissance in France, when the famous Notre Dame Cathedral in Paris was one of hundreds of such tributes to 'our lady'. Durkheim (1938) has depicted the Renaissance as a period of extreme anomie, and many scholars have singled out this period as one of the most important precursors of modernity. The Marian cult was transferred to the New World in its most famous form as Our Lady of Guadalupe – later decreed Our Lady of the Americas – who appeared first on December 9, 1531. The obviously stressful events occurring at that time were associated with the brutal conquest of the Aztecs by the Spanish. More importantly, scholars have found that the Aztecs 'converted' to Catholicism and our lady because she appeared at the same time and place that their pagan goddess used for appearances (Braden 1930)!

In general, the conquest of the New World is marked by numerous appearances, from Santo Domingo to California (see Lovaton 1971 and the many accounts in Sharkey 1952). But then, conquest is not only a stressful (if not brutal) process for all concerned, it also represents the imposition of the initial stages of Western modernity on to primitive culture. Both the conquered and the conquerors turned to the female goddess of the West for succour; the former, because they already recognized her from their own religions, and the latter, because Jesus did not represent all the values they needed to impose modernity on to others against their will.

But it is in France in the nineteenth century that the most famous and memorable appearances of the Virgin Mary occurred.
The first one was Our Lady of Rue de Bac in Paris in 1830, corre-
sponding to the French Revolution in which Charles X was overthrown, and also to a long period of social and economic crises
since 1827. It should be added that a wave of revolutions swept
Europe following the July revolution in France, and of course,
Mary had correctly predicted much bloodshed.

The appearance of Our Lady of Salette in 1846 corresponds to
long-standing economic and political upheavals in Europe, including the potato famine in Ireland, and shortages of food in
France and the rest of Europe. Also, the February Revolution of
1848 took place in Paris, and the Second French Republic was
established. Some years later, Our Lady of Rome in 1854 represented the fall of Rome to Napoleon and another wave of con-
quests, this time within Europe. This was capped by the
appearance of Our Lady of Lourdes in 1858. In addition to the
massive political upheavals that had occurred since Napoleon,
there were several famines in France in the years preceding the
apparitions at Lourdes.

Our Lady of Pontmairn in 1870 in the Alsace-Lorraine region
of France symbolized the turmoil of the Franco-Prussian War, the
Third French Revolution and the establishment of the Third Republic, as well as starvation. (Durkheim had witnessed the German occupation of his home town, Epinal, and must have been
aware of these appearances.) A few years later, Our Lady of Knock
appeared in Ireland in 1879, following the potato famine of 1877,
an outbreak of typhus, and extreme poverty.

Our Lady of Fatima appeared in 1916, and predicted that
'France will suffer'. Many important events led up to this appearance: the First World War, the ascent of Lenin, the ascent of socialism, worker unrest, and massive political upheaval. The
appearances of Our Lady of Noveant in Metz, Lorraine, in
January 1920 corresponded neatly with the return of Lorraine to
France. Her apparitions at Beuraing and Banneaux in Belgium in
1932 corresponded with the ascent of fascism, Mussolini, Hitler,
Stalin, Franco, and communism.

Why so many apparitions in France in the nineteenth century?
Why was sociology born in France at roughly the same time as
these apparitions? The apparitions from Rue de Bac to Fatima

span sociology's career in France from Saint-Simon to Durkheim. The answer to both questions points to France as the *foyer* of modernity during this time period.

Closer to our time, Our Lady of Cuapa in Nicaragua in 1980 dovetails with the socialist revolution and the economic crises that preceded it in Nicaragua (see Vega 1984). Sharkey (1952) goes into seemingly endless examples and instances of her less famous appearances in Europe, the Americas, and Asia, so that I have by no means given an exhaustive account. As of this writing, she is even said to have appeared in Lubbock, Texas, a State that has been the focal point of the severe economic crisis brought on by the savings and loan scandals and failures of the late 1980s.

But her most famous appearances as of this writing have been occurring in the tiny village of Medjugorje in Yugoslavia since 1980. Thus, looking back to the first official and recognized appearance in Paris in 1830 and tracing her appearances to the present, it seems true, as Sharkey (1952: 6) put the matter, that 'our Lady has made more appearances on earth in the past century and a quarter than in any similar period in all history'. Also, she has shifted her appearances from the previous seat of modernity, France, to a country that best symbolizes the violent meeting of East and West, modernity and pre-modernity – Yugoslavia (see Letica 1989). Medjugorje may be regarded as a collective symbol, in the Durkheimian sense, of the kinds of changes we should expect in the next century, as China, India, Africa and other non-Western countries take on modernity and postmodernity. This is in keeping with Pitirim Sorokin's (1957) prediction that Western culture as we know it is dying out and that the next centre of civilization will flow from the East, starting with the Moslem crescent as it touches Europe and moving into Asia.

More importantly, and in keeping with the import of previous Marian apparitions, the apparitions at Medjugorje predated and continue to parallel the social, economic, and political upheaval in the communist countries of Eastern Europe. Very few commentators in 1980 would have guessed that when Mary first appeared in Medjugorje, and called for faith as opposed to reason (as she typically does), she signalled the anti-bureaucratic revolution against communism in Eastern Europe that reached its zenith in 1989. Postmodern discourse, although it pretends to align itself with anti-modern narratives of this sort, completely ignored the symbolic significance of Mary's apparitions.

Still another linkage between postmodern culture and the Marian apparitions is to be found, indirectly, in the sometimes vulgar distortions of the Marian cult found in popular culture. Thus, the singer Madonna achieved international fame in the 1980s, and her song 'Like a Virgin' is instantly recognizable through most of the Western world. MTV (Music Television) frequently portrays females in the symbolic sense of goddesses, sometimes with sado-masochistic overtones. Men's magazines in the 1980s are filled with advertisements to telephone females that they may 'worship', and who in turn will punish them for being 'bad'. Could it be that these perverted representations of female cult worship at the present time are more than an instance of random, postmodern 'hyper-reality'? Could it be that even in countries where the cult of the militant, tough Jesus is still strong, the collective conscience is turning back to primitive female worship?

But Medjugorje deserves a chapter in this sort of discourse for still another reason. Mary's appearances at Medjugorje are a typically *fin de siècle* phenomenon that binds the people who will live though the coming turn of the century with the previous century's revolt against modernity, and subsequent quest for faith. Given the alleged victory of rationalism and positivism in this century, this fact is frankly shocking.

EXPLAINING THE APPEARANCES

I do not mean to imply that modernization must necessarily follow the Western model, although many writers associate modernity with Western culture. On the contrary, I agree with Riesman and Riesman (1967) who note in their analysis of Japan that there exist many paths to modernization. My point is that regardless of what means one uses and the end-points one finally arrives at in modernization, the *process* of modernization in this open-ended Becoming is always stressful. During the stress of this process, any female goddess will serve as the symbol for what is being lost in modernization – the Virgin Mary just happens to be the only one that has survived modernity in the West. (Just compare this state of affairs with the myriad of female goddesses that still animate Hinduism, for example.) Furthermore, in the subsequent analysis, I do not mean to imply any adherence to Catholic theology, only that the Catholics have been more responsible than Protestants for keeping this cult alive, and this cult must be analysed sociologically.

When one considers the essentially abstractionist nature of modernity, it is not surprising that sociologists in general and sociologists of religion in particular have been relatively silent on the cult of the Virgin Mary. Even Max Weber, the most modern sociologist among sociology's precursors (in the pejorative sense of modern) focused on Protestantism in his classic 1904 study of capitalism and religion, and Protestantism tends to shun the Virgin Mary. Durkheim never mentioned the Virgin Mary *per se*, but his 1912 classic on religion lends itself easily to an application to this phenomenon, and he was practically obsessed with primitive religious rites.

Most of the contemporary social scientific literature on the Marian cult takes a narrowly psychological and reductionistic approach (see Byrnes 1988; Carroll 1987). Thus, scholars have analysed the individuals who 'see' the Virgin Mary. Were they psychotic? This is the chief question that is addressed. Psychologists have analysed the Freudian, Oedipal needs on the part of the faithful to 'go along' with these appearances. In all of the psychological explanations, the visionaries and the believers are treated as separate atoms cut off from the rest of society, separated from collective representations, trapped in their own subjectivisms. This is a typically modern effort at explanation.

As illustration, consider the picture on the front cover of one of the many books on Medjugorje. The photograph shows the visionaries hooked up to electrodes and wires of all sorts as scientists measure their vital signs prior to, during, and after the appearances. (The authors never say anything conclusively about the state of mental health of the visionaries.) It is a hideous postmodernist vision. It begs the obvious question why electrodes are not attached to the faithful in the church who are witnessing the visionaries, and why anyone who confesses to religious faith is not hooked up to electrodes. If we were all hooked up to electrodes each time we felt religious, perhaps it would be found that some of us experienced physiological changes in respiration, sweating, heartbeat, and so on – but so what? No doubt I am experiencing some such changes writing this book, and athletes experience it preparing for their sporting events, and everyone undergoes symptoms of stress in any event important to them. This pseudo-scientific approach proves nothing about the objective reality of religious experiences, but it appears 'scientific'. It is postmodernist *kitsch*.

It is interesting in this regard to recall Durkheim's insistence that religion is not an inexplicable hallucination, but a reality that must be taken seriously ([1912] 1965: 251). He adds that 'religion is a system of ideas by which individuals represent to themselves the society of which they are members' and as such is metaphoric and symbolic (257). Religion is an intensity, and it *is* a delirium, 'but if [it] may be said that religion is not without a certain delirium, it must be added that this delirium, if it has the causes which we have attributed to it, *is well-founded*' (258, Durkheim's emphasis).

Preston (1982: 327) reviews the psychological theories that try to correlate the status of female goddesses to the status of women in societies that worship them:

> This is the idea that religious symbolism is an epiphenomenon, a mere projection of psychological or social realities. Thus, if women have low status in a particular society, the same pattern will be echoed at the level of ideology in the relative position of gods to goddesses.

He finds no support for this epiphenomenonalist approach: the status of women is not related in either direction to the status of female icons. I should add that David Riesman informed me that Erich Fromm's doctoral dissertation addressed the status of women in Mexico in relation to the cult of the Virgin Mary, and the results were similar to Preston's.

Durkheim's (1912) approach is superior to these reductionist approaches by virtue of the obvious fact that he treats religious representations as *collective* products. Neither the visionaries nor the faithful, nor society, re-invents religion or the cult of the Virgin Mary anew at each moment of participation. Rather, this cult is handed down *sui generis* (even though we each individualize and privatize it to some extent). Here is still another aspect of the importance of Durkheim's German social realism, exposed by Deploige (1911). The cult of the Virgin Mary is 'objective' and 'real' in the sense that it is imposed upon culture, not projected subjectively by some cranky individuals, because it would be impossible for individuals to re-invent it over and over again. Religion cannot rest on an error and a lie, Durkheim wrote ([1912] 1965: 14).

Catholic theologians offer a very Durkheimian account of the apparitions, albeit unwittingly, without invoking Durkheim, and with the bias of their dogma (see Claudel 1952; Delaney 1959; Klein 1981; Le Blanc 1981; Long 1976; Sharkey 1952). Nevertheless, these theological accounts are of use in the Durkheimian sense of being collective representations. Of these, the most useful, comprehensive, and best written is Don Sharkey's *The Woman Shall Conquer*. Sharkey notes that between 1170 and 1270, the French built eighty cathedrals and over five hundred large churches – in the currency of 1952, seven billion dollars worth of real estate – in honour of the Virgin Mary. He cites the Protestant Revolt against Mary that was occurring at that time as the primary impetus. But in a broader context, it is possible to regard the Protestant Reformation and the subsequent cult of the tough Jesus as another manifestation of modernity, and the recoil to Mary as the tender-hearted mother of an equally tender Jesus as a reaction against modernity. Not just Protestantism, but science and atheism were attacking the Marian cult in particular and traditional religion in general, and this attitude towards Catholicism reached its apex in the nineteenth century: 'The nineteenth century was a time [when] religion was everywhere on the defensive. It was also a time when the Blessed Virgin was very active' (Sharkey 1952: 112).

Sharkey writes that 'when our Blessed Mother looked down at the world of 1830, she saw a world that had revolted against her, against the Church' (1952: 13). Her messages stressed irrational faith as opposed to the rational science that was sweeping Europe. Interestingly, Durkheim ([1912] 1965: 486) also emphasized that faith in science does not differ essentially from religious faith, and that faith is before all else an impetus to action. She advised love and penance as opposed to the then-fashionable ideas that utopia would be produced by science. She said that humankind was sinning, and would be punished for its sins, just as Baudelaire was writing on the decadence of modernity. She always called for penance, asceticism, and prayer, and Durkheim cited these rites as the essence of all religions in his 1912 classic. Above all, she always predicted suffering, and suffering turns out to be one of the major themes of the *fin de siècle*. In sum, the messages of the Virgin Mary since 1830 are vintage examples of the *fin de siècle* spirit, even if these messages were given in the form of religious representations, not scientific discourse or literature.

Without mentioning Medjugorje, Gorbachev, or Glasnost, Sharkey (1952: 3) makes an interesting allusion to the continuities between the coming and previous turns of the century:

> On April 16, 1917, Nikolai Lenin and Leon Trotsky arrived in Petrograd, Russia, to lay plans for the Communist Revolution. Seven months later, on November 7, the Communists took over the government of Russia. This they regarded as but the first step in their sweeping programme of world conquest. 'First Russia, and then the world' was the motto of the godless, religion-hating Communists. Between these two dates the Mother of God made her six appearances at Fatima, in Portugal. At one end of Europe the forces of evil were triumphing. At the other end our Lady was rallying the forces of good for a crusade of prayer and penance. Never were words clearer than those spoken by our Lady at Fatima: 'If my requests are granted, Russia will be converted and there will be peace. Otherwise, Russia will spread her errors throughout the world, provoking wars and persecutions of the Church. Many will be martyred; the Holy Father will have much to suffer; several nations will be destroyed.'

If we decode this theology into secular representations, this passage makes contact with reality. Communism did try to outgrow religion, and in this sense, abstractionist communism ought to be added to the list of distinctly modern phenomena. Many nations *were* destroyed after 1917, but nationalism is staging a comeback. As we witness the supposed death of communism with the coming *fin de siècle* (Brzezinski 1988), it is useful to regard the apparitions at Medjugorje as the harbinger of the end of the era that Lenin began and Stalin consummated.

When Sharkey and other Catholic writers cite the Marian apparitions as signs of hope against secularism, materialism, and general decadence brought on by modernity, their views do not differ essentially from the conclusions reached by many popular secular writers today (witness the writings of Bloom, Bellah, and Bell). The primary difference is that the religious writers end on a note of optimism that 'woman shall conquer', whereas many writers on modernity plunge head-first into nihilism and cynicism. I should add that Durkheim ([1912] 1965: 271) made the claim that 'between the logic of religious thought and that of scientific thought there is no abyss' one of the cornerstones of his work on religion. Durkheim represented the *fin de siècle* belief that even if science strips religion of its speculative functions, religion will not disappear, but will transform itself (478).

AN ELABORATION OF THE DURKHEIMIAN EXPLANATION

One of Durkheim's most distinguishing features as a sociologist is his claim that the past is always linked to the present in an unending chain of collective representations – this, despite modernity's ruthless forgetting of the past. Anthropological evidence abounds to support this claim. I have already remarked that American Indians accepted the Virgin Mary because they recognized her from their own representations. Braden (1930) documents this fact with regard to our Lady of Guadalupe. She appeared on the very hillside that the Goddess Teotenantzin, mother of the Aztec gods, used for her appearances. Moreover, she appeared in the garb of an Indian, and her son Tehuiznahuac is known as the Lord of the Crown of Thorns – the affinities to Jesus Christ are more than a little bit striking.

Preston (1982) reviews a plethora of cross-cultural anthropological studies to suggest that in many developing nations today, women still turn to goddesses to attain pregnancy, goddesses are still invoked in rites meant to ensure good harvests, and that in general, goddesses serve the function of protection. This is not to imply that goddesses lack a destructive, non-nurturant side, as evidenced by Saraswati and Kali in India, for example. Even the Virgin Mary has had some harsh words to say to humankind regarding their just punishments for sins committed. Nevertheless, most cultures have found a need to construct representations of goddesses as *both* virgins and divine mothers.

It is interesting in this regard that Baudelaire (1863) writes that even in modernity, women are and will remain idolized. Fashion, make-up, and jewelry will not disappear with modernity in Baudelaire's scheme of things. On the contrary, these phenomena will increase, despite feminism. Simmel and Durkheim agreed with Baudelaire, as Kandal (1988) demonstrates in his fascinating book *The Woman Question in Classical Sociological Theory*. In fact, Durkheim (1893) believed that the differences between the sexes would become more, not less, distinct with modernization. It is high time to regard these pronouncements by *fin de siècle* thinkers as more than chauvinism. It certainly seems true that despite the feminist movement, women continue to be depicted as holding a mystery for men, and this may stem from an unconscious association of women with fertility and primacy. It is fascinating that the themes of purity and virginity as they pertain to women have not disappeared in postmodern, postfeminist culture: Disney's 'Snow White' and 'Sleeping Beauty' continue to command box-office respect, and the Disney Channel is far more popular than the Playboy Channel on Cable Television.

In fact, as Harry Alpert observed in his unpublished notes, Durkheim regarded religion itself as the 'primal sacral complex', as a symbolic womb. Indeed, Durkheim ([1912] 1965: 255) wrote that 'religion [is] like the womb from which come all the leading germs of human civilization'. In a sense, Durkheim's version of religion is feminine in nature. Durkheim depicts all social institutions as derived from religion, and this is the source of the venerable respect, intensity, and the good and gracious aspects attached to society (239–43). The sentiments that lie at the basis of religion are 'happy confidence' (256).

Additionally, Durkheim (191–3) takes up the topic of sexual totemism, the fact that in primitive societies men and women possess separate totems in addition to the collective tribal totems that they share. Women are said to be sisters descended from a particular ancestor, and the men are brothers descended from a different ancestor. According to Durkheim, 'in regard to the distinct origins assigned to men and to women, it must be said that its cause is to be sought in the separate conditions in which the men and the women live' (193). Even though Durkheim never devotes a chapter to goddesses, a careful, contextual reading of his work leads to the conclusion that sexual totemism arose as a representation of the sexual division of labour, itself a distant forerunner of modernity.

Consider that Durkheim regards totemism in general as 'the religion of an anonymous and impersonal force', without name or history, immanent in the world and diffused in a number of things

(216). On the one hand, this seems to be an asexual definition in that it does not seem to matter whether the gods are male or female; in fact, the totems that Durkheim treats are frequently things – plants, rocks, and asexual animals. On the other, this definition is feminine and pre-modern, because it implies the sacral womb complex, already discussed. Thus, Durkheim seems to imply that the distinction between gods and goddesses does not occur prior to considerable social evolution of the division of labour.

Durkheim treats the 'cumulative veneration of ancestors' (314) as establishing a 'protective' relationship for the faithful. These totemic ideals are created to preserve the authority of tradition *and* to mark the hope of the future (470). Resemblance to sacred images is sought to communicate with the collective ideals that these images symbolize (401). By extrapolation – because Durkheim does not mention it directly – I assume that male and female icons symbolize different social ideals, whether or not these social ideals are always consistently achieved in society. Thus, the Virgin Mary symbolizes certain traditional ideals *as well as* certain ideals pertaining to hope for the future, regardless of the machismo extant in the societies in which she appears, and regardless of the dominance of Protestant religions in modern culture. The primary ideal stressed at Medjugorje is world peace, and this is an ideal to which many Catholics as well as non-Catholics subscribe in the world today.

The apparitions of the Virgin Mary may be linked also to Durkheim's discussion of imitative rites (403). In these rites, the totem is invoked for the sake of the moral comfort afforded by the cult through its regular celebration. The cardinal message received by the participants in imitative rites is that 'it is faith that saves' (ibid.). It is worth repeating that this is an essentially anti-modern message, and it has been repeated by Mary at Medjugorje. As such, it is offensive to both Marxist regimes and neo-positivist scholars who believe that rationality leads to progress.

Finally, Mary's apparitions at Medjugorje may be linked to Durkheim's discussion of piacular rites (435), those that relate to misfortunes (past, present, or future), rites inspired by sentiments of sorrow and fear. Some of these fears have already been mentioned in the preceding chapters, and the chief fear has to do with nuclear war, followed closely by the ability to survive in the dismal economies of communist and formerly communist nations.

In sum, Durkheim's (1912) theory of religion enables one to appreciate Mary's apparitions at Medjugorje as the latest in a series of anti-modernist apparitions that have been occurring at least since 1830 in Paris. The cult of the Virgin Mary involves representative, imitative, and piacular rites simultaneously. This cult represents the mother worship discussed by Preston (1982), and the links to primitive religions discussed by many anthropologists. Armed in this way with Durkheim's theory and some anthropological evidence, we are prepared to venture forth into a specific discussion of Medjugorje and its significance.

THE VIRGIN MARY AT MEDJUGORJE AND THE WEST'S CRISIS OF THE HEART

Since 1980, when the Virgin Mary is said to have first appeared in Medjugorje, Yugoslavia has become something of a Fatima or Lourdes, as well as a typically postmodernist tourist attraction. For the sociologist, it is nothing less than amazing that middle-class, middle-aged persons from America, Germany, Italy, and other industrialized nations (along with some others from developing nations) would travel to a backward and remote village in a poor country just to experience a promised feeling of 'peace', achieve a miracle – or at least experience a postmodernist spectacle of the highest order. They line up in the Church at Medjugorje and touch a statue of the Virgin Mary as if they were touching sacredness itself, their faces expressing awe. (To be sure, some of the pilgrims behave as if they were at Disneyworld.) This is Durkheimian cult-worship as the twentieth century draws to a close, and the excitement generated by this cult is increasing in intensity as of this writing. The amazing thing about all this is that according to Saint-Simon, Comte, and most contemporary sociology textbooks that still pay lip-service to positivism, the human race was supposed to have outgrown all this metaphysics and theology. By now, we were supposed to be firmly entrenched in positivism and rationalism, and to have abandoned the irrational entirely.

Medjugorje is far from being a rare exception to the contemporary illusion of rational progress. It is simply a famous one that caters to tourists, and thereby succumbs to the commercial forces of postmodernism. But the metaphysical phenomenon of Med-jugorje is not essentially different from what might be termed the cult of Jesus in the 'Bible Belt' of the United States, complete with 'Jesus Saves' bumper stickers, open tent revivals where people go to get 'saved' instantly, and other non-positivistic, postmodernist, even superstitious aspects of postmodernist American religion. Nor is it essentially different from Hindu, Moslem, and other tem-ples used throughout modern India to heal everything from men-tal illness (often conceptualized as demon possession) to warts (see Meštrović 1986). Add to this list all the gurus, palm-readers, astro-logers, witches, occult practitioners, and other variations of 'magi-cians' that cater to superstition in the developed as well as developing nations (see O'Keefe 1982), and the positivistic law of rational progress seems to be obviously false. Superstition even reached the White House, where President Reagan, in the last year of his Presidency, was forced to admit that he and his wife believe in astrology. Our postmodernist age needs faith.

Another sign of the postmodern schizophrenia of our times is that while our everyday lives are saturated with magic and super-stition, sociologists continue to write textbooks as well as treatises that espouse Comte and rational progress. This contradiction be-tween scientific concepts (ideology, really) and the perceptions of everyday life is so glaring that it enters the classroom. I am sure that other professors who hold conversations with their students have found, as I have, that many college students today hold to a Creationist version alongside the evolutionist version of the orig-ins of life on earth. None of the sociology majors that I taught would engage in studies of 'root magic' (the belief that a spell or hex can be put on a person through the use of roots) that is to be found all over South Carolina precisely because they are afraid of 'the root'. In general, postmodernist culture allows for, even encourages, such cultural contradictions.

Any of these phenomena are worthy of study in their own right. However, the focus in the remainder of this chapter will be on Medjugorje, and these other magical phenomena that thrive with-in postmodern culture provide a context. The Marian cult at Med-jugorje is a relatively new phenomenon compared to the older cults of Jesus in the United States, various Hindu mythologies in India, and even the other cults of the Virgin Mary in Catholic regions of Europe, which are fairly established by now. Because

Medjugorje is in Yugoslavia, and because Yugoslavia still serves as the boundary between Eastern and Western culture (Letica 1989), pre-modernity and postmodernity respectively, in many ways, the relationship between magic and social structure may make itself more apparent there than it might in a homogeneous culture. Finally, Medjugorje is distant enough from American culture to be exotic, yet close enough (since it is in Europe) to be of interest. And as established previously, it feeds into the collective representations of mother worship that still flow through the subterranean regions of postmodernity.

But the central theme of this chapter and our study of Medjugorje is that it points to the anti-positivist conclusion that despite so-called rational progress and Enlightenment, humanity shall never be rid of metaphysics. Schopenhauer (1818) concluded that the best one can do is to choose between a vulgar versus a sophisticated metaphysics, but that metaphysics is an essential component of human life that feeds the 'will', the 'heart'. Humankind simply must have faith, not just rationality. William James (1902) followed Schopenhauer's lead to conclude much the same in his *Varieties of Religious Experience*. Today, shopping mall bookstores testify to Schopenhauer's conclusion with the proliferation of New Age books, that collection of vulgar metaphysics concerned with astrology, healing crystals, and other crude superstitions.

To be sure, the phenomenon of Medjugorje has already been studied and researched by psychologists, psychiatrists, medical doctors, and theologians. But, as I have mentioned earlier, the starting points in all of these studies have been positivistic and reductionistic, even among the theologians. Thus, the central issue has been whether the 'children' who saw the Virgin Mary (and it must be noted that most of these 'children' are now in their twenties) were sane or insane, honest or dishonest. This issue can never be resolved, and is not even essential to appreciating what is sociologically interesting and important about the phenomena at Medjugorje. Observe that these scientists and theologians assume that a clear and distinct boundary exists between sanity and 'mental illness', hard truths and clear falsehoods. These conceptual distinctions flow from the Enlightenment, but are not terribly helpful. Despite the tremendous apparent popularity of these postmodernist assumptions in their unexamined forms, they are at odds with Freud's pioneering efforts in studying mental illness and the myths that we all live by (along with his distinguished *fin de siècle* colleagues Ribot, Janet, and Wundt). Freud's central thesis is that the dividing line between sanity and insanity is relatively arbitrary, and that in any event, each of us crosses this border every day. We cross into insanity when we dream, when we engage in acts for which we cannot give a rational and purposive account, during the countless daily instances when our behaviour is ruled by irrational *habits* established in childhood, and so on. If Freud's *Psychopathology of Everyday Life* is not convincing in this regard, the sceptical reader need only attempt a thorough inventory of his or her conscious reasons for an hour's worth of behaviour. When one tallies up all the gestures, grimaces, tics, etiquette, fashions, and conventions that one uses without really understanding or conscious reflection, the power of the irrational in daily life should become obvious.

Even if one wants to disregard Freud and the *fin de siècle* thinkers for the sake of argument, one cannot turn to contemporary findings or theories to deduce a preconceived hypothesis on mental illness. The labelling theorists in sociology have made the point that the diagnosis of mental illness depends as much (if not more) on context and the 'social construction of reality' than actual 'symptoms'. Having visions of the Virgin Mary certainly does *not* always qualify one for the diagnosis of mental illness, at Medjugorje or in the rest of the world. Anyone who has witnessed a psychiatric interview at a mental hospital knows that the criteria used by psychiatrists to determine whether or not someone is mentally ill are anything but hard and fast (see Meštrović 1985).

Finally, if for the sake of argument one assumes that by some positivistic standard, the visionaries at Medjugorje are determined to be mentally ill or 'normal', where does that leave the status of the other participants, not to mention the status of religious believers in general? True, even Freud concluded that religion constitutes a collective neurosis, but he did *not* condemn religion (contrary to many false efforts to modernize Freud), and he saw no way to escape entirely the bonds of neurosis. There is no such thing as 'reality', only various representations and myths. In sum, the positivistic programme does not lead to any satisfactory conclusion, and is an intellectual dead-end.

THE ROAD TO MEDJUGORJE

I refer to the 'road' to Medjugorje figuratively as well as literally. To begin with, the Virgin Mary is known in Yugoslavia as *Gospa*, meaning 'Our Lady'. This word is related to but distinct from the word 'gospoda', meaning 'madam' or perhaps 'lady' in the secular sense – the two words are never interchanged. Hereafter I shall refer to the apparitions at Medjugorje in terms of the *Gospa*. Medjugorje is located in a remote corner of the Republic of Croatia, which has traditionally been and continues to be Roman Catholic. Fourteen kilometres from Medjugorje one encounters the border of Bosnia-Hercegovina, which is predominantly Moslem, and definitely pre-modern. Thus, today's *Gospa* emerges out of a fairly long-standing religious as well as political context, and she appears, literally, on the border between East and West. In a recent best-selling book in Yugoslavia, Slaven Letica (1989) argues that the current political crisis of communism in Yugoslavia can be conceptualized as the yearning of Slovenia and Croatia in the West for greater pluralism and democracy versus the Serbian leanings in the East for fascist-like nationalism and monolithic political systems. Is it only a coincidence that Medjugorje is situated on the border of these two opposing political tendencies?

Moreover, these two political tendencies can be found in all of the Eastern European nations that are experiencing crises with communism. Portions of the populations clearly tilt towards liberal social ideals while other portions just as clearly tilt towards revivals of ancient nationalistic hatreds and neo-conservative goals. My point is that much as Paris symbolized modernity in the previous century, and was the city in which Mary began her modern visits to humanity, Medjugorje has become a symbol of postmodernity as the present century draws to a close. It is a tourist spectacle on the dividing line between East and West, the irrational and the rational, heart and mind.

As one drives through the villages and towns of Croatia on the way to Medjugorje and enquires into the names of the Catholic churches that one passes, one discovers that a good many of them are named some kind of *Gospa*. In translation, there is the Church of 'The Little Lady', 'The Lady of the Fields', 'The Croatian Lady', along with seemingly countless variations on this theme. In some ways, the situation seems analogous to the naming of churches in

France during the Renaissance. Moreover, these Croatian churches are old, and the cult of *Gospa* seems to be at least hundreds of
years old. Old-timers told me that prior to Medjugorje, they knew
of many apparitions to many visionaries, and that some competing apparitions are still occurring in nearby Split and Sibenik
(these are covered in the newspapers)! People are also quick to
point out that the Italians 'see the *Gospa* all the time', and that
they're a little bit jealous that Yugoslavia staked out this, famous
one. In Durkheimian terms, the collective representations concerning the Virgin Mary are apparently old and well established
in Croatia, as well as in neighbouring Italy. The establishment of
the Cult in Medjugorje is a clear instance of what sociologists term
the social construction of reality.

Indeed, this cult is carefully circumscribed along religious and
political boundaries in Yugoslavia, and these boundaries are often
equivalent. Thus, the press coming out of Belgrade, which is in
Serbia, is decidedly hostile to the cult of the *Gospa*. For example,
the May 22, 1988 issue of *Duga* (a popular news magazine) carried
a story in which the apparitions of the *Gospa* in Medjugorje were
linked conceptually to the atrocities committed by Croatian Us-
tase against Serbs during the Second World War in the very hills
that the *Gospa* uses for her apparitions. The Serbian press views
the apparitions as disguised Croatian nationalism, and this Serbian view is well known in Yugoslavia. In general, the Serbian
press tends to revive nationalistic wounds from the Second World
War while the Slovenian and Croatian press seeks to emulate
Western European culture.

Unlike the scientists who are interested in the issue of whether
the visionaries are sane or insane, Yugoslav laypersons are interested in the issue of whether the apparitions are a political hoax.
Even among devout, elderly, Catholic women (baba's), one will
encounter cynicism. 'If it's the *gospa*, why doesn't she appear to
me?' one said to me – 'I could use the tourist money'. 'It's a better
tourist attraction than Dubrovnik' said another. There exists a lot
of finger-pointing as to who might be perpetrating the hoax,
collectively and individually, but essentially, Sloterdijk's (1987)
penetrating analysis of cynicism applies to many Yugoslavs.
Contemporary Yugoslavs are as cynical as the Western, anomic
types will ever be.

The Vatican has not sanctioned the apparitions at Medjugorje, but it has not condemned them as a hoax either. The Yugoslav government does not encourage participation in this cult, but it does offer some discouragement. One will not find any road signs leading to Medjugorje anywhere along the way – I had to obtain directions from a priest. When one finally arrives, one is met by uniformed militia checking passports, which is somewhat intimidating. In general, the religiously devout and tourist guides know how to get there despite the cynicism of the general public and the blasé attitude of the government.

Another important contextual dimension is the severe economic and political crisis occurring in Yugoslavia, a crisis that began prior to Medjugorje. It is well known even to those who keep up with leading Western newspapers, and may be summarized as follows. Inflation is running at 2,500 per cent annually. The more Western Republics of Slovenia and Croatia are seeking autonomy from the more backward Republics, and openly resent the fact that political power flows from backward Belgrade. Students, intellectuals, and peasants will tell you that they no longer believe in Marxism or 'the regime' (*vlast*) and that it is only a matter of time before it is toppled. There is some fear of civil war, but that has always been a well-founded fear in Yugoslavia.

Many average persons as well as intellectuals said to me, 'If Ronald Reagan were to run for office in Croatia or Slovenia, he'd be elected in a heartbeat.' The USA, capitalism, and German currency are greatly admired for their material promise, although not for their spiritual value. Empirical support for this perceived malaise and crisis is afforded by recent, staggering increases in the social rates of suicide, alcoholism, and schizophrenia in Yugoslavia, rates that now exceed those found in most of Western Europe and the USA. Yugoslav scholarly journals turn to these signs of malaise and also refer openly to the death of Marxism in their nation.

The figurative road to Medjugorje also includes the optimistic dimension. Prior to visiting Medjugorje to see for myself, many devout persons who had made the pilgrimage said that it transformed their lives, that it gave them peace. Peace is the collective representation associated with Medjugorje, and as I learned later, it is the exact word used by the priests in their sermons. The optimists hope that Medjugorje will alert the world to the need for world peace and for inner, psychic peace. As a cynical counter, I cannot avoid commenting that the indoctrination into the theme of peace reminded me of the constant references to 'fun' on a postmodernist cruise ship. In a typically tourist fashion, one's 'experience' at Medjugorje is carefully pre-packaged.

MEDJUGORJE AS POSTMODERNIST SPECTACLE

Given that Medjugorje is famous, it was somewhat surprising that no signs or markers bearing its name could be found as one approached this tiny village. The tourists are brought in mainly by the buses in any event, so this apparently does not present a problem except for the rare visitor who drives a car into Medjugorje, as I did. After travelling for five hours on a rough and bumpy road that has to be experienced to be believed on a journey that began in Drnis, near Sibenik, I found myself in Medjugorje.

I knew I was in the right place because the unpaved road leading to St James church, where the apparitions now occur, was crowded with parked buses. I parked where I could find a place, which was difficult to find, and began the two hundred metre walk to the church. I had to walk the gauntlet past the souvenir stands run by gypsies and other Yugoslavs, as well as the hot dog stands and small, makeshift cafés. This was the ultimate postmodernist scene, pure kitsch. Statuettes of the *Gospa* and various trinkets were offered by vendors who shouted out to individuals in various languages, guessing their nationalities with seemingly remarkable accuracy. But again, I would add the compassionate viewpoint that many of the tourists who purchased these trinkets seemed to be genuinely moved by their visits, and seemed to *need to purchase a trinket to commemorate the event. In practice, it is very difficult to distinguish postmodernist superficiality from genuine sentimentality.*

I decided to enter the church right away, and put off meeting the priests until later, to see what the completely naive sociologist could discern. I wondered, what does one do at Medjugorje?

Inside the church, a priest was speaking in German, and his speech was being translated simultaneously into Serbo-Croatian by a woman, a few sentences at a time. I later discovered that other priests would give similar speeches in English and Italian. The priest explained precisely what one was supposed to do at

Medjugorje: walk to the top of two nearby mountains where the *Gospa* first appeared (before she moved to the church), then attend the evening rosary at 5.30 p.m. at the church, where she now appears promptly at 6.45 p.m. in the summers and 5.45 p.m. the rest of the year. According to the priest, one was supposed to come away with an overwhelming feeling of peace. He repeated this message seemingly countless times. His audience consisted primarily of middle-aged or older tourists, overwhelmingly foreign and white, slightly more female than male, and colourfully well dressed in the latest styles. If one did not know one was at a religious shrine, one would guess one was on a tour.

The interior of the church is unimposing as far as churches go. In fact, it seemed quite poor. To the left of the simple altar a wooden cross stood with the initials IHS inscribed on top, but unlike most Catholic crucifixes, a figure of the crucified Jesus Christ was *not* hanging on the cross. Across the horizontal beam of the crucifix were written the Croatian words that are translated as 'Jesus Christ, Saviour of the Human Race'. To the right of the altar, but at a level lower than that of the altar, there was a statue of the Virgin Mary. She wore a crown of stars and was dressed in a blue dress, a cream-coloured robe, a dark blue belt, gold necklace, and a bangle. Her hair was long and dark. In front of this statue there were lilies, carnations, and lit candles, but again unlike most Catholic shrines, there was no donation box.

Immediately behind the statue of the Virgin Mary there is a small room wherein (I discovered later) the *Gospa* had made her daily appearances prior to 1987. The location of these appearances was changed, because crowds attempted too diligently to move into the cramped room during the apparitions. Nevertheless, even though she no longer appeared there, a constant line of visitors made their way into this room. Of course, I entered it as well.

In this small room one found a small replica of the layout of the main altar: there was a small altar, with another statue of the Virgin Mary to the right, and another crucifix with the initials INRI to the left. Upon entering the room, most visitors crossed themselves, and knelt immediately on the hard floor. For the women, this behaviour seemed automatic. The men seemed more hesitant, and had to be prodded or instructed by the females as to the 'correct' behaviour. After a moment of silent prayer, the visitors generally walked up to the statue of the Virgin Mary and engaged in some or all of the following behaviours: they touched it, kissed it, hugged it, knelt in front of it, or prayed to it. In addition, some of the visitors would touch the nails in the crucified Christ's feet, but this seemed to be an afterthought, and the statue of the Virgin Mary definitely seemed to offer more of an attraction. Cripples who could not walk to the statue themselves were lifted out of their wheelchairs and carried to it. Sociologically speaking, the participants seemed to be behaving as if they were in the presence of what Durkheim (1912) called the sacred: they treated the room and its artefacts with awe and respect.

Touching a sacred object as part of a ritual is a traditional aspect of participating in its supposed power, of forming a bridge between it and the profane world (Hubert and Mauss 1899). Visitors were told that all of the ground in Medjugorje was sacred, and that some ground was more sacred than other ground. This applied especially to two nearby hills where the *Gospa* had appeared in 1980, and which the visitors were supposed to climb as part of their visit to Medjugorje. In general, at Medjugorje one was supposed to touch sacred objects and walk on sacred ground – a very primitive schedule for modern persons of a few generations ago to follow, but one that postmodern persons seemed to accept with ease.

My interview with the priest in charge of the daily programme at Medjugorje revealed the following. The visionaries now experience the apparitions under lock and key in the back of the church in the choir loft. At most, this priest and five or so selected visitors are allowed to witness an apparition. This was done to alleviate the problem of crowd control during apparitions, he explained. Moreover, not all of the 'children' who originally experienced the visions as a group continue to do so. Essentially, the visionaries take turns having the visions, because the visions interfere too much with their lives. 'They are not saints', the priest said of the visionaries. I asked him to elaborate, and he said that they do not lead necessarily exemplary lives from the Catholic point of view, nor have they chosen to devote their lives to the Church by becoming priests or nuns. In fact, one of them opened a guest house for the tourists.

I asked the priest to account for the fact that this group of visionaries are 'not saints' compared to the 'children' of Lourdes and Fatima. Not surprisingly, he said that God works in mysterious ways, and that the particular medium chosen for the sacred message is not as important as the message itself. I enquired further into the messages from *Gospa*. He answered that only one of the visionaries actually receives the messages, at the rate of one per month, and then not always consciously and directly. Sometimes this particular visionary draws a picture, or puts down a few lines on a piece of paper, and the priest interprets the messages. Some of the messages are still secret, even from the priest.

I was granted permission to witness an apparition under lock and key. It was a small group, indeed: one male visionary (who did not say a word to us as we waited for the service to begin) three male members of the clergy, a married couple, the priest I had interviewed, and myself. One Oriental priest brought a small vial of holy water contained in a kitsch, plastic figurine of the Virgin Mary, and placed it next to the small statue of Mary that was present in the choir loft. I determined that the apparition was expected to add an extra dose of holiness to the already holy water. The praying of the rosary began on schedule below, and we all knelt. A minute before the Virgin Mary was supposed to appear, the visionary checked his watch, and then, at the exactly designated time, he knelt in what was supposed to be ecstasy and had his vision. It did not last more than two minutes. The woman in our group was crying, and the others in the group exhibited behaviour that Durkheim would have said indicated that they thought they were in the presence of the sacred. The crowd in the church below, as well as outside (I could see both crowds by means of a window or the loft) looked to the choir loft at the exactly designated time, and remained silent during the apparition.

At the conclusion of the apparition, the crowds continued praying, but the visionary was whisked away by the priest, in a noticeable rush, down the stairs and outside. The visionary made his way quickly into the cornfields behind the church and the paths they hid. I do not think most people recognized him, or knew of this arrangement. The most striking aspect of the apparitions at Medjugorje is their strict orchestration. The Virgin Mary, in keeping with abstract, Protestant modernity, is now punctual, methodical, predictable, and as dependable as the trains in France. Weber's rationalization and bureaucratization of the irrational extends to the experience of the sacred in modern times. It shows just how far we have come since the previous turn of the century.

The typical visitor spends a day and one night in Medjugorje. Once he or she has climbed the designated hill tops, prayed through an apparition, and listened to a sermon, the experience is officially over. One can purchase the official manual of prayer titled *Pray With the Heart* for Catholic guidance and prayer to accompany the experience (see Barbaric 1988). My reading of this manual from the Durkheimian perspective indicates that it espouses the themes of asceticism, prayer, and pessimism that connect Durkheimian sociology of religion with Catholic dogma. This is not all that surprising given Schopenhauer's admiration for the philosophy inherent in Catholic dogma, as well as Schopenhauer's influence on Durkheim. In any event, the concluding chapter in this manual of prayer tells the visitor to take home these Durkheimian–Catholic messages:

> We know one thing: at home you have your own Krizevac, your own hill of the cross, your own cross and suffering. You left it at home and it is waiting for you. But have no fear ... your hill of the cross at home is standing and waiting for you, often built out of troubles and sufferings for which you are neither responsible nor to blame. Build a smaller hill next to it right away, build your own Hill of Apparitions, your own Tabor.... Remember well! Our Lady has taken Christ's words seriously. She goes with you up to your Krizevac, up to your Calvary.
>
> (Barbaric 1988: 148)

IMPLICATIONS

In 1818 Schopenhauer castigated Protestantism for vulgarizing the essentially pessimistic message of Christianity that life is a vale of tears. Without using the word modernity, Schopenhauer was clearly criticizing an abstractionist, hyper-optimistic, aspect of modernity as it is refracted through Protestantism long before Baudelaire arrived on the scene. But apart from what he considered to be vulgar Protestantism, Schopenhauer felt that all modern religions were unconsciously reflecting increasingly pessimistic themes. In 1912, Durkheim refracted Schopenhauer's observation by concluding that as religions evolve from primitive to modern, they reflect more, not less, asceticism, suffering, and pessimism. From 1980 to the present, the apparitions of the Virgin

159

Mary in Medjugorje have reflected these Durkheimian and Scho-penhauerian themes for non-sociologists and non-philosophers. The Virgin Mary teaches that the world is sinful, and that one should pray, turn away from materialism, and nurture faith.

Postmodernism latched on to the Medjugorje phenomenon and transformed it into a spectacle. It became a tourist attraction in which the essentially serious and pessimistic message that the Virgin Mary gives is drowned out by kitsch souvenirs and the overall kitsch setting. Essentially, one can have as much fun at Medjugorje in one's search for inner peace as at any shopping mall searching for the right 'look'.

Nevertheless, despite the obvious postmodernist overtones, I have followed the *fin de siècle* lead in apprehending religion as a system of collective representations that betray something about the state of 'collective conscience' of a particular society. As in psychoanalysis, society is the patient, and religious beliefs, rites, and symbols are the symptoms. This was the essence of the method followed in Wundt's 'folk psychology' as it influenced Durkheimian sociology. I am suggesting that this approach is far more useful in apprehending the import of religion within post-modernity than contemporary approaches that engage in reduc-tionism, subjectivism, and epiphenomenalism.

Thus, female goddesses versus male gods symbolize different aspects of a given society's collective consciousness. From anthro-pological evidence it seems safe to conclude that female sacred figures were more prominent in primitive societies, and that male gods arrived late on the scene. Moreover, with the rise and development of Protestantism, and its subsequent emphasis on the militant Jesus, the only remaining female goddess in modern Christianity, the Virgin Mary, has been gradually but relentlessly eclipsed. Social scientific study ought to address whether (1) this masculinization of divinity is taking place more rapidly even in developing countries and religions, like Hinduism, as these modernize; (2) how the social character of societies dominated by male divinity, namely Protestant and Moslem cultures, differs from cultures in which female divinity figures still play a promi-nent role. This kind of research has not taken place because it assumes the Durkheimian idea that society is a Being *sui generis*, derived from *fin de siècle* Germany, and this idea is completely alien to modernity.

The issue of what cultural values are associated with the Prot-estant cult of Jesus versus the Catholic cult of Mary will become increasingly important as communism continues to dissolve in the remainder of this century. The USSR and Eastern Europe are closer, symbolically and culturally, to the values symbolized by Mary than the Protestant Jesus. After all, the Madonna dominates various Orthodox sects. As the USA and the USSR try to undo the Cold War, they will do so through the values of their respective religious cults. The cult of Jesus seems to represent modern, ab-stractionist, militant values that were actually commensurate with some atheistic elements of former communist regimes. Now that the indigenous religions of the East are returning to their former positions of strength, it may be that some of the pre-modern values systems will return as well. The cult of Mary, or the cult of a female goddess in general, may dominate Eastern European and Soviet thinking as communism continues to dissolve. Is it a co-incidence that *Time*'s 'Man of the Decade', Mikhail Gorbachev, espouses the Marian value of world peace much more forcefully than George Bush, who holds that disarmament is not warranted by recent changes?

I have proposed the hypothesis that modern and postmodern societies turn to female divinity during times of extreme stress. From the Renaissance to 1830 France to Medjugorje, the Virgin Mary appears during times of social, political, and economic up-heaval as if humanity is turning collectively to its mother and the representations that surround motherhood. Does something simi-lar occur in Hindu and other cultures during their times of stress? To the best of my knowledge, this question has never been ad-dressed formally.

This chapter also leads one to re-examine the role of mother-hood within modernity and postmodernity. Statistics indicate that with modernity, fewer women give birth to fewer children, and that they delay childbirth as long as possible. Feminism, instead of seeking to civilize and humanize males, has sought to give females equal footing in a world of masculine values. In the next century, will both sexes be equal in relation to Protestant, abstract, subjec-tivist values, and if so, will their cynical children be satisfied with their modern lives? What will happen to mother worship, a theme that has dominated human culture for thousands of years? Per-haps the day will come when it will be seen as something alien, like the figure of Isis and Horus in a museum. One can imagine Wendy, the character in 'Peter Pan' who acts as mother to the lost children of Neverland, as the historical equivalent of Isis for historians and anthropologists in the twenty-first century.

Chapter Nine

POSTMODERN DEREGULATION AND ECONOMIC ANOMIE

In his *Condition of Postmodernity*, David Harvey (1989) cites the year 1972 as the beginning of a 'sea-change' of economic and political change that finally dissolved the old-fashioned, modern, Fordist philosophy into the Reagan, postmodernist, voodoo economics of deregulation. He refers to postmodern economics of the 1980s as 'economics with mirrors' because it is far more dependent upon images, imagery, and imaginary money than the old-fashioned economics of the inner-directed era. It is not entirely clear why the year 1972 should be singled out as the beginning of a process that Baudelaire cited as far back as 1863. And Harvey's brilliant analysis of the political and economic problems caused by postmodernism does not point to any alternative nor anything like a solution to these problems.

Harvey is probably correct to caricature Ronald Reagan as the penultimate postmodernist President. Reagan's 'teflon' coating (no criticisms would stick to him), his ever-pleasing personality and charm, and his conservative, nostalgic values are a clear reflection of major tenets of postmodernist cultural values. Ronald Reagan preached deregulation and tax cuts even as he increased both regulation and taxes for most of the US population, without their strong objection. From a Durkheimian perspective, one would note that Reagan achieved these typically postmodernist, contradictory aims less due to his personal charisma than to the fact that he was the perfect social product to ride the wave of postmodernism that is sweeping this century to a close. His legacy includes the Stock Market crash of 1987, several subsequent 'mini-crashes', a complete erosion of confidence on the part of individual investors, the dramatic rise of corporate buy-outs, the domination of airport 'hubs' by a few airlines, and other phenomena that essentially benefited the rich and hurt the average person.

Still, Reagan seemed to get along amicably with Gorbachev, and it is interesting that Gorbachev, too, rode on a collective sentiment that rebelled at bureaucracy. When one looks beneath Gorbachev's charm and charisma, one finds drastic economic and political problems that have ensued in the USSR since the inception of Glasnost. In fact, if one attempts to isolate the social philosophy that underlies Reagan's, Gorbachev's, and the end of this century's economic policies, it seems to be the optimistic belief that less government interference will eventually improve economic performance and the life of the average person. It is a belief in Adam Smith's invisible hand all over again, without explicit acknowledgement. Time will tell if this postmodernist optimism is correct.

But it is certain that this optimistic belief applied to economic life is far from original or in any way new. Bureaucracies and bureaucratic structures have been assailed many times in many different cultural contexts, from Hitler to the Bolsheviks as far back as Max Weber's own timid criticisms of the irrationality of excessive bureaucratic rationality. Meanwhile, far in the background of the Western cultural landscape, there lies the Judeo-Christian tradition which depicts the human person as being inherently wicked and selfish, and consequently, in need of constant regulation. Time and time again, various dogma and philosophies have tried to rebel at this religious philosophy, and postmodernism is merely the most recent attempt. Durkheim's sociology is interesting in this regard in that it integrates a distilled version of the Judeo-Christian world view into a sociological analysis of economic institutions.

These are the postmodernist contradictions that concern us in the present chapter: postmodernism espouses deregulation and anti-bureaucratic sentiments at the same time that conservative ideology calls for more regulation and bureaucracy. Durkheim (1893), Freud (1930), Elias (1982), and a host of other thinkers have found that the civilizing process entails more, not less, regulations, restrictions, and constraints of all sorts. Postmodern philosophies purport to rebel at these narratives of constraint, but they fail to address the question of what will replace the constraints. and of course, the problem of human nature is left hanging by postmodernist thinkers: do postmodern humans need constraint or not?

AN OVERVIEW OF DURKHEIM'S POLITICAL AND ECONOMIC PHILOSOPHY

I have referred already to Durkheim's (1887) reports on his study trip to Germany. What must be stressed is that in these reports, Durkheim attacked British and French classical economists of his day, and praised German economists who were still writing in a Hegelian, Schopenhauerian, Romantic vein (see Mirowski 1987; Riba 1985). The gist of Durkheim's critique is the German *fin de siècle* idea that *laissez-faire* economics is an invitation to moral and economic catastrophe that leads to suffering for the entire social body, not just those who are heavily involved in business affairs. Modernity and postmodernity have transformed most of society along economic interests such that economic catastrophes suddenly affect every person in some way. This strange idea from the previous turn of the century is more relevant than ever as we prepare for the next turn of the century.

Durkheim's 1887 essays were the opening salvo in a long and sustained effort to criticize capitalist *and* socialist systems of economics and government (followers of both Reagan and Gorbachev would benefit from reading Durkheim, if for no other reason than to expose themselves to an intelligent counterargument). He repeated, refined, and refashioned his argument in *The Division of Labor (1893)*, *Suicide* (1897), and *Professional Ethics* (1950). Essential to his argument is the seemingly strange concept 'anomie', a Greek word charged with German, Romantic, *fin de siècle* meanings that imply the derangement of human passions as the result of enlightenment. Thus, in the opening lines of his famous second preface to the *Division of Labor in Society*, Durkheim makes clear that his book is primarily about anomie in general and economic anomie in particular:

> We repeatedly insist in the course of this book upon the state of juridical and moral anomie in which economic life actually is found. Indeed, in the economic order, occupational ethics exist only in the most rudimentary state.... Moreover, most of these

precepts are devoid of all juridical character, they are sanctioned only by opinion, not by law; and it is well known how
indulgent opinion is concerning the manner in which these
vague obligations are fulfilled. The most blameworthy acts are
so often absolved by success that the boundary between what is
permitted and what is prohibited, what is just and what is un-
just, has nothing fixed about it, but seems susceptible to almost
arbitrary change by individuals. An ethic so unprecise and in-
consistent cannot constitute a discipline. The result is that all
this sphere of collective life is, in large part, freed from the
moderating action of regulation.

(Durkheim [1893] 1933: 1–2)

The layperson living in the age of postmodernism is well aware
of the problems that Durkheim cites above. After all, the media
are saturated with stories of corruption in the business profession,
and 'insider trading' is so common, it is not always considered a
crime even among businessmen. Yet contemporary sociologists
have ignored or otherwise completely obscured Durkheim's intentions in this classic. *The Division of Labor* is *not* typically read as
a treatise on anomie. The term anomie is well known but misunderstood by social scientists, and almost completely unknown
by the public. It is tragic that anomie, a term that is helpful in
understanding the impact of modern economics on social life, has
been relegated to an obscure status. This sense of tragedy is com-
pounded now that the Marxist concept of alienation is losing relevance as Marxism loses adherents all over the world.

Durkheim's phrase 'economic anomie' is not even used by contemporary sociologists! The bulk of anomie research since Durkheim's death has focused on anomie as the cause of crime and
delinquency, not the relationship of anomie to Wall Street, the
lack of business ethics, and white-collar crime. It is easy to explain
this oversight. Durkheim's concept of anomie implies the tyranny
of unbridled passions imposed upon humans, and postmodernity,
in its abstractionism, has turned a deaf ear to the notion of passion. In keeping with the premises established in the opening
chapters of this book, we shall read Durkheim's comments on
economic anomie in the context of the *fin de siècle* spirit. This
contextual reading highlights Durkheim's proposed project to engage in the scientific study of morality that singles out economic

anomie as the major culprit in the public debasement of morality.

While sociologists have ignored Durkheim's concept of economic anomie, the popular press has certainly mirrored Durkheim's *fin de siècle* observations in the 1980s, albeit without invoking Durkheim. The news is saturated with reports of insider trading scandals, the decline of business ethics, and analyses of the purportedly new ethic of success at any cost, and all this in the midst of an ongoing yet completely atheoretical debate on regulation versus deregulation of the business community. To pick one out of several such stories as illustration, on January 19, 1989, the news broke concerning an FBI sting operation that had uncovered widespread and routine 'shaving' of prices in the Chicago Futures Market, but this is one in a long list of such scandals. Magnet (1986: 65) summarizes well the public's perception of such scandals:

> What is this – the business news or the crime report? Turn over one stone and out crawls Boesky's tipster; investment banker Dennis Levine, dirt clinging to his $12.6 million insider-trading profits. Turn over another and there's a wriggling tangle of the same slimy creatures, from minute grubs like the Yuppie Gang to plump granddads like jailed former Deputy Defense Secretary Paul Thayer. A shovel plunged into the ground above General Electric recently disclosed a bustling colony industriously faking time sheets to overcharge the government on defense contracts. Almost everywhere you look in the business world today, from the E.F. Hutton check-kiting scheme to the Bank of Boston money-laundering scandal, you glimpse something loathsome scuttling away out of the corner of your eye.

Durkheim had foreshadowed both the seemingly new yet typically postmodernist, success-at-any-cost 'ethic', as well as the lack of a formal code of ethics in the business profession:

> There is a professional ethic of the lawyer and the judge, the soldier and the priest, etc. But if one attempted to fix in a little more precise language the current ideas on what ought to be the relations of employer and employee, of worker and manager, of tradesmen in competition, to themselves or to the public, what indecisive formulas would be obtained! Some generalizations, without point, about the faithfulness and devotion workers of all sorts owe to those who employ them, about

the moderation with which employers must use their economic advantages, a certain reprobation of all competition too openly dishonest, for all untempered exploitation of the consumer; that is about all the moral conscience of these trades contains.

(Durkheim [1893] 1933: 2)

Durkheim's remarks are still on the mark regarding the state of business ethics as we approach the next *fin de siècle*. How could his observations have been ignored for these many years?

But Durkheim's theoretically grounded concept of economic anomie goes further than predicting the sordid sequence of scandals that saturates our daily papers. It points to deeply rooted antecedents as well as consequences that affect the entire social body, not just those who work in the business sectors. This 'total' approach to the study of the economic impact on the social body is precisely what Durkheim gleaned from his 1885 sojourn to Germany, and one of the ideas that Deploige (1911) claims that Durkheim stole from Germany. It is certainly an important idea. Durkheim writes ([1893] 1933: 2–4):

It is this anomic state that is the cause, as we shall show, of the incessantly recurrent conflicts, and the multifarious disorders of which the economic world exhibits so sad a spectacle.... That such anarchy is an unhealthy phenomenon is quite evident, since it runs counter to the aim of society, which is to suppress, or at least to moderate, war among men.... A form of activity which has assumed such [an anomic] place in social life evidently cannot remain in this unruly state without resulting in the most profound disasters. It is a notable source of general demoralization. For, precisely because the economic functions today concern the greatest number of citizens... it follows that as that world is only feebly ruled by morality, the greatest part of their existence takes place outside the moral sphere.... If in the task that occupies almost all our time we follow no other rule than that of our well-understood interest, how can we learn to depend upon disinterestedness, on self-forgetfulness, on sacrifice? In this way, the absence of all economic discipline cannot fail to extend its effects beyond the economic world, and consequently weaken public morality.

Bellah et al. (1985) and Bloom (1987) have attacked the malignant form of individualism that Durkheim described in the previous turn of the century, albeit without invoking Durkheim, without linking this anomic individualism to economic institutions, and without distinguishing it – as Durkheim does – from the more healthy kind of individualism that Durkheim felt would characterize future societies. Bellah et al. and Bloom have captivated the popular consciousness in the 1980s, and their works have given rise to numerous book reviews and debates, yet their solutions to the perceived problem seem unsatisfactory. Bellah et al. advocate a conservative return to a previous era of republicanism, whereas Bloom openly calls for a return to a kind of ethnocentrism in place of the cultural relativism that he attacks – both sentiments are out of sync with the liberal, democratic tradition of American society (see Hall 1987).

By contrast, Durkheim's ([1893] 1933: 37) explicit call for a reconciliation of liberal individualism characteristic of modernity with the social solidarity characteristic of pre-modernity remains largely unheeded and unknown: 'How can [the individual] be at once more individual and more solidary?' That still seems to be a crucial question for postmodernist social philosophers to answer. Habermas (1987) claims that he wants to find alternatives to neo-conservative and nihilistic reactions to modernity as well, but it is not clear how his intersubjective communication can achieve this goal. Yet Durkheim's solution clearly relies on the *fin de siècle* emphasis on the irrationalist 'cult' of the individual as part of his solution.

Other non-theoretical statements on the current crisis in Western business and economic institutions also reflect Durkheim's concerns without invoking Durkheim, and thereby unwittingly attest to his profound relevance to the present and the future. Hundreds of articles cite the demoralizing effects of the Stock Market crash of 1987 on enrollment in business schools, consumer confidence, and donations to education and religion. Seligman (1988: 50) notes that 'the rate of depression over the last two generations has increased roughly tenfold', and attributes this increase in psychopathology to the phenomenon of 'rising expectations' found in economic as well as other social and personal aspects of life. Seligman's analysis of rising expectations is remarkably similar to Durkheim's depictions of anomie as a state of limitless desires in general social life, and the pathogenic effects of this state.

Other popular literature has begun to question the 'efficient market hypothesis', the belief among economists that the markets and individuals behave according to rational principles (Etzioni 1988). But none of these analyses have penetrated into the underlying philosophical assumptions concerning human nature that inform capitalist economic theory or liberalism (Hall 1987). In short, modern economic theory is still informed by Enlightenment notions of human nature at the expense of *fin de siècle* assumptions that depicted human passions as being far more tyrannical and inexorable.

Thus, the Brady Commission's investigation of the Stock Market crash of 1987 faulted the use of computers and other mechanisms in trading without addressing social, psychological, or philosophical issues. The Brady Commission's report has been generally criticized for its failure to investigate underlying causes of the crash, but no theoretically grounded alternatives have been found. I believe that these alternatives lie in German *fin de siècle* economic theory that Durkheim reported in his 1887 essays on German philosophy.

Durkheim ([1893] 1933: 3) observes that modern society tends to be predominantly industrial, whereas in previous eras, economic life was made secondary to religious or political life. It is interesting that even in Weber's portrait of the Puritan Work Ethic, financial success was secondary to serving the glory of God. What contemporary person would choose a 'calling', much less a profession, for the glory of God? For Durkheim, the economic sphere of life, which is the source of immorality, has become penultimate in social life, and transforms all our other actions. Durkheim adds that 'only the scientific functions seem to dispute their [economic functions] place, and even science has scarcely any prestige save to the extent that it can serve practical occupations, which are largely economic' (3).

Durkheim's observations are still relevant to the postmodernist age. Even science has been reduced to economic considerations when one considers that most government supported basic research in the USA has been linked either to perceived technological needs or war, both of which involve pecuniary interests. Consider that the social sciences have been given and have maintained a developing world status relative to the natural sciences since the inception of the National Science Foundation in the United States following the Second World War. Harry Alpert observed that sociology was deliberately excluded from funding considerations at first, and was admitted for consideration much later. Many sociological research grants following the Second World War focused on the American soldier's performance and morale at the expense of other areas of research. It is well known that research grants at major universities are 'padded', and that the university takes a huge chunk of the granted money for 'overhead'.

Not only educational and scientific institutions, but most other modern social institutions are run as businesses. Contemporary churches hire secretaries, purchase word processors, and invest in stocks. Charities use only a fraction of the money they collect for the intended needy persons that motivated contributions – advertising, secretarial, and administrative costs must also be paid. Even the family as an institution is affected by economic considerations. One can scarcely think of a Western social institution that is not motivated primarily by economic considerations, and consequently, that is unaffected by economic anomie.

The norm of financial success at any cost has permeated a host of other social institutions and functions, from science to private relationships, thereby transferring what Durkheim calls the 'habit' of feeble morality into the core of public life: 'Naturally, we are not inclined to thwart and restrain ourselves; if, then, we are not invited, at each moment, to exercise this restraint without which there is no ethic, how can we learn the *habit* [of morality]'? (Durkheim [1893] 1933: 4, emphasis added).

The most deleterious effect of this immorality that Durkheim cites is the injustice experienced by the exploited and weaker social classes, and the ensuing conflicts this sense of injustice produces:

To be sure, the strongest succeed in completely demolishing the weakest, or in subordinating them. But if the conquered, for a time, must suffer subordination under compulsion, they do not consent to it, and consequently this cannot constitute a stable equilibrium. Truces, arrived at after violence, are never anything but provisional, and satisfy no one. Human passions

171

stop only before a moral power they respect. If all authority of this kind is wanting, the law of the strongest prevails, and latent or active, the state of war is necessarily chronic (3).

A retrospective examination of history since Durkheim's time – the world wars, the almost constant state of smaller wars, race and other riots, trade wars, even the war between the sexes – reveals that Durkheim's deliberately vague use of the word 'war' applies to the effects of all sorts of perceived injustices, from international to domestic.

This brings us back to the so-called problem of social order, still touted as *the* problem of sociology. As Durkheim made clear, above, one can have social order without justice, but only temporarily. The abuses of the 'law of justice' that stem from the unfettered will of postmodern times submit persons to the law of the strongest (economically), not tranquility or even equilibrium. For Durkheim, it is lack of justice, not just social order, that is the central problem of modern economic institutions: 'Just as ancient peoples needed, above all, a common faith to live by, so we need justice' (388). He felt that justice could be conceptualized as a social fact such that 'at every moment of history there is a dim perception, in the moral consciousness of societies, of the respective value of different social services, the relative reward due to each, and the consequent degree of comfort appropriate on the average to workers in each occupation' ([1897] 1951: 249).

Durkheim certainly adopted the Hegelian idea that a strong State government was necessary to regulate and restrain human passions. At the same time, he argued resolutely against any government tendencies towards totalitarianism. How is this apparent paradox to be explained? Unlike some Marxists and communists, Durkheim did not envision the State as the avant-garde of law and order, immune from the will of the people, an instrument in the hands of the few that would 'break a few heads to make an omelette' (Mao's famous line cited by Harvey 1989: 16, apparently with some approval). Rather, the State was to be an 'organ' intimately related to and communicating with the people: it was to be the 'brain' to the 'heart' (the nation). It may well be the case that such a strong, but communicative, friendly State would *not* deteriorate into totalitarianism. No one knows for certain because Durkheim's political theory has not been given a wide hearing.

Nevertheless, in the 1980s, the governments of the United States, Great Britain, and Canada in particular, and many Western governments in general, had systematically 'deregulated' many industries and areas of economic life. Similarly, many governments in Eastern Europe had completely dismantled many former branches of power. While the State had been weakened in both cases, it is not clear that communication with the people improved. In the USA, the poor became poorer under the Reagan Administration – their voices were not heard. In Eastern Europe, so many voices emerged, clamouring, when totalitarian regimes were removed, that anarchy often ensued. For Durkheim, complete, unregulated submission to the unbridled 'will of the people' is an invitation to anomie and public malaise. For Reagan, Thatcher, and Mulroney, the politics of deregulation are part of a conservative swing in opinion that swept and kept them in power for many years. Yet Durkheim's poignant comments on government regulation speak to us today ([1897] 1951: 255):

> Actually, religion has lost most of its power. And government, instead of regulating economic life, has become its tool and servant. The most opposite schools, orthodox economists and extreme socialists, unite to reduce government to the role of a more or less passive intermediary among the various social functions. The former wish to make it simply the guardian of individual contracts; the latter leave it the task of doing the collective bookkeeping.... On both sides nations are declared to have the single or chief purpose of achieving industrial prosperity; such is the implication of the dogma of economic materialism, the basis of both apparently opposed systems. And as these theories merely express the state of opinion, industry, instead of being still regarded as a means to an end transcending itself, has become the supreme end of individuals and societies alike. Thereupon the appetites thus excited have become freed from any limiting authority. By sanctifying them, so to speak, this apotheosis of well-being has placed them above all human law. Their restraint seems like a sort of sacrilege.

Durkheim's observations on economic anomie, malignant individualism, and injustice are unwittingly reflected in many contemporary writings, thereby attesting, indirectly, to the relevance and importance of Durkheim's thought for modern reflections on the Stock Market and social problems stemming from the economic structure. The most pressing and controversial modern social problems centre on the lack of business ethics, the selfishness of the so-called 'me generation', and the rise of rampant hyper-individualism. But contemporary commentators do not know where to turn for theoretical scaffolding to find a proposed solution. Interesting parallels even exist between the panic of 1893, which Durkheim witnessed, and the Stock Market crash of 1987 (Hale 1988). The advantage of Durkheim's observations over current reflections is the *fin de siècle* context that Durkheim invokes.

PERCEIVING ECONOMIC ANOMIE

Already it should be apparent that there is something terribly wrong, if not silly, about the way that Durkheim's relevant observations on economic anomie have been simply ignored by contemporary sociologists. For example, conventional wisdom leads one to expect that the Stock Market crash of 1987 has had a devastating and long-lasting impact on the US population as a whole as well as other populations in the world. Indeed, many other countries in the world suffered similar financial catastrophes following October 19, 1987. Something similar is true for other economic catastrophes since the previous turn of the century. What is surprising about society's as well as sociologists' response and the subsequent attempts to understand the impact of these crashes in general, and the Stock Market crash of 1987 in particular, is the lack of a recourse to theoretical or conceptual frameworks within which the crash can be assessed methodologically and understood. In keeping with Sloterdijk's (1987) analysis of contemporary cynicism, it seems that government, corporate, and other civic leaders simply keep previous policies intact, and wait for a given economic catastrophe to recede into memory.

Because it is completely beyond the scope of this chapter to treat the many economic catastrophes since the previous turn of the century, I shall focus on the Stock Market crash of 1987 as an illustration. Even the focus on 1987 will have to be necessarily brief.

To illustrate further the relevance of Durkheim's concept of economic anomie, and to point to the continuities in his work, let us turn for the moment from his *Division of Labor* (1893) to his equally classic *Suicide* (1897). Along the lines established above, Durkheim wrote in 1897 in *Suicide* that 'the sphere of trade and industry' is the one in which anomie exists in a chronic state ([1897] 1951: 254). Durkheim adds (256):

> Such is the source of the excitement predominating in this [business] part of society, and which has thence extended to the other parts. There, the state of crisis and anomy is constant and, so to speak, normal. From top to bottom of the ladder, greed is aroused without knowing where to find ultimate foothold. Nothing can calm it, since its goal is far beyond all it can attain. Reality seems valueless by comparison with the dreams of fevered imaginations; reality is therefore abandoned.... We may even wonder if this moral state is not principally what makes economic catastrophes of our day so fertile in suicides.

This enshrinement of greed eventually leads to economic catastrophes – even the popular media knows that – but the catastrophes in turn affect the entire social body. This latter idea, self-consciously borrowed by Durkheim from Germany, is not invoked by social scientists or laypersons, and is worth studying. Durkheim writes (252):

> In the case of economic disasters, indeed, something like declassification [*déclassement*] occurs which suddenly casts certain individuals into a lower state than their previous one. Then they must reduce their requirements, restrain their needs, learn greater self-control.... But society cannot adjust them instantaneously to this new life and teach them to practice the increased self-repression to which they are unaccustomed. So they are not adjusted to the condition forced on them, and its very prospect is intolerable; hence the suffering which detaches them from a reduced existence even before they have made trial of it.

A similar *déclassement* occurred in Eastern Europe in the 1980s as people's standard of living fell drastically in a relatively small space of time. Even though Eastern European economic aspirations were never on par with aspirations in the rest of Europe or the USA, the basic principle is the same. Economic anomie occurs when people's material desires override their real conditions, and economic anomie eventually produces a variety of other forms of anomie – political, domestic, religious, and so on. Moreover, many of the empirical indicators of economic anomie that Durkheim (241–58) mentions in his famous section of *Suicide* devoted to economic anomie may be found preceding and following the Stock Market crash of 1987, and could easily be subjected to an empirical test.

For example, Durkheim (242) cites bankruptcies as an index of anomie. *The Wall Street Journal* reports that bankruptcies have been at their highest rate in recent years immediately before and following the Stock Market crash of 1987. As of 1989, the United States is experiencing the most costly bail-out of bankrupt savings and loan institutions in its history. David Riesman has remarked that bankruptcies, for institutions as well as individuals, have become so commonplace that society no longer assigns the stigma to them that it used to a few generations ago. The cause of most bankruptcies, individual and corporate, is obvious: unrestrained, narcissistic greed that is not mindful of the will of others.

Durkheim also mentions that 'When the price of the most necessary foods rises excessively, suicides generally do the same' (244). He referred to the price of wheat, rye, and steam boilers in his day in this context, which seem to correspond to a tremendous surge in prices for soybeans, wheat, and corn preceding the Stock Market crash of 1987. As of 1989, the price of these commodities on the Chicago Futures Exchange has been the highest in American history. Also in the section of *Suicide* devoted to economic anomie, Durkheim (244) cites the increase in private wealth, annexations of wealth, and the amassing of wealth into a few concentrated areas as important indexes of anomie. This corresponds to findings that in recent years Western wealth has been concentrating in the upper classes, corporate takeovers have been on a dramatic and unprecedented increase, and the unequal distribution of wealth seems to be on the rise.

In a footnote Durkheim (249) even mentions that suicide increases when income tax laws are changed. Harry Alpert (1938a), in particular, focused on the implicit theory of rising expectations found in Durkheim's writings on anomie, but subsequent Durkheimian scholars have tended not to follow Alpert's lead. Nevertheless, immediately preceding the Stock Market crash of 1987, the United States underwent one of the most drastic changes in income tax laws in its history, and this must have had a dramatic impact on people's desires for material wealth.

Other indicators of anomic 'disturbances of the collective order' with regard to economic life can be gleaned from Durkheim's 1897 study: sharp increases in the Dow Jones Industrial Average serve as rough equivalents to Durkheim's focus on the sharp stimulus to trade and industry (243); a comparison of the number of world expositions and world trade fairs before and after the crash (244); the proportion of media coverage devoted to the changing tax laws and luxury tax laws compared to previous years (249); the increase in media coverage of deregulation (255); the increase in the number of laws favouring deregulation (255); the increase in the rate of novelty shops (255); the increase in the number of businesses devoted to hedonism, exotic pleasures, and what Durkheim calls 'a thirst for novelties, unfamiliar pleasures, and nameless sensations' (256).

The social rates of novelty and sex shops and other indicators of the distribution of pornography, found in the 1986 Attorney General's Commission on Pornography Report, would serve as one of several excellent sources of indicators for what Durkheim apparently intended with his reference to the need for novelties. But for empirical proof, one needs only consider the fact that in contemporary, postmodern Western culture, there exist towns and sites in cities whose only industry is the tourist industry. These 'tourist traps' thrive on selling kitsch. This might be somewhat understandable, even if offensive, at traditionally popular tourist attractions like the Taj Mahal or the Acropolis. But there now exist imitations of these and other historical sites – for example, the replica of the Acropolis in Nashville, Tennessee, and the imitation of a Swiss Alpine Village in Helen, Georgia, both in the United States.

THE POSTMODERNIST RESPONSE TO DURKHEIM'S CONCEPT OF ANOMIE

It has not yet been determined formally whether, in fact, suicide rates or other measures of symptomatology in the United States and other major industrial nations increased dramatically before, during, or after the Stock Market crash of 1987. I have suggested that indicators to test this hypothesis can be found in many diverse sources of data. Similarly, it would be interesting to examine various rates of symptomatology in the USSR and Eastern Europe prior to and following the prolonged political and economic crises of the 1980s. The data for such a project may not be as readily available, but in both cases, it is the lack of theoretical scaffolding that is the major obstacle.

It is important also to account for the similarities between Durkheim's concept of anomie and many *fin de siècle* German concepts like it. For example, anomie is essentially similar to Schopenhauer's notion of the 'will' as the bottomless abyss of human desires. This insatiable, tyrannical 'will' became Simmel's (1971) concept of 'life' in opposition to forms, discussed in the opening chapters. It is also remarkably similar to Freud's 'id' and dualistic Eros that leads to civilization and its discontents; Tönnies's opposition between the 'natural will' of *Gemeinschaft* and the 'artificial will' of *Gesellschaft*; even Nietzsche's conflict between Apollonian and Dionysian forces.

Apart from these specific similarities, there exist remarkable similarities between Durkheim's critique of modern economic institutions and similar critiques by Simmel in his *Philosophy of Money* (1978) as well as Marx's well-known analyses of capitalism. All three of these thinkers posit that the manner in which modern individuals relate economically determines, to various degrees, how they will relate to each other in all other areas of social life. For this reason, Simmel likens the money economy to prostitution. Durkheim's critique is no less penetrating than these German critiques. Additionally, and unlike Marx, Durkheim (1928) criticizes socialism as well as capitalism from the *fin de siècle* perspective. Yet, Durkheim continues to be referred to as a neo-conservative, status quo functionalist!

However, the probable reason why these sources and conceptual linkages have been neglected is ideological: Abstractionist postmodernity precludes an examination of a concept that is antithetical to it, and that invokes the insatiability of human desire – anomie. Anomie is caught in the present-day ruthless forgetting that is essential to modernity. The Stock Market crash of 1987 occurred at a time when sociological theory was moving away from the concept of anomie in general and Durkheim's version of anomie in particular (see Besnard 1987; Orru 1987). And similarly for the political and economic crises in Eastern Europe in the 1980s. The state of intellectual anomie within the social sciences has precluded an empirical assessment of Durkheim's theory of anomie.

For example, in a recent work on the usage of the concept of anomie since Durkheim, Philippe Besnard (1987) argues that the concept of anomie has been used by sociologists as an ornament, a professional badge. He argues convincingly that Merton (1957) and the neo-functionalists have vulgarized Durkheim's original meaning of anomie. But surprisingly, Besnard concludes that the concept of anomie should be dropped entirely from the sociological vocabulary. Orru (1987) arrives at a similar conclusion, that anomie has so many divergent meanings, it has no one meaning. Sociologists are trapped by a nihilism of their own design.

There does not exist any realistic hope for supposing that Durkheim's concepts of anomie in general and economic anomie in particular will ever be resurrected in a meaningful and useful way. Abstractionist postmodernity is too well entrenched. But this pathetic state of affairs does not negate the import of the concept of economic anomie for comprehending the impact of postmodern economic institutions, in the West as well as the East, as the present century draws to a close. I have given sufficient empirical illustrations, above, to conclude that only a sleepwalker would be content with the rationalist models used today to apprehend economic functions, capitalist or socialist. Tiryakian has summarized the matter well (1988: 393):

After the severe erosion of confidence in America in the morality of 'insiders' in the public and the financial sectors, stemming from Watergate, Irangate, and the economic scandals of Wall Street, the ultimate sociological concern of Durkheim is one that should be seen as of contemporary relevance.

DURKHEIM'S REMEDY FOR ECONOMIC ANOMIE

'But, the evil observed, what is its cause and what can be its remedy'? Durkheim ([1893] 1933: 4) asks in his *Division of Labor*. His reply is that something he calls the 'corporation' must be restored in the workplace, a solution he repeats in the conclusion of *Suicide* (1897) as well as *Professional Ethics and Civic Morals* (1950). Part of the problem in appreciating his solution is that the word 'corporation' conjures up precisely the heartless, overly rational

179

images of the postmodern corporation that Durkheim fights against. In addition, positivistic misreadings of Durkheim could not incorporate his explicit comparisons between his version of the corporation and religious versions, as well as the religious flavour of the family. The gist of Durkheim's solution is that through modernization, the 'heart' element of the workplace has been lost, and it must be restored.

Durkheim observes that in ancient times, 'above all, the corporation was a religious organization. Each one had its particular god whose cult was celebrated in a special temple when the means were available' ([1893] 1933: 11). It is well known that for Durkheim (1912), religion embodies notions of the sacred. And as Pickering (1984) has demonstrated, the sacred, for Durkheim, carries connotations of spontaneous attraction, warmth, awe, respect, and other elements of the 'heart'. In addition, the corporation or workplace as he conceived it would be a society, as opposed to the disunified aggregate of individuals that make up the contemporary workplace. Society, for Durkheim, always carries this element of heart, because 'it is not only a moral authority which dominates the life of its members; it is also a source of life *sui generis*. From it comes a warmth which animates its members, making them intensely human, destroying their egotisms' ([1893] 1933: 26) – this is an obviously Hegelian, Schopenhauerian idea.

Durkheim also draws an interesting parallel between the dissolution and evolution of the family with the corporation. First, by virtue of being a society, the family is 'a group of individuals who find themselves related to one another in the midst of political society by a particularly strong community of ideas, of sentiments and interests' (16). Second, the corporation was 'formed on the model of domestic society' (17) and even 'substituted for the family' (18).

To understand the full implications of the parallel that Durkheim draws, one must be mindful of his scattered writings on the family, found especially in his reviews in *L'Année sociologique*. According to Marcel Mauss, the family was a favourite topic for Durkheim, even though he never wrote a definitive text on it. In any case, it is instructive to invoke one of these reviews by Durkheim as illustration, his review of Marianne Weber's *Wife and Mother in Legal Development* (1904). Durkheim argues that the evolution of the family from matriarchy through patriarchy to present-day egalitarianism parallels: (1) the evolution from mechanical to organic solidarity, treated at length in his *Division of Labor*; (2) the evolution of the ideal of moral individualism, the new 'cult of the individual' that would eventually replace the religions of former times; and (3) the anomic form of the family, an aberration in which men and women gain equality in 'public life' at the expense of an impoverished 'domestic life'. Let us examine this argument in more detail.

For Durkheim, the family, like society, is supposed to be the *foyer* of life. Robert Hall (1988: 117) explains that the *foyer* was one of Durkheim's favourite images and that 'the *foyer* was originally the fireplace or hearth, then generally a source of heat and by analogy a center of activity, a focus of interest, or a hotbed of intrigue'. In the context of the present discussion, Durkheim claims that, ideally, the modern family ought to function as the *foyer* for the religious respect, passion, and other emotions derived from the notions of the sacred and the heart. Yet the dissolution of 'domestic life' because of divorce, egoism, the working status of both partners, and other factors throws water on this 'hearth' and thereby dampens the progress of moral individualism, and lessens any real progress that has been made with regard to the subjugation of women. Rather than coldly equalize men and women *vis-à-vis* 'public life', Durkheim proposed that both men and women should be *humanized vis-à-vis* the home while keeping their respective individualisms in public as well as domestic life. This thoroughly Schopenhauerian argument is certainly intriguing, and seems to be more than a little bit relevant to the current crisis of the family.

Contemporary research findings substantiate Durkheim's prediction that the amount of time the average Western family interacts per day can be measured in minutes, not hours. Durkheim is implying that the modern arrangement of a working couple who devote themselves more to public than domestic life is not a family properly speaking, because for many hours in the day, family life does not 'circulate' and is literally non-existent, as he notes in *Suicide* (Durkheim [1897] 1951: 202). The modern *foyer* has been reduced to a pilot light that barely flickers, and family members are absorbed almost wholly in 'public life'. Research also indicates that men and women in the West have opted for this disjunction of domestic and private lives due to economic necessity, not rational choice: it is impossible for most families to maintain the middle-class standard of their parents unless both parents work. It is again apparent that economic interests are penultimate in postmodern culture, as Durkheim suggested, and that in this case, economic anomie contributes to domestic anomie. In addition, it should be noted that since Durkheim's death, social rates of divorce, suicide, delinquency, and other indicators of family malintegration in Western societies have certainly not decreased. Even if one wants to disagree with Durkheim, his pessimistic assessment deserves to be taken seriously, and to be tested empirically.

Suppose that efforts were made to maintain the family and the workplace as the religious *foyers* of moral life, as Durkheim intended. First, how would one go about achieving such aims? How would the doctrines of liberalism and individualism be modified to make them attractive to large numbers of modern persons who suffer the ill effects of the present arrangements, domestically and publicly? These are the questions that Durkheim's assessment leads one to consider.

In any case, Durkheim seems to be correct to assert in his *Division of Labor* that the present arrangement is pathogenic:

> Perhaps now we shall be better able to explain the conclusions we reached at the end of our book, *Le Suicide*. We were already proposing there a strong corporative organization as a means of remedying the misfortune which the increase in suicides, together with many symptoms, evinces. Certain critics ... have seen only an utilitarian association whose effect would at best bring order to economic interests, whereas it must really be the essential element of our social structure. The absence of all corporative institution creates, then, in the organization of a people like ours, a void whose importance it is difficult to exaggerate. It is a whole system of organs necessary in the normal functioning of the common life which is wanting. Such a constitutive lack is evidently not a local evil, limited to a region of society; it is a malady *totius substantiae*, affecting all the organism.... It is the general health of the social body which is here at stake.
> ([1893] 1933: 29)

Rough approximations of what Durkheim might have intended exist in the Japanese system in which the workplace bears some resemblance to Durkheim's corporation. And the Swedish system of giving both the husband and wife lengthy periods of time off from work, with pay, to be with the newborn child and each other, is an interesting example of maintaining the *foyer* of domestic life. Other isolated examples can be found, but none have been related to theory, and none have been part of an organized effort on the part of societies to restore morality in the modern world.

Finally, care must be taken not to conclude that Durkheim's sentiments express a misplaced Romanticism. Such a faulty conclusion would only feed the rampant cynicism that precludes a consideration of the solutions proposed by Durkheim and some of his contemporaries (see Sloterdijk 1987). Prior to writing his *Division of Labor* Durkheim had reviewed Tönnies's *Community and Society* (1887). Durkheim agreed with Tönnies's thesis overall, but took issue with him precisely on the question whether the future held in store only the malignant 'rational will' of *Gesellschaft*. Durkheim was more Schopenhauerian than Tönnies in his approach – even though he noted specifically the influence of Schopenhauer on Tönnies's thesis – in that he felt that modern forms of solidarity were as much a manifestation of the 'natural will' as Tönnies maintained was present only in primitive societies. In other words, Durkheim felt that the present-day utilitarian, rational arrangements of the workplace and family were *aberrations* that could be repaired, not the normal forms that these institutions were destined to become in postmodern culture. This intriguing explanation of modernity shall be examined in further detail in the next chapter.

Thus, it is not true that Durkheim wants to restore the past based on some conservative or Romantic biases. Rather, he sought to purify and distinguish what he thought should have been the normal forms of the modern development of the workplace and family from the anomic forms that predominate. In contradistinction to positivistic and Enlightenment assumptions, he felt that religious sentiments should become more, not less, important for future societies, and that the positivistic structure itself is anomalous.

Chapter Ten

CIVILIZATION AND ITS DISCONTENTS, AGAIN

The theme of civilization and its discontents is the most dominant theme found in *fin de siècle* artistic as well as social scientific literature (Ellenberger 1970). From Melville to Mann, from Freud to Toynbee, scores of writers used the term 'civilization' as a synonym for modernity, and despite noting some of its benefits compared to primitive life, condemned it overall. Yet this easily verifiable fact has been distorted by the postmodernist dogma of boosterish optimism concerning so-called progress. Even though the rejection of Enlightenment narratives is a key component of postmodernist philosophy, as a rule, postmodernist writers never go as far in criticizing bourgeois civilization as the previous *fin de siècle* thinkers did. Here is another instance of hypocrisy and shallow rhetoric in postmodernist culture that actually hides a bourgeois mentality.

To be sure, exceptions to this rule exist. Norbert Elias (1982) has revived Freud's notion that civilization necessarily implies self-restraint, and therefore some degree of discontent. Bloom (1987) has exposed the pessimism of *fin de siècle* writers concerning civilization with the aim of exposing the superficiality of 1980s USA culture. Notwithstanding these and a few other exceptions, the general rule in contemporary social scientific textbooks is to pay lip-service to a naive version of progress that is a throwback to the Enlightenment. And even Elias, Bloom, and others who wish to achieve a sober reappraisal of the present in relation to the previous *fin de siècle* are not as clear as they might be on the question *why* civilization *must* lead to discontent.

For example, anyone who has lived for any length of time in a so-called developing nation will probably not want to trade his or her bourgeois discontent for the squalor and unsanitary life of the peasant. And as noted in the opening chapters, the Durkheimians were against romanticizing the past. Primitive societies seem to have their share of discontent, so why criticize modernity or post-modernist boosterism? On the other hand, were postmodernism optimism genuine, why does so much of postmodernist culture focus on violence, apocalyptic themes of saving the world from destruction, brutality, and other forcefully pessimistic (albeit camouflaged with fun) themes.

Then there is the philosophical problem of whether discontent stems from self-restraint, as Elias and Freud maintained, or the lack of such self-restraint, as Schopenhauer and Durkheim claimed, or some mysterious combination of both insights.

Good reasons exist to suppose that something new might be learned in relation to these problems from Durkheim's *Division of Labor*, a text that is never invoked in such discussions. This is because Durkheim's classic continues to be misread as a defence of Enlightenment theories of naive progress (Lukes 1985). But much evidence has already been presented that it might be read as something other than a defence of neo-Kantian, positivist theories of rationalist progress. Even the most cursory glance at the broad outlines of Durkheim's thesis in *Division of Labor* indicates that it simply does not fit anything like Comte's, the utilitarian, or other Enlightenment writings based on the progress of reason. Rather, like Schopenhauer and many *fin de siècle* writers, Durkheim ([1893] 1933: 249) pessimistically concludes that as human-kind 'advances' with civilization and the division of labour, 'the general happiness of society is decreasing'. Given Ellenberger's (1970) analysis of the *fin de siècle* spirit that gave rise to Freud's (1930) *Civilization and Its Discontents*, and many other gloomy works like it, it seems unlikely that Durkheim would have written an optimistic work that completely contradicted his times.

Apart from questioning the historical accuracy of the misreadings of Durkheim's thought as a derivative of Enlightenment philosophies, it is possible to question the efficacy of these rationalist readings to explain the origins and nature of social problems within postmodernity, as well as their solutions. For example, consider Merton's (1957) extension of the Parsonian understanding of the 'problem of social order', widely cited in functionalist treatments of social problems, especially with regard to anomie. Merton claims that he wants to move away from the Freudian-like perspective in which social disorder is understood as the result of the ungoverned id and other biological tendencies – what Rochberg-Halton (1988) calls the life concept. But to the extent that Merton ascribes his conceptualization of anomie to Durkheim – which he does at times – one must account for the fact that Durkheim's concept of the dualism of human nature has many affinities with the Freudian view that Merton rejects. It must, since Freud's thought is admitted to be, in large measure, a refraction of Schopenhauer's philosophy. But the question which begs an answer in the Parsonian–Mertonian version of the 'problem of social order' is this: Where do the desires that lead to disorder originate in their positivist and overly rationalist scheme of things? The answer seems to be that any theory that denies the life-concept cannot account for the id-like, desiring, 'lower' pole of the dualism of human nature, and therefore cannot really account for social disorder.

In his historical study of French *fin de siècle*, Eugen Weber (1987: 4) notes that the social problems which beset Durkheim's age are still with us. The most glaring of these are the recurrent problems, scandals, and demoralization that stem from what Durkheim termed the essentially amoral character of modern economic institutions, addressed in the previous chapter. And these social problems are still being apprehended in terms of outmoded, outdated positivistic and optimistic concepts of human nature derived from the Enlightenment. Even the Mertonian version of anomie as 'normlessness' is derived from the Enlightenment, and is problematic for that reason. Moreover, the Mertonian version links anomie conceptually to crime and delinquency in society's deviant subcultures, not, as Durkheim intended, to economic life that lies at the core of society's modern institutions.

A distinguishing aspect of Schopenhauer's philosophy in relation to postmodernity is that the 'will to life' is fuelled, unleashed, and exacerbated by science, knowledge, and general enlightenment, rather than restrained by these phenomena of progress ([1818] 1969b: 573):

Awakened to life out of the night of unconsciousness, the will finds itself as an individual in an endless and boundless world,

186

among innumerable individuals, all striving, suffering, and err-
ing... its desires are *unlimited*, its claims inexhaustible, and every
satisfied desire gives birth to a new one. No possible satisfaction
in the world could suffice to still its craving, set a final goal to
its demands, and fill the *bottomless pit* of its heart. (Emphasis
added.)

It is suggestive that in his famous characterization of anomie,
Durkheim uses some of Schopenhauer's exact phrasing and that
throughout *Suicide*, he also attacks civilization as the major culprit
in understanding the origins of anomie (Durkheim, [1897] 1951:
247):

Irrespective of any external regulatory force, our capacity for
feeling is in itself an insatiable and bottomless abyss. But if
nothing external can restrain this capacity, it can only be a
source of torment to itself. Unlimited desires are insatiable by
definition ... being unlimited, they constantly and infinitely sur-
pass the means at their command; they cannot be quenched.
Inextinguishable thirst is constantly renewed torture.

In essence, Schopenhauer turned the Enlightenment understanding of human nature – in which the mind is granted a superior position in relation to the heart – upside down. Durkheim did
not deviate significantly from this Schopenhauerian formula.
Central to this formula is the assumption that 'will' and 'idea' develop in parallel as well as in opposition, thereby making their
antagonism more fierce. Enlightenment restricts emotional life at
the same time that it expands the horizon of objects of desire. This
is the primary, albeit paradoxical, reason why civilization leads to
discontent for Schopenhauer and Durkheim, not just because civilization leads to restraint, as Freud and Elias argue. But this argument requires careful elaboration.

THE RATIONAL VERSUS THE NATURAL WILL DEPICTED BY TÖNNIES

In 1889 Durkheim reviewed Ferdinand Tönnies's classic *Community and Society* ([1887] 1963). Tönnies posited a social evolution
from the more primitive 'community' *(Gemeinschaft)* to the more
recent 'society' *(Gesellschaft)* that is anything but an example of the

benign effects of rational progress. Tönnies reflects Schopenhauer in his terminology by contrasting the 'natural will' of community with the 'rational will' of society, but reflects him even
further in the substance of his argument. Tönnies even referred
to Schopenhauer by name in *Community and Society*. Alpert
([1938a] 1961: 188) noted but did not elaborate on the fact that
Durkheim ([1889] 1978: 115) remarked on Schopenhauer's in-
fuence on Tönnies. For the purposes of this chapter, the polemic
between Tönnies and Durkheim in the context of Schopenhauer's
philosophy illuminates the manner in which Durkheim fashioned
his own version of *fin de siècle* pessimism relative to Tönnies's own
extremely gloomy assessment of modernism in conjunction with
an extremely romantic vision of the past.

To phrase the issue somewhat differently, the polemic between
Tönnies and Durkheim – hardly ever invoked by scholars – is important for highlighting the contrast between two aspects of the
fin de siècle spirit, romanticism and cynicism.

For Tönnies, the more primitive 'natural' will is fluid, soft,
warm, deep, and good. By contrast, he describes the modern rational will as artificial, mechanical, hard, cold, superficial, and evil.
The argument that fills in this great opposition is difficult to summarize – even Durkheim acknowledges that – because it is a very
original extension of Schopenhauer, Marx, and other proponents
of the *fin de siècle* spirit. Nevertheless, it seems that Tönnies approached the problem of human evil along an avenue that
Schopenhauer had opened.

The introduction of rationality into *Gemeinschaft* is depicted by
Tönnies as the beginning of dissolution: 'All rational will contains
something false and unnatural', forced, tendentious and heartless
([1887] 1963: 127). It isolates one from the group and thereby
gives rise to a calculated egoism, and 'the more perfectly egoistic
one is, the more indifferent he is towards the weal and woe of
other people' ([1887] 1963: 130). Compassion is sytematically
eradicated from the community. Rational, isolated, modern humanity is poised against nature as well as other 'naked' wills:

> The forms of rational will set the individual as giving and re-
> ceiving against the whole of nature. Man tries to control nature
> and to receive from it more than he himself is giving. But with-
> in nature he is confronted with another rational will which

aspires to the same, i.e., with another individual who is to gain by his losses.

([1887] 1963: 140)

Tönnies seems to draw on Schopenhauer's notion of an enlightened will that foreshadowed Durkheim's concept of anomie. Thus Tönnies writes that 'increase in knowledge means increase and multiplication of desires' ([1887] 1963: 161). It is worth repeating that this is the gist of Schopenhauer's rebellion against the Enlightenment. According to Tönnies, 'as women enter the struggle to earn a living' they develop a calculating, rational will, and they 'become enlightened, coldhearted, conscious' ([1887] 1963: 166). As a result, the original meaning of the family is perverted: 'The family becomes an accidental form for the satisfaction of natural needs' (168). Neighbourhood and friendship are supplanted by special interest groups, businesslike morality, and legalistic relationships. The dissolution of the family signalled the demise of *Gemeinschaft*, which in turn 'meant the victory of egoism, impudence, falsehood, and cunning, the ascendancy of greed for money, ambition and lust for pleasure.... And this process can never be considered completed' (202). We have observed in the previous chapter that Durkheim refracted many of Tönnies's sentiments on women and the family in his own writings on these subjects.

Tönnies describes modern society in severe terms: dry, hard, cold, cruel, abstract, artificial, business-like, full of deceit: 'The lie becomes a characteristic element of *Gesellschaft*' (165). In line with the Schopenhauerian distinction between the mind and the heart, Tönnies explicitly aligns *Gemeinschaft* with the heart and *Gesellschaft* with the 'brain' (131).

In his review, Durkheim claims that he agrees with Tönnies overall. In *The Division of Labor in Society*, Durkheim, too, would eventually refer to anomie as an 'evil' that causes humans to suffer needlessly ([1893] 1933: 5). Durkheim, too, would point to the economic institutions as being essentially amoral, and to economic anomie as the originator of most of the other varieties of anomie. The only essential difference is that Durkheim would not allow that the future inevitably held in store only the perverted, malignant form of the modern social will that Tönnies described. Durkheim ([1889] 1978: 121) writes in his review:

189

But the point at which I will differ with him [Tönnies] is in his theory of *Gesellschaft*. If I have properly understood his thought, *Gesellschaft* is characterized by a progressive development of individualism, the dispersive effects of which can be prevented only for a time and through artificial means by the action of the state. It is essentially a mechanical aggregate.... Now, I believe that the life of great social agglomerations is every bit as natural as that of small aggregates. It is neither less organic nor less self-contained.... We would need an entire book to prove this.

Durkheim eventually wrote this book, *The Division of Labor in Society*. It contains all the themes that Tönnies takes up – solidarity, individualism, decadence, dissolution, the State, etc. – in addition to anomie, but from a slightly different vantage point. Both thinkers were inspired by Schopenhauer, but ended up in different theoretical arenas. Durkheim was far less romantic than Tönnies about the past, and less severe about the future, yet equally pessimistic overall.

DURKHEIM'S PESSIMISM IN *THE DIVISION OF LABOR*

In his *Division of Labor in Society*, Durkheim asks: 'But in fact, is it true that the happiness of the individual increases as man advances'? and replies, 'nothing is more doubtful' ([1893] 1933: 241). Durkheim (337) adds:

This does not mean that civilization has no use, but that it is not the services that it renders that makes it progress. *It develops because it cannot fail to develop*. Once effectuated, this development is found to be generally useful, or, at least, it is utilized ... we must notice that the good it renders in this direction is *not* positive enrichment, a growth in our stock of happiness, but only repairs the losses that it has itself caused. (Emphasis added.)

Durkheim never really defines civilization. He admits that it is almost impossible to define. He refers to it vaguely as all the things that go into what we call the 'higher' things in life, and he locates its origin in bourgeois, urban culture. There can be no doubt that he uses civilization as a synonym for modernity. Like Schopenhauer (1818), Freud (1930), and a host of other *fin de siècle* writers, at times he seems to condemn it overall, or he is at least very critical of certain portions of it. Durkheim alludes to the concentration of unhappiness and immorality in centres of civilization. *The Division of Labor* is sprinkled with bitter comments of this sort. For example, Durkheim ([1893] 1933: 50) writes:

> The average number of suicides, of crimes of all sorts, can effectively serve to mark the intensity of immorality in a given society. If we make this experiment, it does not turn out creditably for civilization, for the number of these morbid phenomena seems to increase as the arts, sciences, and industry progress.

Durkheim adds that 'far from serving moral progress, it is in the great industrial centres that crimes and suicides are most numerous' (51). Towards the end of the book, he adds that 'the true suicide, the sad suicide, is in the endemic state with civilized peoples' (247). This type of suicide is even distributed geographically like civilization' (247). 'Civilization is concentrated in the great cities, suicide likewise' (247). One is reminded here of Walter Benjamin's (1973) analysis of Baudelaire to the effect that 'modernism must be under the sign of suicide'. Durkheim even goes so far as to note a benefit of *not* being overly exposed to civilization:

> Woman has had less part than man in the movement of civilization. She participates less and derives less profit. She recalls, moreover, certain characteristics of primitive natures. Thus, there is about one fourth the suicides among women as among men ([1893] 1933: 247).

Schopenhauer made the claim that the modern individual is subject to the disconcerting alternative between pain and boredom, a well-known aspect of his thought. Similarly, Durkheim asserts that in modern times 'if we are open to more pleasures, we are also open to more pain', including boredom (242), and adds:

> Assuredly, there is a host of pleasures open to us today that more simple natures knew nothing about. But, on the other hand, we are exposed to a host of sufferings spared them, and it is not at all certain that the balance is to our advantage. Thought, to be sure, is a source of joy which can be very intense, but, at the same time how much joy does it trouble! For a solved problem, how many questions are raised without solution! For a cleared-up doubt, how many mysteries come to disconcert!

Indeed, if the savage knows nothing of the pleasures of bustling life, in return, he is immune to boredom, that monster of cultivated minds.

Durkheim arrives at the conclusion that 'there is, then, no relation between the variations of happiness and the advances of the division of labor' (250). He adds immediately that 'this proposition is of the utmost importance'. Its consequence is that sociologists must not try to assess the change and development of societies in relation to human happiness or the lack of it: 'Social science must resolutely renounce these utilitarian comparisons in which it has too often been involved' (250). Yet post-Durkheimian sociology has ignored Durkheim's conclusion, and opted for the very utilitarian comparisons that Durkheim criticized.

It is obvious that boredom and the need for almost constant distraction have become more, not less, problematic with the development of postmodern culture. Cruise ships, classrooms, television programmes, and a host of other postmodern phenomena seem almost desperate in their attempts to keep the viewer, customer, or spectator constantly amused and distracted. Inner-directed solitude is hardly permitted in the tyranny of postmodern social structure. What could be the reason, except the terrible fear of boredom – and this, despite all the images, channels, idols, and diversity offered by postmodernist culture!

POSTMODERNITY AND RELIGION

With regard to the implicit relationship between postmodernity and religion, Schopenhauer was among the first to posit 'the fundamental difference of all religions in the question whether they are ... optimistic or pessimistic' ([1818] 1969b: 170). The more modern the religion, the more its dogma expresses pessimism. This intriguing alternative to Marxist and Freudian views on religion as mere epiphenomena illuminates further the problem of civilization and its discontents.

Durkheim follows Schopenhauer's lead almost exactly, rejecting the typical classifications of religion on the basis of theism, beliefs, animism, or even the need to believe in a divinity ([1912] 1965: 39–50). Durkheim also concludes that the essence of modern religions is that they are pessimistic (354).

192

For both Schopenhauer and Durkheim, religion is essentially a system of representations or concepts 'calculated with reference to the mental capacity of the great mass of people' (Schopenhauer [1818] 1969b: 168). As Durkheim put the matter: 'Religion is in a word the system of symbols by means of which society becomes conscious of itself; it is the characteristic way of thinking of collective existence' ([1897] 1951: 312). The pessimistic collective representations of modern religions reflect the pain and suffering that stem from progress and enlightenment in other areas of social life.

This exacerbation of the will through enlightenment is another theme that Schopenhauer attributes to Christianity as contrasted with ancient Judaism. As support for his general proposition that 'the more intense the will, the more glaring the phenomenon of its conflict, and hence the greater the suffering', Schopenhauer ([1818] 1969a: 395) cites passages like Ecclesiastes 1: 18. 'He that increaseth knowledge increaseth sorrow' (310). Schopenhauer adds: 'In proportion as knowledge attains to distinctness, consciousness is enhanced, pain also increases ... the person in whom genius is to be found suffers most of all' (310).

Durkheim even follows Schopenhauer's focus on asceticism as the solution to the problem of the enlightened will, which perceives more objects of desire on its horizon as it becomes more cultivated. Note that for Freud and Elias, this asceticism is, in contrast to Schopenhauer and Durkheim, the source of discontent in modernity. But for Durkheim, asceticism is also necessary for social life to exist in the face of ever-increasing anomie ([1912] 1965: 356).

Thus, in a 1914 essay intended to serve as a sequel to his *The Elementary Forms*, Durkheim offers a sobering appraisal of optimistic theories of progress in relation to religion:

But, unfortunately, history is far from confirming these optimistic hopes. It seems that, on the contrary, human malaise continues to increase. The great religions of modern man are those which insist the most on the existence of the contradictions in the midst of which we struggle. These continue to depict us as tormented and suffering, while only the crude cults of inferior societies breathe forth and inspire a joyful confidence. For what religions express is the experience through which humanity has lived.

(Durkheim [1914] 1973: 156)

Durkheim asserts that 'we are thus condemned to live in suffering', and that compared to animals, 'man alone is normally obliged to make a place for suffering in his life' (154).

In *Suicide*, Durkheim writes ([1897] 1951: 366):

> From certain indications it even seems that the tendency to a sort of melancholy develops as we rise in the scale of social types. As we have said in another work, it is a quite remarkable fact that the great religions of the most civilized peoples are more deeply fraught with sadness than the simpler beliefs of earlier societies.

The other work to which Durkheim refers is his *Division of Labor*, in which he asks, 'Is it not very remarkable that the fundamental cult of the most civilized religions is that of human suffering'? ([1893] 1933: 243). There exists an unmistakable affinity between Durkheim's pessimistic sentiments on religion and modern Western societies, and Schopenhauer's ([1818] 1969b: 603–46) many allusions to the pessimism inherent in Christianity, Western thought, and the Bible.

This is an important point to consider since most contemporary social theorists tend to view Western thought as the exemplification of an optimistic *Zeitgeist* (Bailey 1958). On the contrary, Schopenhauer ([1818] 1969a: 326) would have us consider that from Hinduism, Buddhism, and Plato on through Christian dogma, the West has been reflecting a deep-seated, albeit unconscious perception of suffering:

> I cannot here withhold the statement that *optimism*, where it is not merely the thoughtless talk of those who harbour nothing but words under their shallow foreheads, seems to me to be not merely an absurd, but also a really *wicked*, way of thinking, a bitter mockery of the unspeakable sufferings of mankind. Let no one imagine that the Christian teaching is favourable to optimism; on the contrary, in the Gospels, world and evil are used almost as synonymous expressions.

As noted in chapter 5, it is undeniable that both the Catholic and Protestant versions of Christianity focus on the cross, a symbol of torture, as their emblem. To be sure, important differences exist between Protestant and Catholic dogma, and some of these differences reflect the more modern tendencies of Protestantism (its abstractionism, and disdain for Catholic rituals, idols, traditionalism, and emphasis on the concrete). Even Schopenhauer's polemic against Protestantism as a bastardization of Christianity (as he understood it) is problematic. Is Protestantism an example of normal modernity or is it an abnormal aberration of modernity? Regardless of the answer one arrives at, one should note Durkheim's own polemic against Protestantism, and the fact that he isolated this religion as one of the main causes of suicide ([1897] 1951). In short, Durkheim's and Schopenhauer's pronouncements on religion and modernity are more complex than my summary indicates.

Nevertheless, compared to Marxist, Weberian, Freudian, and other dominant perspectives on religion, Schopenhauer's and Durkheim's versions seem distinct – and relevant. History has proven that Marx was wrong about the death of religion in modernity. Religion is clearly enjoying a great revival in the USSR and Eastern Europe as we approach the next *fin de siècle*. Weber's thesis about the relationship between Protestantism and capitalism continues to be debated and misunderstood. Whatever the outcome of this debate, no one really believes that capitalism or modernity must necessarily be built on Protestantism. And Freud's arrogant treatment of religion in his *Future of an Illusion* cannot explain why religion continues to gain importance as humanity grows older, because Freud felt that religion served childish needs of dependence.

Durkheim's neglected understanding of religion presents scholars with the following propositons. Religion is *not* the opium of the people, nor a mere epiphenomenon of other psychological or social needs. Rather, it is essentially a system of ideas that symbolize the collective conscience of society. It reflects our collective inner state to ourselves. The interesting problems Durkheim has presented for future study, as yet unacknowledged by scholars, are: whether modern religions are truly more pessimistic than 'primitive' ones, how this can be ascertained, and what it implies for the future of religion in postmodern societies.

STRESS AND MODERN HEROISM

It must be kept in mind that shallow, boosterish optimism is an important aspect of postmodernity. Thus far, I have used the division of labour and religion as illustrations of contemporary pessimistic representations that persist, albeit unconsciously, despite postmodernity's optimism. But the most obvious sign that pessimism persists, if not thrives, within postmodernity is the concept of stress. Recall Walter Benjamin's observation that for Baudelaire, the ordinary person becomes a hero, because modernity is so difficult to endure. Stress is the modern (and postmodern) person's opportunity to be a hero. I am referring to 'stress' as a collective representation, in the Durkheimian sense, a word that is fairly new in Western languages, but that most Westerners believe that they understand. My point is that the persistence of the concept of stress bespeaks the theme of civilization and its discontents as humanity approaches the next *fin de siècle*, despite postmodernity's official rhetoric of kitsch optimism.

There exists a hiatus in meanings attributed to the concept of stress between the forerunners of the stress concept – Hans Selye and Walter Cannon – and its use in contemporary positivistic literature (see Meštrović 1985; Meštrović and Glassner 1983). For Selye and Cannon, a stressor is anything that produces stress, such that 'normal life events may turn otherwise inconsequential conditioning factors into potent stressors' (Selye 1978: 370). In other words, stressor effects depend not so much upon what we do or what happens to us, but on the way we respond to life's events. Anything can *become* stressful, and this seems to be especially true in modern societies. Selye and Cannon, who were still saturated with the *fin de siècle* spirit, even went as far as to claim that society as a whole can act as a stressor depending upon the ways that society is arranged. Walter Cannon (1963: 313) phrased the matter beautifully: 'The homeostasis of the individual human being is largely dependent on social homeostasis.' It must be noted that this seems to be another version of the German social realism that Durkheim is accused to have stolen and imported into France.

By contrast, contemporary stress research today relies on the individualistic, subjectivist version of 'stressful life events'. Stress is determined largely by asking subjects to recall specific events that have been listed on something that resembles a laundry list, from death of a loved one to vacations. But it is well known that events that are stressful for one person may be beneficial to another, whether that event is marriage, divorce, death, or anything else on the official list of stressful life events. The current paradigm seems to make unwitting use of the host-pathogen model of disease, which was the very model that Selye and Cannon argued against! Contemporary stress research is almost exclusively psychological in its orientation, and ignores completely the notion that societal disarrangements can act as originators of stress.

Thus, even the concept of stress has been vulgarized in post-modern culture. In keeping with the tenets of postmodernity, stress is conceptualized as a particular event that happens to specific individuals. To avoid stress, individuals must avoid these events. In practice, this is impossible, because everyone will experience eventually most of the events listed as 'stressful life events'. Even so, contemporary research results suggest that although most studies have found a correlation between life events and symptoms, the results are not consistent, and the correlations are low. Furthermore, the 'symptoms' range from depression to suicide and cancer, yet contemporary research manages to correlate these symptoms with events in a hyper-abstractionist manner. That is, stress research almost never touches on the mood and feelings of the persons experiencing stress: cynicism, exasperation, weariness, disillusionment, ennui, and other states found in the writings of Durkheim, Freud, and other *fin de siècle* intellectuals.

The aims of contemporary stress research are rationalist and pragmatic, to predict and control the environment or who will succumb to illness. It should be noted carefully that the initial impetus for contemporary stress research arose out of a perceived need to study the effects of prolonged stays in submarines by American sailors following the Second World War. In a typically postmodernist fashion, Selye and Cannon were used as ornament by stress researchers, because their *fin de siècle* depictions of stress were never taken seriously, or really understood.

Selye's solution to stress was what he called the philosophy of 'altruistic egoism' or earning the gratitude of others (1978: 449). In line with Schopenhauer, Durkheim, Sorokin, and other thinkers who drew on the *fin de siècle* spirit, Selye felt that a life of self-interest tempered by compassion would minimize the inevitable effects of stress brought on by modernity. Contemporary stress research does not even address the issue of moral philosophy as it pertains to stress. Nevertheless, one might characterize the social philosophy of the current paradigm as 'raw egoism' (to distinguish it from Selye's altruistic egoism), since persons are seen as objects to be used as supports, and there exists no notion of giving to others. In other words, the current paradigm assumes the vulgar Darwinian notion of survival of the fittest: avoid stressors, use other people for social support, and don't worry about compassion. It is an extension of the vulgar, me-generation aspect of postmodernist culture.

When considered as a collective representation, the concept of stress may be traced back further than Selye and Cannon, past Freud and Durkheim, to Baudelaire's notion of the ordinary person as hero. Stress is the symbol of modernity *par excellence*, even though this is not at all apparent from current literature. It is interesting that Durkheim referred to the word 'tension' (a word that bears some etymological resemblance to 'stress', the Latin *strictere*) by predicting that the tension felt by individuals will 'increase with the growth of civilization' ([1914] 1973: 163). Indeed, the modern layperson *feels* tense almost as often as he or she feels cynical. In large American cities, one will find bus stop benches with the following words painted on them: 'Tired? Tense? Nervous?' The anthropologist or sociologist should view these contemporary representations as important signs of the times in which we live.

I have referred to Durkheim's notion of anomie several times in slightly different contexts in the past three chapters. Still another dimension of anomie is relevant to the present context – the medical dimension. Durkheim describes the effects of anomie with words that reverberate in the writings of Selye as well as the postmodern collective consciousness: disenchantment, fatigue, impatience, overexcitation, agitation, malcontent, distress, misery, malady, affliction, and torment. The symptoms of anomie seem to overlap to some extent with the symptoms of stress. In *Suicide*, Durkheim did nothing less than accuse Western post-industrial societies of suffering from a collective derangement (anomie) that had been established as a rule. Baudelaire, Freud, Durkheim, Selye, and other *fin de siècle* forerunners of the stress concept were not clear on the issue of how much modern stress can be avoided or repaired, but they were clear in arguing that modernization itself is the root cause.

Thus, in the search for the crossroads at which contemporary appraisals of the *fin de siècle* became vulgar misunderstandings, the concept of stress deserves a special place. Persons living in the postmodernist age routinely feel tired, impatient, overexcited, and tormented, and feel that way most of the time. Everybody feels like a hero just for living. Is the situation worse now than it has been in the past? Will it get still worse as Durkheim (1914) had predicted? If the answer to these questions is in the affirmative, then what can humankind do collectively to remedy the situation? The purpose of this chapter has been to expose the importance of these questions, which are imperfectly appreciated or not appreciated at all in much contemporary literature.

CONCLUSIONS

These and other questions that flow from a *fin de siècle* reading of texts are no less important than they were in the 1890s. If social scientists continue to assume the Parsonian and economic model of human behaviour as being essentially rational without empirical verification, and this assumption turns out to be incorrect, the coming *fin de siècle* may hold in store more than the normal share of social malaise. Even without formal empirical investigations, anyone who keeps up with the news knows that the world today mirrors Baudelaire's, Tönnies's, Durkheim's, and Selye's pessimistic observations more closely than the abstractions found in Parsons's still influential *Structure of Social Action* (1937) or, closer to our times, the equally optimistic and overly rationalistic writings of Habermas (1987).

Rather than discuss the merits of rationalist versus irrationalist explanations of human malaise on ideological grounds, or worse yet, ignore the irrationalist *fin de siècle* thinkers, one should turn to empirical research to settle the questions that Durkheim's classics raise. Does enlightenment lead to economic anomie (from the previous chapter), other kinds of anomie, added stress, and discontent? In Schopenhauerian terms, do knowledge, education, and other sorts of enlightenment expand the horizon of desires and unleash the will? If Durkheim and Schopenhauer are correct, what can be done about it? Can asceticism be taught, and will it contain anomie to some extent? Surely the social sciences have progressed sufficiently since Durkheim's time to settle these issues, and surely the issues are important. But for such empirical research to take place, the essentially *fin de siècle*, pessimistic nature of Durkheim's and other sociological works must be recognized and acknowledged by scholars.

Apart from empirical concerns, it is important to attend to the humanistic import of the theme of civilization and its discontents, for individuals as well as collectivities. We all know that 'growing up' entails a loss of innocence, although few wish to dwell on the magnification of such results in the modern world. Consider that Western children today are forced to learn about AIDS, cocaine, sexual activity, pregnancy, and other phenomena at increasingly younger ages. Dating starts earlier for every generation, and fashion consciousness has now penetrated to the crib. Infants are even entered into beauty pageants! By the time adulthood is reached, it is no longer the 'big deal' it used to be (complete with rites of passage, formal or informal), as it is said in the USA. Cynicism, disillusionment, and ennui strike more and more of these enlightened individuals in postmodern societies, and at increasingly younger ages.

Humanity itself, considered as a collective being in the Durkheimian sense, has lost its collective innocence as it emerged from childhood. Oswald Spengler (1926) in his *Decline of the West*, Pitirim Sorokin (1957), and a few others have taken their cue from Durkheim and other *fin de siècle* intellectuals in this regard. The essential message is that as societies become older, the collective representations that symbolize pessimism, cynicism, and discontent of all sorts multiply and gradually increase. I have tried to argue that this pessimistic message from the previous *fin de siècle* is relevant as we enter the next *fin de siècle*, and it must be addressed, openly and soberly. The veneer of shallow optimism cannot possibly sustain an ageing humanity, and the underlying morbidity breaks through the veneer in the form of ghastly statistics that depict various social problems from increasing suicide rates to vast amounts of cocaine use.

Chapter Eleven

CONCLUSIONS
The coming fin de siècle and postmodernism

Is postmodernism an extension of modernity or a reaction against it? It seems that as the present century draws to a close, postmodernism elaborates on modernity more than it rebels against it. Much like modernity, postmodern culture entails a ruthless forgetting, repression, or other kind of obfuscation of genuinely irrational cultural elements. In our postmodern age, the concept of the unconscious is not invoked to explain human behaviour. The role of compassion in morality is almost completely overlooked. The power-hungry, militant values associated with the cult of Jesus have almost completely eclipsed the tender-hearted values associated with humanity's ancient female cults. Works by artistic and intellectual giants from the previous *fin de siècle* are invoked only to the extent that they can be forced to fit an abstractionist version of their works. Thus, Durkheim and Weber are known through Parsons's 'rational social action' paradigm more than they are known in relation to the context of the *fin de siècle* spirit. If one were to invoke cultural standards from the previous turn of the century, one would conclude that the coming *fin de siècle* will occur in the midst of a cultural desert. Frustration and cynicism have increased, and these have led to empirically observable increases in aggressive behaviour, from suicide to genocide. Most of the social problems that troubled leading intellectuals from the previous *fin de siècle* have multiplied in magnitude and scope in the coming *fin de siècle*.

Even the rationalizations that were used to excuse and forget social ills in the previous century have been perfected. The vampire-like capitalist barons (as Marx called them) of that era excused their exploitation by noting that they kept the workers out of idleness, and therefore out of the devil's clutches. Nowadays, the exploiters do not need to resort to such excuses. They can publish memoirs, because the secret of success at any costs is of intense interest to the public. The credo of postmodern culture seems to be captured by the words of the popular song, 'Don't Worry, Be Happy'. Ronald Reagan became the penultimate postmodernist hero, mocked by liberals for his bungling, 'What, me worry?' attitude, but immensely popular not only in the USA but in many places around the world. One could state, in a Durkheimian fashion, that the postmodernist age produced Ronald Reagan. One can scarcely imagine a brooding, serious, Lincoln type of President getting elected in the USA as this century draws to a close.

What various theorists have referred to thus far as postmodernist culture or philosophy can be summed up aptly as extensions of old-fashioned Durkheimian anomie, Riesman's other-directedness, Baudelaire's institutions of dandyism, Sorokin's sensate culture, and other well-known conceptualizations that have been reviewed in this book. Postmodernity is not something new or original, nor is it nearly as 'nice' as it is sometimes purported to be.

But Gorbachev and the values he represents seem to be something different. Gorbachev has been likened to Abraham Lincoln in Europe and the USSR, and is commonly regarded as a politician that comes along only once in a few centuries. He seems to fit Riesman's inner-directed typology, and he *does* worry. His value-orientation seems to fit the values that flow from the cult of the Madonna and her desire for peace more than the values associated with the Protestant Jesus. At least as of this writing, there is no good reason to suspect his anti-bureaucratic sentiments.

In fact, the real wave of postmodernity may not yet have been born, or may exist only in a state of infancy. And it may not originate in the USA or Western Europe, but in the USSR and Eastern Europe. The so-called death of communism in the 1980s signifies a genuine rebellion against an important narrative left over from the Enlightenment. While the debris has not yet settled, it seems evident that socialist sentiments of human concern for fellow humans have not been overthrown in the revolution against communism.

One looks in vain for genuine elements of the 'heart' in the USA or Western European versions of postmodernity. What one will find instead are commercialism, vulgarization, exploitation, and the old-fashioned class structure. But Eastern Europe is showing many more signs of what used to be called the heart in the previous *fin de siècle*. Not all of it is 'nice' nor benign, but much of it seems to be genuinely irrational. Thus, religion is staging a dramatic comeback. Nationalism, and worse, fundamentalism, populism, ethnocentrism, and ethnic identity are erupting from Siberia to the borders of Germany. Dictatorships are being overthrown, and the 'will of the people' sometimes spills over into an irrational desire for revenge against the former masters. The Soviets and the Eastern Europeans are still far from understanding the tourist industry and how to mass-produce kitsch that foreign visitors will want to consume.

Among social theorists witnessing this genuine spectacle, Jürgen Habermas has emerged as one of the most popular voices. He warns against postmodernity's unwelcome ties with neo-conservative ideology, and seeks to complete the Enlightenment project. He does not see that the West's neo-conservative ideology is an extension of the very project he proposes to complete. Neo-functionalists and neo-Marxists make the same mistake: all of these theorists assume that the mind can override the heart, and that transnational, non-religious, non-emotional social integration is not only possible, but desirable. The communist experiment in such heartless social order suggests, instead, that there exist definite limits to the power of hyper-rational tyrannies to control the 'will' of the people.

To the extent that there exists a postmodernist culture, it shares some significant traits with hyper-rational communism, and may eventually suffer the same fate. Both are derived from an extreme version of the Enlightenment. Much like communism, postmodern culture has its slogans, rationalizations, and collective plans (based on the model of shopping malls and tourism). The image of Mickey Mouse adorns as many public places in the USA as images of Tito adorn public places in Yugoslavia. If one can argue that the communist appeals to brotherhood and self-sacrifice masked exploitation on the part of the avant-garde, one could just as well argue that postmodernist appeals to fun mask a commercial motive and old-fashioned exploitation on the part of the bourgeoisie. It would be interesting to compare and contrast Eastern European versus Western European and American cynicisms, and their development, in relation to these hyper-rational cultural systems. It may be the case that Western cynicism still has a long way to go before kitsch postmodernism is ever overthrown, because it is currently immensely popular. Still, Sloterdijk (1987) has made his point concerning the extent of postmodern cynicism in the West.

Which force will prevail as the century draws to a close? Will MTV, which is currently broadcast live from England into Eastern Europe, be the first step in the vulgar commercialization and transformation of that inner-directed culture into a Western-like land of kitsch? Or will Gorbachev's Madonna-like pleas for peace finally penetrate into American consciousness? Will the current, vulgar version of postmodernism be transformed into a genuine re-examination of the evil side of Enlightenment narratives? Or will Eastern Europe and the USSR become the next tourist traps and super shopping malls?

The *fin de siècle* concept has been used as a foil to examine issues discussed under the rubric of postmodernity, and to cast these issues into a new light. The end of the century signals an end as well as a beginning, pessimism as well as optimism and hope, ennui and disgust at dead forms as well as excitement at the new signs of 'life' that are emerging. The *fin de siècle* concept is an archetype, a symbol that is relived each time the end of a century occurs. As such, we share many commonalities with our ancestors who underwent this anniversary. Many of these common, collective representations have been examined. At the same time, ours is a unique age, and despite links to the past, the future is always new. In the remaining sections, I intend to offer a brief sense of closure to some of these aspects of the *fin de siècle* spirit that have been discussed.

ANOMIE AND POSTMODERNISM

Durkheim's original usage of the concept of anomie (as opposed to Merton's and other sociological usages) casts an entirely new light on the concept of postmodernism. Simply put, postmodernism *is* the institutionalization of anomie in the core of culture and across many social institutions, from religion to the family.

Durkheim's understanding of anomie as a state of infinite desires that is exacerbated by enlightenment is rooted in Schopenhauer's philosophy of the will, which in turn symbolized the *fin de siècle* spirit, according to Simmel (1907). More importantly, it is a concept that one can use to account for the many characteristics that are frequently cited in describing postmodern culture, from the narrative of being opposed to narratives to a delight in cultural excrement.

Throughout this book, I have emphasized that for Durkheim, anomie is inevitable, and it holds a benign as well as an evil aspect. Let us review each of these points in turn. Anomie is inevitable, because without it, there would be no progress, and in turn, all progress produces some degree of anomie. Thus, Durkheim describes the process by which modernization sensitizes individuals to stimuli of all kinds that our ancestors tended to ignore (a process akin to Simmel's and Elias's descriptions of the civilizing process). The postmodern person values hygiene, quiet, civilized manners, and aesthetic niceties that our ancestors could scarcely imagine. This desire for things that used to be considered luxuries, coupled with irritation at the status quo, leads to innovation in all fields – one invents new ideas and technology only when one is dissatisfied, which is to say, anomic. Yet each new achievement in ideas or material goods leads eventually to ennui and a renewed desire to innovate. For Durkheim, this process is inexorable.

Anomie's positive side is that it is thrilling and exciting, even seductive. Perhaps this aspect of anomie can explain part of the 'fun' aspect of postmodernity, at least prior to the routinization of fun. When old narratives are challenged in anomic acts, one is closer to what Simmel termed 'life' as opposed to the forms that are used to apprehend 'life'. Stimuli that used to be assimilated blandly, that were reified, or otherwise reduced in internal intensity, are augmented and experienced more intensely during anomic states. No doubt this is the secret of the postmodernist spectacle (again, with the caveat that such spectacles can be made routine). Our ancestors experienced such periods of what Durkheim called 'collective effervescence' during traditional rites, holy days, or revolutions. Postmodernists actively seek and even purchase the opportunity to experience such spectacles.

But there exists a very real, dark side to anomie that writers on postmodernity do not like to admit. Excitement is followed by

satiation, boredom, ennui, and an increased hunger for excitement. For example, when television was first introduced into
homes, the choice of a few channels sufficed to satisfy viewers.
Today, the postmodernist viewer can scarcely be satisfied without
a vast array of channels supplied by cable or a satellite dish, and
even then, often feels bored after 'zapping' through all of them at
rapid speed with a 'remote control'. This picture of zapping
through images on television can be transferred to the zapping
through images in 'real' life. Postmodernists routinely demand
greater choices in careers, lovers, and most other 'things' in their
lives, and after 'zapping' through these in their lives, often feel
bored and insatiable again.

In sum, anomie can be likened to an addiction. One is reminded of Durkheim's ominous pronouncement that anomie is
like the bottomless abyss of emotions, and Schopenhauer's claim
that the 'will' is inherently insatiable. The more one obtains, de-
vours, and consumes, the more one wants. In the end, the hunger
never goes away, and cynicism seems to increase due to this very
fact. This is an unwelcome conclusion, but it seems easy enough
to verify. Countries in which postmodern culture has taken root
most strongly are also the ones in which suicide rates, drug addiction, alcoholism, and other indicators of an insatiable, deranged
will have also taken root. Also, postmodernist films, music, and
other cultural artefacts betray an ever-increasing preoccupation
with violence, sex, and aggression of many kinds, all indicators
that the postmodern self is bored, and demands an increase in the
quantity of stimulation.

Does there exist a limit to the amount of stimulation that the
human organism can tolerate? Are the nations that now stand on
the brink of postmodernity (Eastern Europe) and modernity
(developing nations) doomed to experience the anomie and cynicism that now afflicts Western Europe and the USA? Can one have
the positive aspects of anomie without the negative aspects? These
are the kinds of questions to which the present application of the
concept of anomie to postmodernity leads.

OPTIMISM VERSUS PESSIMISM

Although optimism and pessimism are always intertwined in
everyday life, it is possible to isolate the two as ideal types for the

purposes of discussion. From the outset, I have followed the lead of numerous authors who have concluded that essentially, and especially among the intellectuals and artists, the previous turn of the century's 'spirit' was essentially pessimistic. The following elements of this pessimistic ethos seem particularly important. There is no real progress, because every step in the direction of apparent progress produces new problems. Western civilization is in a period of disintegration and decline. Humans are more non-rational or irrational than rational in their behaviour. Society is composed of non-rational, easily influenced masses. Scientific truth and knowledge may be harmful for society while myth and superstition may be beneficial. Durkheim, Sorokin, Schopenhauer, Nietzsche, T.S. Eliot, and numerous other thinkers have been invoked to illustrate various aspects of these pessimistic themes.

In sharp contrast, the ideal type of the optimistic *Zeitgeist* which preceded the previous *fin de siècle*, may have begun to emerge again at the close of the previous *fin de siècle*, and definitely ruled the early and middle parts of the present century's intellectual life: There is progress. Social evolution is linear. Western civilization is moving continually towards greater heights. Humans are rational, or at least capable of being so, and this is desirable. Scientific truth and knowledge are beneficial for society, while myth and superstition are harmful. A society represents a harmony of interests. From Parsons to Habermas, this *Zeitgeist* definitely animates mainstream sociological theorizing.

One could hypothesize that a dominance of optimistic versus pessimistic representations in a given society at a given period of time is related in some fashion to the degree of anomie in that society. In the present analysis, I am unable to resolve this issue. It is offered for further study. Also, I am unable to resolve whether any relationship exists between the dominance of one or the other *Zeitgeist* and humanity's distance from a turn of the century. In other words, one is not in a position to predict that pessimism dominates during any transition period known as the *fin de siècle* – massive amounts of historical and empirical data would be needed to draw any such conclusion. Furthermore, it is not immediately apparent at what stage in the modernizing or Elias's civilizing processes optimism or pessimism tend to dominate. But such grand theorizing was never an aim in this book.

However, it is possible to conclude that what passes as postmodernism in many contemporary writings seems to represent the optimistic *Zeitgeist*, at least on the surface, despite the rhetoric of rebellion against Enlightenment narratives. It is important to observe that postmodernist narratives do not typically question progress, do not harp on disintegration, do not conclude that myth is more important than science, and in general, do not seriously adopt positions contained in the pessimistic *Zeitgeist*. And yet, postmodernist culture will attempt to shock and horrify. It will use myth, and it will seem to be anti-scientific at times. Pessimistic themes will be touched. Sado-masochism, death, disease, pestilence, and other depressing topics are offered to the postmodernist consumer culture as entertainment. But the endings of postmodern films, music, and treatises are nevertheless predictably up-beat. A happy face is always painted, the status quo is maintained, and rationality's sovereignty is never questioned. Hence, the conclusion that postmodernity, at least at present, is an extension of, and not a reaction against, modernity.

It may well turn out to be the case that postmodernity will turn more pessimistic as the present century draws closer to a close. Perhaps the current, hypocritical, vulgar state of postmodernist culture will turn to a genuine period of William James's 'twice-born' pessimism, and consequent re-examination of modernist assumptions. Nevertheless, at the present time, I believe that one is in a position to disagree with those theorists who depict postmodernity as a threat to modernity. On the contrary, current postmodernity is descended from modernity and the optimistic *Zeitgeist*. The pessimistic *Zeitgeist*, to the extent that it is relevant to postmodern culture, is an unconscious component, and is never primary.

RATIONALISM VERSUS IRRATIONALISM

A major theme of this book has been that postmodernism is essentially 'heartless', that it is an extension of modernity's hyper-rationalism. This conclusion may stir up fears of the irrational that are frequently used to buttress modernity and postmodernity. To be sure, irrationalism has its dark sides, especially excessive nationalism and ethnocentrism. On the other hand, it has a kind face – compassion. More importantly, excessive rationalism also has an evil side, a tendency to condone cruelty of every sort in the name of some glorified, utopian ideal. In the not-so-distant days when communism ruled Eastern Europe, Marxism stood for the view that nothing was beyond rational explanation, no matter how much the supposedly bourgeois West wanted to cling to its pessimism, metaphysics, and irrationalist reliance on faith. This Marxist faith in reason was used to justify all kinds of brutalities on the part of the avant-garde, and many Western, Marxist intellectuals agreed that 'to make an omelette, one has to break a few eggs'. My aim has been to expose this dark side of rationality.

I have tried to demonstrate that starting with Schopenhauer, many *fin de siècle* intellectuals felt that there existed definite limits to rational explanations. The irrational was accepted as an important aspect of humanity, ranging from the concept of the unconscious to the mysterious quality of compassion. And contrary to the Marxists, Durkheim apparently felt that every 'egg' (individual) was important, and should not be harmed in any way, even as various societal 'omelettes' were being prepared.

Many difficult questions were not resolved in this book, and perhaps they are so difficult that they will not be resolved for some time. Is a morality based on compassion viable? Were our ancestors more or less compassionate than we are? Can compassion be taught?

However, it is evident that postmodernist culture holds to the Enlightenment belief that morality is essentially rational, not irrational. And signs that morality based on rationality has its limits are all around us. Historically, rational calculation has not, and in the future may not be able to instil a desire in individuals to act in concert and with concern for humanity's common fate on this globe. Rather, as scores of *fin de siècle* thinkers have noted, rationality is more likely to counsel egoism, wickedness, and the kinds of selfishness that eventually leads to mutual self-destruction.

Thus, an important conclusion of the present study is that the nature and role of compassion needs to be examined as humanity contemplates the fate of the planet. Values associated with the cult of Jesus that were instrumental in establishing Protestant, capitalist, postmodernist culture need to be contrasted with values associated with the cult of the Madonna that seem to be animating Eastern Europe, the Soviet Union, and the fringes of Western culture at present.

IMPLICATIONS

As we enter the next century and millennium, a critical examination of history since the previous *fin de siècle* may help humanity
avoid some of the tragic errors that have been committed collectively in this century. I have argued that the penultimate error has
been the collective repression of the heart in favour of excessive
intellectualism, the mind. The role of sociology in guiding modern
societies through the next millennium needs to be re-examined as
well, because sociology is just as excessively abstractionist as the
rest of culture. Contemporary humanity needs Durkheim's vision
of sociology as the science of morality – with all of its overtones of
compassion and desire to be ethical – more than ever, despite the
fact that hardly any contemporary sociologist invokes this vision.
Communism is dying, Marxism is in turmoil, anomie is rampant,
and the West needs a new faith – but sociology itself is in a state of
crisis.

This desperate need for faith as opposed to cynicism is evident
from reading most treatises on modernity, and I have used Sloterdijk's (1987) analysis as an intriguing illustration. But David Riesman had foreshadowed this modern crisis of faith even as he wrote
his *Lonely Crowd* in the relatively innocent 1950s. Thus, Riesman's
other-directed type is the postmodern type in infancy. Other-
directed as well as postmodern inside-dopesters conclude that
since they can do nothing to change the world, they might as well
gossip about it, and try to understand it without being able to do
anything about it (this may be one possible explanation for the
phenomenal popularity of Cable News Network and the whole
postmodernist cult of news-watching). Modern persons can be as
fatalistic and feel as powerless about their futures as the slaves that
Durkheim describes in his illustration of fatalism. Riesman echoes
Baudelaire's description of the dandy when he writes that the inside-dopester's goal is 'never to be taken in by any person, cause,
or event' (1950: 200). He echoes Durkheim and foreshadows
Sloterdijk when he writes that 'no matter how politically active the
inside-dopester may appear, he is essentially passive – a self-
conscious puppet tolerantly watching and making sure that the
strings that move him do not touch his heart' (201).

The fanaticism associated with Marxism at the beginning of this
century betrayed an ardent faith, mistaken or not, of its followers.

When one considers the fact that Marxism took root in undeveloped or developing nations in the main, it is obvious that it convinced people not by reasons, but through its appeal to the heart. The fact that hyper-rational communism inspired faith and took root in cultures based on faith (especially Buddhist Cambodia) is an excellent illustration of postmodernist contradiction that eventually and finally broke down. Nor surprisingly, many of those who are leading the opposition against communism are former communists who are just as ardent in their opposition. The cynical West looks on with some degree of jealousy that it cannot feel that strongly about capitalism as a moral cause.

An important theme of this book has been that abstractionist postmodernity has imposed a ruthless forgetting upon humanity. In particular, the fact that sociology was born in the Romantic era has been forgotten. Saint-Simon's, Schopenhauer's, and other *fin de siècle* emphases on the heart as opposed to the mind have been repressed. The social sciences in general and sociology in particular have fallen victim to this collective amnesia. The end result is that the social sciences, like the postmodern societies they purport to study, are mired in an ideological bias that has rephrased most human problems in terms of excessive rationality.

I have indicated that the term postmodernism is used by some to denote rejection of the great narrative of the Enlightenment, and by others as its extension. It is to be doubted whether this fundamental confusion will be resolved any time soon. For the purposes of the present study, the term postmodernism is not really essential for understanding the future of modernity. It is one more bit of unnecessary jargon imposed upon humanity by intellectuals who suffer from excessive rationalism. It obscures more than it illuminates. The essential point is that what has been called modernity entails the seemingly deceptive triumph of the mind over the heart, and that the *fin de siècle* project involves restoring the balance back to the rightful primacy of the heart. In sum, the Enlightenment 'project' is an illusion. Actually, it died long ago, and had been discredited after its death during the previous turn of the century. All the concern expressed by postmodern theorists with this 'project' constitutes an anomic aberration, a long-standing collective neurosis that stems from repression of the irrational. The proof is that while intellectuals write about completing the Enlightenment project, the rest of humanity turns to irrationalities of every sort to satisfy its collectively hungry heart – religion, nationalism, cults, love songs, the totemism of sports, New Age books, live-sex acts, and all kinds of sentiment thrive in postmodernist culture. When will the Holy Inquisition of Science, as Unamuno called it, be over, when the irrational can be discussed openly? The task in the next millennium is to confront and tame the irrational, and reach the goal of a cosmopolitan society of humankind. My suggestion is that the best way to achieve these hopeful goals is to re-examine the legacy of the previous *fin de siècle* as we prepare ourselves for the next one.

REFERENCES

Abrams, P. (1988) Notes on the Difficulty of Studying the State. *Journal of Historical Sociology* 1: 58–89.

Alexander, J.C. (1988) *Durkheimian Sociology: Cultural Studies.* Cambridge: Cambridge University Press.

Alpert, H. (1937) France's First University Course in Sociology. *American Sociological Review* 2: 311–17

—— ([1938a] 1961) *Émile Durkheim and His Sociology.* New York: Columbia University Press.

—— (1938b) Operational Definitions in Sociology. *American Sociological Review* 3(6): 855–61.

—— (1939a) Émile Durkheim and Sociologismic Psychology. *American Journal of Sociology* 45(1): 64–70.

—— (1939b) Explaining the Social Socially. *Social Forces* 17(3): 361–5.

—— (1940a) Reviews of *De Durkheim à Bergson* by J. Vialatoux; *L'Évolution Pedagogique en France*, by É. Durkheim; and *Annales Sociologiques*, edited by J. Ray, *American Sociological Review* 5: 129–31.

—— (1940b) Célestin Bouglé (1870–1940). *Journal of Social Philosophy* 5(3): 270–3.

—— (1941) Émile Durkheim and the Theory of Social Integration. *Journal of Social Philosophy* 6(2): 172–84.

—— (1951) Reviews of *Suicide: A Study in Sociology* by É. Durkheim and *The Rules of Sociological Method* by É. Durkheim, *American Sociological Review* 10: 565–7.

—— (1960) Review of *Montesquieu and Rousseau: Forerunners of Sociology* by É. Durkheim, *American Sociological Review* 25: 972–5.

—— (1973) Review of *Émile Durkheim: His Life and Work* by Steven Lukes, *Contemporary Sociology* 12: 198–200.

Althusser, L. (1982) *Montesquieu, Rousseau, Marx: Politics and History,* translated by Ben Brewster. London: Verso.

Bailey, J. (1988) *Pessimism.* London: Routledge.

Bailey, R.B. (1958) *Sociology Faces Pessimism: A Study of European Sociological Thought Amidst a Fading Optimism.* The Hague: Martinus Nijhoff.

Baillot, A. (1927) *Influence de la philosophie de Schopenhauer en France (1860–1900)*. Paris: J. Vrin.

Barbaric, S. (1988) *Pray With the Heart: Medjugorje Manual of Prayer*. Zagreb: Tisak.

Barnouw, D. (1988) *Weimar Intellectuals and the Threat of Modernity*. Bloomington: Indiana University Press.

Baudelaire, C. ([1863] 1965) *The Painter of Modern Life and Other Essays*, translated by J. Mayne. New York: Phaidon.

—— ([1869] 1970) *Paris Spleen*, translated by Louise Varese. New York: New Directions Books.

Bauman, Z. (1987) *Legislators and Interpreters: On Modernity, Post-Modernity, and Intellectuals*. Ithaca, N.Y.: Cornell University Press.

Bearak, B. (1989) Stilling the Voices: Officials Dismiss Marian Messages at Lubbock Church. *Houston Chronicle* June 3, 1989.

Bell, D. (1976) *The Cultural Contradictions of Capitalism*. New York: Basic Books.

—— (1977) *The Coming of Post-Industrial Society: A Venture in Social Forecasting*. New York: Basic Books.

Bellah, R.N., Madsen, R., Sullivan, W.M., Swidler, A., and Tipton, S.M. (1985) *Habits of the Heart*. Berkeley: University of California Press.

Bender, T. (1978) *Community and Social Change in America*. New Brunswick, N.J.: Rutgers University Press.

Bendix, R. (1970) Sociology and the Distrust of Reason. *American Sociological Review* 35: 831–42.

Benjamin, W. (1968) The Work of Art in the Age of Mechanical Reproduction. pp. 219–66 in *Illuminations*, edited by Hannah Arendt. New York: Harcourt, Brace & World.

—— (1973) *Charles Baudelaire: A Lyric Poet in the Era of High Capitalism*, translated by H. Zohn. London: NLB Press.

Bergson, H. ([1932] 1954) *The Two Sources of Morality and Religion*, translated by R.A. Audra and C. Brereton. Garden City, N.J.: Doubleday.

—— (1944) *Creative Evolution*. New York: Modern Library.

Berman, M. (1982) *All That Is Solid Melts into Air: The Experience of Modernity*. New York: Simon & Schuster.

Besnard, P. (1987) *L'anomie: Ses usages et ses fonctions dans la discipline sociologique depuis Durkheim*. Paris: Presses Universitaires de France.

Bloch, E. ([1938–1947] 1986) *The Principle of Hope*. Cambridge: MIT Press.

Bloom, A. (1987) *The Closing of the American Mind*. New York: Simon & Schuster.

Bouglé, C. (1896) *Les Sciences sociales en Allemagne*. Paris: Alcan.

—— (1909) Darwinism and Sociology. pp. 465–76 in *Darwin and Modern Science*, edited by A.C. Seward. Cambridge: Cambridge University Press.

—— (1918) *Chez les prophètes socialistes*. Paris: Alcan.

—— (1926) *The Evolution of Values*, translated by Helen Sellars. New York: Henry Holt & Co.

—— (1930) The Present Tendency of the Social Sciences in France. pp. 64–83 in *The New Social Science*, edited by Leonard D. White. Chicago: University of Chicago Press.

—— (1935) *Bilan de la sociologie française contemporaine*. Paris: Alcan.

—— (1938) *The French Conception of 'Culture Générale' and Its Influences Upon Instruction*. New York: Columbia University Press.

Bowler, P.J. (1988) *The Non-Darwinian Revolution: Reinterpretation of a Historical Myth*. Baltimore: Johns Hopkins University Press.

Braden, C.S. (1930) *Religious Aspects of the Conquest of Mexico*. Durham, N.C.: Duke University Press.

Brzezinski, Z. (1989) *The Grand Failure: The Birth and Death of Communism in the Twentieth Century*. New York: Scribner's.

Byrnes, J.F. (1988) Explaining the Mary Cult: A Hypothesis and Problems. *Journal of Religion* 68: 277–85.

Cahoone, L.E. (1988) *The Dilemma of Modernity: Philosophy, Culture, and Anti-Culture*. Albany, N.Y.: SUNY Press.

Calinescu, M. (1987) *Five Faces of Modernity*. Durham: Duke University Press.

Camic, C. (1986) The Matter of Habit. *American Journal of Sociology* 91: 1039–87.

Camus, A. (1955) *The Myth of Sisyphus and Other Essays*. New York: Random House.

Cannon, W. (1963) *The Wisdom of the Body*. New York: Norton.

Carlisle, R.B. (1988) *Saint-Simonianism and the Doctrine of Hope*. Baltimore: Johns Hopkins University Press.

Carroll, M.P. (1985) The Virgin Mary at LaSalette and Lourdes: Whom Did the Children See? *Journal for the Scientific Study of Religion* 24: 56–74.

—— (1987) *The Cult of the Virgin Mary: Psychological Origins*. Princeton: Princeton University Press.

Cartwright, D. (1984) Kant, Schopenhauer and Nietzsche on the Morality of Pity. *Journal of the History of Ideas* 45: 83–98.

—— (1987) Kant's View of the Moral Significance of Kindhearted Emotions and the Moral Insignificance of Kant's View. *Journal of Value Inquiry* 21: 291–304.

—— (1988a) Schopenhauer's Axiological Analysis of Character. *Revue Internationale de Philosophie* 41: 18–36.

—— (1988b) Schopenhauer on Suffering, Death, Guilt, and the Consolation of Metaphysics. In E. Luft (ed.), *Schopenhauer: New Essays in Honor of His 200th Birthday*. Lewiston, N.Y.: Mellen Press.

—— (1989) Schopenhauer as Moral Philosopher – Towards the Actuality of his Ethics. Paper presented at the bicentennial of Schopenhauer's birth.

Chateaubriand, C. ([1805] 1957) *Atala-René*, translated by Irving Putter. Berkeley: University of California Press.

Clark, P. (1975) Suicide, société et sociologie: De Durkheim à Balzac. *Nineteenth-Century French Studies* 3: 200–12.

Claudel, P. (1952) *Le Symbolisme de la Salette*. Paris: Gallimard.

Clifford, J. (1981) On Ethnographic Surrealism. *Comparative Studies in Society and History* 23: 539–64.

—— (1988) *The Predicament of Culture: Twentieth-Century Ethnography, Literature, and Art*. Cambridge: Harvard University Press.

Clinch, B.J. (1906) Our Lady of Guadalupe. *American Catholic Quarterly Review* 31: 240–57.

Cortese, A.J. (1984) Moral Judgment in Chicano, Black and White Young Adults. *Sociological Focus* 7: 189–99.

—— (1989) *Ethnic Ethics: The Restructuring of Moral Theory*. Albany: SUNY Press.

Davy, G. (1927) *Émile Durkheim*. Paris: Louis-Michaud.

Delaney, J. (1959) *A Woman Clothed With the Sun: Eight Great Appearances of Our Lady in Modern Times*. New York: Doubleday.

Dent, N.J.H. (1989) *Rousseau*. London: Basil Blackwell.

Denzin, N.K. (1988) *Blue Velvet: Postmodern Contradictions. Theory, Culture and Society* 5(2–3): 461–74.

Deploige, S. ([1911] 1938) *The Conflict Between Ethics and Sociology*, translated by Charles C. Miltner. London: B. Herder Book Co.

Descombes, V. (1980) *Modern French Philosophy*, translated by L. Scott-Fox and J.M. Harding. Cambridge: Cambridge University Press.

Doroszewski, W. (1932) Quelque remarques sur les rapports de la sociologie et de la linguistique: Durkheim et F. de Saussure. *Journal de Psychologie* 30: 82–91.

Dubos, R. (1959) *The Mirage of Health*. New York: Harper & Row.

Durant, W. (1961) *The Story of Philosophy*. New York: Simon & Schuster

Durkheim, É. ([1885] 1978) Review of Albert Schaeffle's *Bau und Leben des Sozialen Korpers*. pp. 93–114 in *Émile Durkheim on Institutional Analysis*, edited by M. Traugott. Chicago: University of Chicago Press.

—— ([1887] 1976a) La Science positive de la morale en allemagne. pp. 267–343 in *Textes*, edited by V. Karady, Vol. 1. Paris: Les Éditions de Minuit.

—— ([1887] 1976b) L'avenir de la religion. pp. 149–65 in *Textes*, edited by V. Karady, Vol. 2. Paris: Les Éditions de Minuit.

—— ([1887] 1976c) La Philosophie dans les universités allemandes. pp. 437–86 in *Textes*, edited by V. Karady, Vol. 3. Paris: Les Éditions de Minuit.

—— ([1889] 1978) Review of Tönnies's *Community and Society*. pp. 115–22 in *Émile Durkheim on Institutional Analysis*, edited by M. Traugott. Chicago: University of Chicago Press.

—— ([1892] 1965) *Montesquieu and Rousseau: Forerunners of Sociology*. Ann Arbor: University of Michigan Press.

—— (1893) *De la Division du travail social*. Paris: Alcan.

—— ([1893] 1933) *The Division of Labor in Society*, translated by George Simpson. New York: Free Press.

—— ([1893] 1984) *The Division of Labor in Society*, translated by W.D. Halls. New York: Free Press.

—— (1895) *Les Règles de la méthode sociologique*. Paris: Alcan.

—— ([1895] 1938) *The Rules of Sociological Method*, translated by D. Soloway. New York: Free Press.

—— ([1895] 1982) The Rules of Sociological Method. pp. 31–163 in *Durkheim: The Rules of Sociological Method and Selected Texts on Sociology and Its Method*, edited by S. Lukes. New York: Free Press.

—— ([1897] 1951) *Suicide: A Study in Sociology*, translated by John A. Spaulding and George Simpson. New York: Free Press.

—— ([1897] 1963) *Incest: The Nature and Origin of the Taboo*, translated by E. Sagarin. New York: Stuart Lyle.

—— ([1900] 1973) Sociology in France in the Nineteenth Century. pp. 3–22 in *Émile Durkheim on Morality and Society*, edited by R. Bellah. Chicago: University of Chicago Press.

—— (1906) The Determination of the Moral Fact. In *Sociology and Philosophy*, 35–79. New York: Free Press.

—— (1908) Remarks in L'inconnu et l'inconscient en histoire. *Bulletin de la Société Française de Philosophie* 8: 217–47.

—— ([1912] 1965) *The Elementary Forms of the Religious Life*, translated by J. Swain. New York: Free Press.

—— ([1913] 1960) Pragmatism and Sociology. pp. 386–436 in *Émile Durkheim, 1858–1917*, edited by K. Wolff. Columbus, OH: Ohio State University Press.

—— ([1914] 1973) The Dualism of Human Nature and Its Social Conditions. pp. 149–66 in *Émile Durkheim on Morality and Society*, edited by R. Bellah. Chicago: University of Chicago Press.

—— ([1920] 1978) Introduction to *Morality*. pp. 191–202 in *Émile Durkheim on Institutional Analysis*, edited by M. Traugott. Chicago: University of Chicago Press.

—— ([1922] 1958) *Education and Sociology*, translated by Sherwood Fox. Glencoe, Ill.: Free Press.

—— (1924) *Sociologie et Philosophie*. Paris: Alcan.

—— ([1924] 1974) *Sociology and Philosophy*, translated by D.F. Pocock. New York: Free Press.

—— ([1925] 1961) *Moral Education*, translated by Everett K. Wilson and Herman Schnurer. Glencoe, Ill.: Free Press.

—— ([1928] 1958) *Socialism and Saint-Simon*, translated by Charlotte Sattler. Yellow Springs, Ohio: Antioch Press.

—— ([1938] 1977) *The Evolution of Educational Thought*, translated by Peter Collins. London: Routledge & Kegan Paul.

—— ([1950] 1983) *Professional Ethics and Civic Morals*, translated by Cornelia Brookfield. Westport, Conn.: Greenwood Press.

—— ([1955] 1983) *Pragmatism and Sociology*, translated by J.C. Whitehouse. Cambridge: Cambridge University Press.

Durkheim, É. and Mauss, M. ([1902] 1975) *Primitive Classification*, translated by R. Needham. Chicago: University of Chicago Press.

Eksteins, M. (1989) *Rites of Spring: The Great War and the Birth of the Modern Age*. New York: Houghton Mifflin.

Elias, N. (1982) *The Civilizing Process*. Oxford: Basil Blackwell.

Ellenberger, H. (1970) *The Discovery of the Unconscious*. New York: Basic Books.

Emerson, R.W. (1960) *Selections From Ralph Waldo Emerson*. Boston: Houghton Mifflin.

Etzioni, A. (1988) *The Moral Dimension: Toward a New Economics*. New York: Free Press.

Fauconnet, P. (1920) *La Responsabilité: Étude Sociologique*. Paris: Alcan.

Featherstone, M. (1988) In Pursuit of the Postmodern: An Introduction. *Theory, Culture and Society* 5(2–3): 195–216.

Filloux, J. (1970) *La Science sociale et l'action*. Paris: Presses Universitaires de France.

—— (1977) *Durkheim et le socialisme*. Paris: Droz.

Foucault, M. (1972) *The Archaeology of Knowledge*, translated by A. Smith. New York: Pantheon.

Fox, M. (1980) *Schopenhauer: His Philosophical Achievement*. Totowa, N.J.: Barnes & Noble.

Frank, R. (1988) *Passions Within Reason: The Strategic Role of the Emotions*. New York: W.W. Norton.

Fraser, N. and Nicholson, L. (1988) Social Criticism Without Philosophy: An Encounter Between Feminism and Postmodernism. *Theory, Culture and Society* 5(2–3): 373–98.

Freud, S. ([1916] 1974) *Introductory Lectures on Psychoanalysis*. New York: W.W. Norton.

—— ([1924] 1974) Letter to *Le Disque Vert*. In *The Standard Edition of the Complete Psychological Works of Sigmund Freud*, edited by J. Strachey, Vol. 19. New York: W.W. Norton.

—— ([1925] 1959) *An Autobiographical Study*. New York: W.W. Norton.

—— ([1930] 1961) *Civilization and Its Discontents*. New York: W.W. Norton.

—— ([1933] 1965) *New Introductory Lectures on Psychoanalysis*. New York: W.W. Norton.

Frisby, D. (1984) *Georg Simmel*. London: Tavistock.

—— (1986) *Fragments of Modernity: Theories of Modernity in the Work of Simmel, Kracauer and Benjamin*. Cambridge: MIT Press.

—— (1989) Simmel and Leisure. pp. 75–91 in *Leisure for Leisure*, edited by C. Rojek. New York: Routledge.

Fromm, E. (1955) *The Sane Society*. Greenwich: Fawcett.

—— (1962) *Beyond the Chains of Illusion*. New York: Simon & Schuster.

Gay, P. (1986) *The Bourgeois Experience. Vol. 2. The Tender Passion*. New York: Oxford.

Giddens, A. (1987) *Social Theory and Modern Sociology*. Stanford: Stanford University Press.

Gilligan, C. (1982) *In a Different Voice*. Cambridge: Harvard University Press.

Gisbert, P. (1959) Social Facts in Durkheim's System. *Anthropos* 54: 353–69.

Goodwin, P. (1967) Schopenhauer. pp. 325–32 in *The Encyclopedia of Philosophy*, edited by P. Edwards, vol. 7. New York: Macmillan.

Goranov, K. (1970) *The Historical Life of Art*. Sofia, Bulgaria: Bulgarian Communist Party Publishing House.

Gorbachev, M.S. (1986a) *The Challenge of Our Time: Disarmament and Social Progress*. New York: International Publishers.

—— (1986b) *The Coming Century of Peace*. New York: Richardson & Steirman.

—— (1987) *Perestroika: New Thinking for Our Country and the World*. New York: Harper & Row.

Gouldner, A. (1958) Introduction. pp. v–xxviii in *Socialism and Saint-Simon*, by Émile Durkheim. Yellow Springs, Ohio: Antioch Press.

—— (1970) *The Coming Crisis of Western Sociology*. New York: Basic.

Greenwood, S. F. (1989) Structuring a Transpersonal Sociology of Religion. Unpublished Master's Thesis, University of Maine.

Grunbaum, A. and Wesley, S. (1988) *The Limitations of Deductivism*. Berkeley: University of California Press.

Guitton, J. (1959) *The Modernity of Saint Augustine*. Baltimore: Helicon Press.

Guyau, J.-M. ([1885] 1907) *Esquisse d'une morale sans obligation ni sanction*. Paris: Alcan.

—— ([1887] 1909) *L'irreligion de l'avenir*. Paris: Alcan.

Habermas, J. (1970) *Toward a Rational Society*. Boston: Beacon.

—— (1975) *Legitimation Crisis*. Boston: Beacon.

—— (1981) Modernity Versus Postmodernity. *New German Critique* 22: 3–14.

—— (1987) *The Philosophical Discourse of Modernity*. Cambridge: MIT Press.

Halbwachs, M. ([1912] 1974) *La Classe ouvriere et les niveaux*. London: Gordon & Breach.

—— (1918) La doctrine d'Émile Durkheim. *Revue philosophique* 85: 353–411.

—— (1925) Les Origines puritaines du capitalisme. *Revue d'histoire et de philosophie religieuses*. 5: 132–57.

—— ([1930] 1978) *The Causes of Suicide*. London: Routledge & Kegan Paul.

—— (1935) *Sources of Religious Sentiment*. New York: Free Press.

—— ([1938] 1960) *Population and Society: Introduction to Social Morphology*, translated by Otis Dudley Duncan and Harold W. Pfautz. Glencoe, Ill.: Free Press.

—— (1939) Individual Conscience and Collective Mind. *American Journal of Sociology* 44: 812–22.

—— (1958) *The Psychology of Social Class*, translated by Georges Friedman. Glencoe: Free Press.

Hale, D. (1988) The Panic of 1893: Historical Precedent to the 1987 crash is Not 1929. *Across the Board* 25 (Jan.): 24–32.

Hall, J.A. (1988) *Liberalism: Politics, Ideology, and the Market.* Chapel Hill: University of North Carolina.

Hall, R.T. (1987) *Émile Durkheim: Ethics and the Sociology of Morals.* New York: Greenwood Press.

Hamlyn, D. (1980) *Schopenhauer.* London: Routledge & Kegan Paul.

Harvey, D. (1985) *Consciousness and the Urban Experience.* Baltimore: Johns Hopkins University Press.

—— (1989) *The Condition of Postmodernity.* London: Basil Blackwell.

Hayek, F.A. (1988) *The Fatal Conceit: The Errors of Socialism.* Chicago: University of Chicago Press.

Hazelrigg, L. (1989) *Social Science and the Challenge of Relativism.* Volume 1. Tallahasee: Florida State University Press.

Hegel, G.W.F. ([1899] 1965). *The Philosophy of History.* New York: Dover.

Hertz, R. ([1907–1909] 1960) *Death and the Right Hand.* Aberdeen: Cohen & West.

Hitler, A. (1940) *Mein Kampf.* New York: Reynal & Hitchcock.

Hodson, C.E. (1971) Nuestra Señora de Guadalupe: Appearance Before an Indian. *Catholic World* 54: 727–34.

Hollis, M. (1987) *The Cunning of Reason.* Cambridge: Cambridge University Press.

Holton, R.J. (1987) The Idea of Crisis in Modern Society. *The British Journal of Sociology* 38: 514–31.

Horkheimer, M. (1947) *The Eclipse of Reason.* New York: Oxford University Press.

Horowitz, I.L. 1987. Disenthralling Sociology. *Society* 24: 48–55.

Hubert, H. and Mauss, M. ([1899] 1964) *Sacrifice: Its Nature and Function.* Chicago: University of Chicago Press.

—— ([1904] 1972) *A General Theory of Magic.* New York: W.W. Norton.

Hunter, J.D. (1983) *American Evangelicalism: Conservative Religion and the Quandary of Modernity.* New Brunswick, N.J.: Rutgers University Press.

Inkeles, A. (1983) *Exploring Individual Modernity.* New York: Columbia University Press.

James, W. ([1890] 1950) *The Principles of Psychology.* New York: Dover.

—— ([1896] 1931) *The Will to Believe, and Other Essays in Popular Philosophy.* New York: Longmans.

—— ([1902] 1961) *The Varieties of Religious Experience.* New York: Collier Books.

—— (1948) *Essays in Pragmatism.* New York: Hafner Publishing.

Janaway, C. (1989) *Self and World in Schopenhauer's Philosophy.* New York: Oxford.

Janik, A. and Toulmin, S. (1973) *Wittgenstein's Vienna.* New York: Simon & Schuster.

Jay, M. (1988) *Fin de Siècle Socialism and Other Essays.* London: Routledge.

Joas, H. (1984) Durkheim et le pragmatisme. *Revue française de sociologie* 25: 560–81.
—— (1985) *George Herbert Mead: A Contemporary Re-examination of his Thought.* Cambridge: MIT Press.
Jones, E. (1981) *The Life and Work of Sigmund Freud.* Vols 1–3. New York: Basic Books.
Judovitz, D. (1988) *Subjectivity and Representation in Descartes: The Origins of Modernity.* Cambridge: Cambridge University Press.
Jung, C.G. (1961) *Memories, Dreams, Reflections.* New York: Pantheon.
—— (1973) *Man and His Symbols.* New York: Dell.
Kaern, M. (1985) Georg Simmel's Sociology of Als-Ob. Doctoral dissertation, University of Pittsburgh.
Kaern, M., Phillips, B.S., and Cohen, R.S. (1990) *Georg Simmel and Contemporary Sociology.* Boston: Kluwer.
Kallen, H.M. (1932) *Judaism at Bay: Essays Toward the Adjustment of Judaism to Modernity.* New York: Bloch Publishing.
Kandal, T.R. (1988) *The Woman Question in Classical Sociological Theory.* Miami: University Presses of Florida.
Kant, I. ([1788] 1956) *Critique of Practical Reason.* Indianapolis: Bobbs-Merrill.
—— (1963) *On History.* Indianapolis: Bobbs-Merrill.
Käsler, D. (1988) *Max Weber.* Chicago: University of Chicago Press.
Katz, J. (1988) *Seductions of Crime: Moral and Sensual Attraction in Doing Evil.* New York: Basic Books.
Kellner, D. (1988) Postmodernism as Social Theory. *Theory, Culture and Society* 5(2–3): 239–70.
Klein, J.H. (1981) *Thunder in the Valley.* Boston: St Paul Editions.
Knapp, P. (1985) The Question of Hegelian Influence Upon Durkheim's Thought. *Sociological Inquiry.* 55: 1–15.
Kohlberg, L. (1984) *Essays in Moral Development.* San Francisco: Harper & Row.
Kojeve, A. (1969) *Introduction to the Reasoning of Hegel,* translated by J. Nichols. New York: Basic Books.
Kraljevic, S. (1984) *The Apparitions of Our Lady at Medjugorje.* Chicago: Franciscan Herald Press.
Lalande, A. ([1926] 1980) *Vocabulaire technique et critique de la philosophie.* Paris: Presses Universitaires de France.
—— (1960) Allocution. pp. 20–3 in *Centenaire de la naissance d'Émile Durkheim.* Paris: Annales de l'Université de Paris.
Lamartine, A. (1890) *Raphaël, or Pages of the Book of Life at Twenty.* Chicago: A.C. McClung & Co.
Larson, M.A. (1927) *The Modernity of Milton.* Chicago: University of Chicago Press.
Lash, S. (1990) *The Sociology of Postmodernism.* London: Routledge.
Laurentin, R. and Rupcic, L. (1984) *Is the Virgin Mary Appearing at Medjugorje?: An Urgent Message for the World Given in a Marxist Country,* trans. by Francis Martin. Washington, DC: The Word Among Us.

Le Blanc, M.F. (1981) *Cause of Our Joy*. Boston: St Paul Editions.

Le Bon, G. (1901) *The Crowd*. Dunwoody, GA: Norman S. Berg, Publishers.

Letica, S. (1989) *Cetvrta Jugoslavija*. Zagreb: Dnevnik.

Levett, A. (1989) Psychological Trauma: Discourses of Childhood Sexual Abuse. Doctoral dissertation, University of South Africa.

Levy, A. (1904) *Stirner et Nietzsche*. Paris: Société Nouvelle.

Lévy-Bruhl, L. (1890) *L'Allemagne depuis Leibniz*. Paris: Hachette.

—— (1895) La Crise de la métaphysique en Allemagne. *Revue des Deux Mondes* 15: 341–67.

—— (1899) *The History of Modern Philosophy in France*. Chicago: Open Court Publishing.

—— (1903a) *La morale et la science des moeurs*. Paris: Alcan.

—— (1903b) *The Philosophy of Auguste Comte*, translated by Kathleen de Beaumont-Klein. London: Swan Sonnenschein & Co.

—— (1905) *Ethics and Moral Science*. London: Archibald Constable & Co.

Lindsey, H. (1970) *The Late Great Planet Earth*. Grand Rapids, MI.: Zondervan.

Logue, W. (1983) *From Philosophy to Sociology*. De Kalb: Northern Illinois University Press.

Long, V. (1976) *The Mother of God*. Chicago: Franciscan Herald Press.

Lovaton, L. (1971) La Virgen de las Mercedes en la isla de Santo Domingo. *Journal of Inter-American Studies*. 13: 53–61.

Love, N. (1986) *Marx, Nietzsche, and Modernity*. New York: Columbia University Press.

Luft, E. (1988) *Schopenhauer: New Essays in Honor of his 200th Birthday*. Lewiston, N.Y.: Mellen.

Lukács, G. (1980) *The Destruction of Reason*, translated by Peter Palmer. Atlantic Highlands: Humanities Press.

Lukes, S. (1982) Introduction. pp. 1–27 in *Durkheim: The Rules of Sociological Method and Selected Texts on Sociology and Its Method*, edited by S. Lukes. New York: Free Press.

—— (1985) *Émile Durkheim: His Life and Work*. Stanford, CA: Stanford University Press.

Lyotard, J. (1984) *The Postmodern Condition*. Minneapolis: University of Minnesota Press.

McSwain, J. (1988) *Rethinking the Origins of Modernity: The Renaissance Origins of Modernity*. Baton Rouge: Louisiana State University Press.

Magee, B. (1983) *The Philosophy of Schopenhauer*. New York: Oxford University Press.

Magnet, M. (1986) The Decline and Fall of Business Ethics. *Fortune* 114, Dec. 8, 65–71.

Mann, T. ([1939] 1955) Introduction. pp. iii–xxiii in *The Works of Schopenhauer*, edited by W. Durant and T. Mann. New York: Frederick Ungar Publishers.

Manschreck, C. (1976) Nihilism in the Twentieth Century: A View From Here. *Church History* 45: 85–96.

Marcus, S. (1984) *Freud and the Culture of Psychoanalysis: Studies in the Transition From Victorian Humanism to Modernity.* Boston: Allen & Unwin.

Margolis, J. (1989) *Pragmatism Without Foundations.* London: Basil Blackwell.

Martinez, B. (1982) *Apparitions of Our Blessed Mother at Cuapa, Nicaragua.* Washington, N.J.: World Apostolate of Fatima.

Masaryk, T. ([1883] 1970) *Suicide and the Meaning of Civilization.* Chicago: University of Chicago Press.

Mauss, M. (1906) Review of Wilhelm Wundt's *Volkerpsychologie. L'Année Sociologique* 2: 53–68.

—— ([1950] 1979a) *Sociology and Psychology.* London: Routledge & Kegan Paul.

—— ([1950] 1979b) *Seasonal Variations of the Eskimo: A Study in Social Morphology.* London: Routledge & Kegan Paul.

Meillet, A. (1906) Comment les mots changent des sens. *L'Année sociologique* 9: 1–39.

Menand, L. and Schwartz, S. (1982) T.S. Eliot on Durkheim: A New Attribution. *Modern Philology* 79: 309–15.

Merriman, J.M. (1975) *1830 in France.* New York: New Viewpoints.

Merton, R.K. (1957) *Social Theory and Social Structure.* New York: Free Press.

Meštrović, S.G. (1982) *In the Shadow of Plato: Durkheim and Freud on Suicide and Society.* Unpublished doctoral dissertation, Syracuse University.

—— (1985) A Sociological Conceptualization of Trauma. *Social Science and Medicine* 21: 835–48.

—— (1986) Magic and Psychiatric Commitment in India. *International Journal of Law & Psychiatry* 9: 431–49.

—— (1988a) *Émile Durkheim and the Reformation of Sociology.* Totowa, N.J.: Rowman & Littlefield.

—— (1988b) The Social World as Will and Idea: Schopenhauer's Influence Upon Durkheim's Thought. *The Sociological Review* 36: 674–705.

—— (1989a) Rethinking the Will and Idea of Sociology in the Light of Schopenhauer's Philosophy. *The British Journal of Sociology* 40: 271–93.

—— (1989b) Moral Theory Based on the Heart Versus the Mind: Schopenhauer's and Durkheim's Critiques of Kantian Ethics. *The Sociological Review* 38: 431–57.

—— (1989c) The Theme of Civilization and Its Discontents in Durkheim's Division of Labor. *Journal for the Theory of Social Behaviour* 19: 443–56.

—— (1989d) Simmel's Sociology in Relation to Schopenhauer's Philosophy. In M. Kaern (ed.) *Georg Simmel and Contemporary Sociology.* Boston: Kluwer.

REFERENCES

Meštrović, S.G. and Brown H.M. (1985) Durkheim's Concept of Anomie as Dérèglement. *Social Problems* 33: 81–99.
Meštrović, S.G. and Cook, J. (1988) On Childism as Prejudice. *Psychiatric Forum* 14: 34–41.
Meštrović, S.G. and Glassner, B. (1983) A Durkheimian Hypothesis on Stress. *Social Science and Medicine* 17: 1315–27.
Mill, J.S. (1968) *Auguste Comte and Positivism*. Ann Arbor, MI: University of Michigan Press.
Mirowski, P. (1987) The Philosophical Bases of Institutionalist Economics. *Journal of Economic Issues* 21: 1001–37.
Mosca, G. (1939) *The Ruling Class*, translated by H. Kahn. New York: McGraw-Hill.
Mounin, G. (1975) *La Linguistique du XXe siècle*. Paris: Presses Universitaires de France.
Mudragei, S. (1979) The Problem of Man in the Irrationalist Teachings of Soren Kierkegaard. *Voprosy Filosofii* 33: 76–86.
Munch, R. (1988) *Understanding Modernity: Toward a New Perspective Going Beyond Durkheim and Weber*. London: Routledge.
Murphy, J. (1989) *Postmodern Social Analysis and Criticism*. New York: Greenwood Press.
Nandan, Y. (1977) *The Durkheimian School: A Systematic and Comprehensive Bibliography*. Westport, Conn.: Greenwood Press.
Nelson, B. (1981) *On the Roads to Modernity*. Totowa, N.J.: Rowman & Littlefield.
Nietzsche, F. ([1874] 1965). *Schopenhauer as Educator*. South Bend, Ind.: Gateway.
—— ([1901] 1968) *The Will to Power*. New York: Random House.
—— (1968) *The Portable Nietzsche*, translated by W. Kaufmann. New York: Viking Library.
Norman, D. (1988) *The Psychology of Everyday Things*. New York: Basic Books.
Odell, C.M. (1986) *Those Who Saw Her: The Apparitions of Mary*. Boston: Our Sunday Visitor.
Oizerman, T. (1977) The Rational and the Irrational. Voprosy Filosofii 31: 82–95.
O'Keefe, D.L. (1982) *Stolen Lightning: A Social Theory of Magic*. New York: Random House.
Orru, M. (1987) *Anomie: History and Meanings*. London: Allen & Unwin.
Pareto, V. ([1931] 1963) *The Mind and Society*. New York: Dover.
Park, R.E. and Burgess, W.E. (1921) *Introduction to the Science of Sociology*. Chicago: University of Chicago Press.
Parsons, T. (1937) *The Structure of Social Action*. Glencoe: Free Press.
Pearce, F. (1989) *The Radical Durkheim*. London: Unwin Hyman.
Pelletier, J.A. (1985) *The Queen of Peace Visits Medjugorje*. Worcester, MA: Assumption Publications.
Piaget, J. ([1932] 1965) *The Moral Judgement of the Child*. New York: Free Press.

Pickering, W.S.F. (1979) *Durkheim: Essays on Morals and Education.*
London: Routledge & Kegan Paul.
—— (1984) *Durkheim's Sociology of Religion: Themes and Theories.* London:
Routledge & Kegan Paul.
Pinkney, D.H. (1972) *The French Revolution of 1830.* Princeton:
Princeton University Press.
Popper, K.R. ([1934] 1961) *The Logic of Scientific Discovery.* New York:
Science Editions.
Preston, J.J. (1982) *Mother Worship.* Chapel Hill, N.C.: University of
North Carolina Press.
Renouvier, C. (1892) Schopenhauer et la metaphysique du
pessimisme. *L'Année philosophique* 3: 1–61.
Riba, T. (1985) Romanticism and Nationalism in Economics.
International Journal of Social Economics 12: 52–68.
Ribot, T. (1874) *La Philosophie de Schopenhauer.* Paris: Librairie Gerner
Baillière.
—— (1896) *The Psychology of Attention.* Chicago: Open Court.
Riesman, D. ([1950] 1977) *The Lonely Crowd.* New Haven:
Yale University Press.
Riesman, D. and Riesman, E.T. (1967) *Conversations in Japan:
Modernization, Politics, and Culture.* Chicago: University of Chicago
Press.
Rochberg, G. (1988) News of the Culture or News of the Universe?
Annals of the AAPSS 500: 116–26.
Rochberg-Halton, E. (1986) *Meaning and Modernity: Social Theory in the
Pragmatic Attitude.* Chicago: University of Chicago Press.
—— (1988) *Cultus* and Culture. Paper presented to the Third
German–American Theory Conference, Bremen, West Germany.
—— (1990a) Review of James Clifford's *The Predicament of Culture.*
Contemporary Sociology, 18: 934–6.
—— (1990b) Never the Twain Shall Meet? Commentary in *The
American Sociologist* 20:24–5.
Roche, J.P. (1974) *Sentenced To Life.* New York: Macmillan.
Rojek, C. (ed.) (1985) *Capitalism and Leisure Theory.* London: Tavistock.
—— (ed.) (1989) *Leisure for Leisure.* New York: Routledge.
Rooney, L. and Faricy, R. (1984) *Mary, Queen of Peace: Is the Mother of
God Appearing in Medjugorje?* New York: Alba House.
Rose, E. (1965) *Faith From the Abyss: Hermann Hesse's Way From
Romanticism to Modernity.* New York: New York University Press.
Rundell, J.F. (1987) *Origins of Modernity: The Origins of Modern Social
Theory from Kant to Hegel to Marx.* Madison: University of Wisconsin
Press.
Rutler, G.W. (1987) *Beyond Modernity: Reflections of a Post-modern
Catholic.* San Francisco: Ignatius Press.
Saussure, F. ([1916] 1959) *Course in General Linguistics*, translated by
W. Baskin. New York: Philosophical Library.
Schopenhauer, A. ([1813] 1899) *On the Fourfold Root of the Principle of
Sufficient Reason and On the Will in Nature.* London: G. Bell & Sons.

—— ([1818] 1969a) *The World as Will and Representation*, translated by E. Payne. Vol. 1. New York: Dover Press.

—— ([1818] 1969b) *The World as Will and Representation*, translated by E. Payne. Vol. 2. New York: Dover Press.

—— ([1841] 1965) *On the Basis of Morality*. Indianapolis: Bobbs-Merrill.

—— (1985) *Early Manuscripts (1804–1818)*. Oxford: Berg.

Segady, T.W. (1987) *Values, Neo-Kantianism and the Development of Weberian Sociology*. New York: Peter Lang.

Seligman, M. (1988) Boomer Blues: With Too Great Expectations, the Baby Boomers are Sliding into Individualistic Melancholy. *Psychology Today* 22 (October): 50–5.

Selye, H. (1978) *The Stress of Life*. New York: McGraw-Hill.

Sharkey, D. (1952) *The Woman Shall Conquer: The Story of the Blessed Virgin in the Modern World*. Milwaukee: Bruce Publishing Co.

Sica, A. (1988) *Weber, Irrationality, and Social Order*. Berkeley: University of California Press.

Simmel, G. (1893) *Einleitung in die Moralwissenschaft*. Leipzig.

—— ([1907] 1986) *Schopenhauer and Nietzsche*. Amherst: University of Massachusetts Press.

—— (1971) *On Individuality and Its Social Forms*. Chicago: University of Chicago Press.

—— (1977) *Problems of the Philosophy of History: An Epistemological Essay*. New York: Free Press.

—— (1978) *The Philosophy of Money*. London: Routledge & Kegan Paul.

—— (1980) *Essays on Interpretation in Social Science*. Totowa, N.J.: Rowman and Littlefield.

Sivric, I. (1989) *The Hidden Side of Medjugorje*. Notre Dame, Canada: Psilog.

Sloterdijk, P. (1987) *Critique of Cynical Reason*, translated by Michael Eldred. Minneapolis: University of Minnesota Press.

Soja, E. (1989) *Postmodern Geography*. London: Routledge.

Sorokin, P. (1947) *The Ways and Power of Love*. New York: American Book Company.

—— (1957) *Social and Cultural Dynamics*. New York: American Book Company.

—— (1963) *A Long Journey: The Autobiography of Pitirim A. Sorokin*. New Haven, Conn.: College and University Press.

Spencer, H. (1864) *First Principles*. New York: D. Appleton.

Spengler, O. ([1926] 1961) *The Decline of the West. Vol. 1. Form and Actuality*, translated by Charles F. Atkinson. New York: Alfred A. Knopf.

—— ([1928] 1961) *The Decline of the West. Vol. 2. Perspectives on World-History*, translated by Charles F. Atkinson. New York: Alfred A. Knopf.

Tarde, G. (1969) *On Communication and Social Influence*. Chicago: University of Chicago Press.

Tiryakian, E.A. (1966) A Problem for the Sociology of Knowledge: The Mutual Unawareness of Émile Durkheim and Max Weber. *European Journal of Sociology* 7: 330–6.

—— (1988) Durkheim, Mathiez, and the French Revolution: The Political Context of a Sociological Classic. *European Journal of Sociology* 29: 373–96.

Tönnies, F. ([1887] 1963) *Community and Society*, translated by C. Loomis. New York: Harper & Row.

Topel, A. (1966) On the Sociology of Petty Bourgeois Thinking. *Deutsche Zeitschrift für Philosophie* 14: 963–77.

Turner, S. (1986) *The Search for a Methodology of Social Science: Durkheim, Weber, and the Nineteenth Century Problem of Cause, Probability, and Action*. Dordrecht: D. Reidel.

Unamuno, M. ([1913] 1954) *The Tragic Sense of Life*. New York: Dover.

Urbach, P. (1987) *Francis Bacon's Philosophy of Science*. Chicago: Open Court.

Vaihinger, H. ([1924] 1935). *The Philosophy of As If*. London: Routledge.

Vattimo, G. (1988) *The End of Modernity: Nihilism and Hermeneutics in Postmodern Culture*. Baltimore: Johns Hopkins University Press.

Vega, P. (1984) *The Apparitions of Our Blessed Mother in Cuapa, Nicaragua*. St Paul, Minn.: American Franciscan Press.

Vendreys, J. (1921) Le Caractère social du langage et la doctrine de Ferdinand de Saussure. *Journal de Psychologie* 18: 617–24.

Weber, E. (1987) *France, Fin de Siècle*. Cambridge: Harvard University Press.

Weber, M. ([1904] 1958) *The Protestant Ethic and the Spirit of Capitalism*, translated by T. Parsons. New York: Scribner's.

Whewell, W. ([1847] 1967) *The Philosophy of the Inductive Sciences*. London: Frank Cass & Co.

Whimster, S. and Lash, S. (1987) *Max Weber, Rationality and Modernity*. Boston: Allen & Unwin.

White, S.K. (1988) *The Recent Work of Jürgen Habermas: Reason, Justice, and Modernity*. Cambridge: Cambridge University Press.

Williams, R. (1983) *The Year 2000*. New York: Pantheon.

Wirth, L. (1938) Urbanism as a Way of Life. *American Journal of Sociology* 44: 1–24

Wolff, K. (1983) *Beyond the Sociology of Knowledge*. Lanham, MD: University Press of America.

—— (1988) Anomie and the Sociology of Knowledge in Durkheim and Today. *Philosophy & Social Criticism* 14: 51–68.

Wundt, W. (1907) *The Principles of Morality and the Departments of the Moral Life*. New York: Macmillan.

Zijderveld, A.C. (1979) *On Clichés*. London: Routledge & Kegan Paul.

Znaniecki, F. ([1934] 1968) *The Method of Sociology*. New York: Octagon Books.

NAME INDEX

Baudelaire, Charles xi-xii, 20,
23–6, 30, 69, 75–8, 80–2,
87–91, 125, 143, 196, 199, 210;
his definition of modernity 22
Bell, Daniel 5, 24, 27
Bellah, Robert N. 27, 169
Benjamin, Walter xii, 2, 20, 23,
30, 75, 87, 191
Bergson, Henri 35, 68–9, 80–1,
110–1,
Bloom, Allan xi, 27, 55, 67, 95–7,
169, 184
Bouglé, Célestin 30–3, 35, 43, 55,
90, 99, 112

Camus, Albert 11
Chateaubriand, C. 76–8, 89
Comte, Auguste 6, 30, 37, 75,
95–9, 101–2, 148

Darwin, Charles 30–5, 115
Deploige, Simon x, 43, 54–5,
99–110, 168
Dickens, Charles 47
Durkheim, Émile viii, xi, xiii,
28–9, 32–4, 43–6, 75–8, 83–6,
88–94, 139, 143–8, 157–62,
176–8, 180–3, 188, 191, 194–7,
210; German influence on his
thought 95–107; his liberal
thought 8, 31, 120–69, 182;
nicknamed 'Schopen' 117;

Schopenhauer's influence on
his sociology 109, 135, 159; and
Simmel's sociology 54–74, 176;
and social realism 18, 24,
98–102, 105, 142

Elias, Norbert 16, 18, 23–6, 130,
164, 184
Eliot, T.S. 40–3
Ellenberger, Henri 8, 68, 88, 95,
109
Emerson, Ralph W. 46
Espinas, Alfred 99

Freud, Sigmund 3, 17, 62, 68–70,
87, 151, 164, 190–2
Fromm, Erich 23, 142

Gorbachev, Mikhail 6–9, 144,
161–4, 202

Habermas, Jürgen xi, 14–16, 20,
22, 27–8, 81, 108, 112, 116,
169,
Halbwachs, Maurice 30–5
Hartmann, Eduard von 85–6,
89–90, 97
Harvey, David 20, 163–5
Hegel, G.F.W. 16, 22, 42, 100–1,
172
Hertz, Robert 40
Hesse, Hermann

SUBJECT INDEX

Socialism and Saint-Simon 5–6, 42, 102, 123
Sociology and Philosophy 62, 121–3, 126
State 172–3, 190
stock market crashes 10, 14, 169, 173–8
stress 4, 195–9
suffering 57, 84–8, 189
suicide 5, 10–11, 23, 75, 78, 85–93, 191, 197
Suicide 44, 57, 85–9, 123, 175–81, 187, 194,
syphilis 9, 10, 46

unconscious 67–9, 207–8
utilitarianism 61, 124

Virgin Mary 10, 14–15, 136–62
Volkerpsychologie 55–6, 95–7, 109

will 22, 60–2, 64, 67–70, 88, 178, 193
will to life 44, 57–9, 62, 73, 90, 186